AN AMERICAN SOLDIER IN THE GREAT WAR
The World War I Diary and Letters of Elmer O. Smith

Published by Hellgate Press
(An imprint of L&R Publishing, LLC)

Hellgate Press
PO Box 3531
Ashland, OR 97520
email: sales@hellgatepress.com

Editor: Harley B. Patrick
Interior design: Michael Campbell
Cover design: L. Redding

Cover photo: The formal military portrait of Private Elmer O. Smith in uniform was likely taken in June 1917. It appeared in the post-war book of photographs of servicemen from the Lansing, Michigan area, entitled, *Honor Roll and Complete War History of Ingham County in the Great World War, 1914-1918.*

Library of Congress Cataloging-in-Publication Data
Smith, Elmer O., 1897-1968.
An American soldier in the Great War : the World War I diary and letters of Elmer O. Smith : Private First Class, 119th Field Artillery Regiment, 32nd Division / edited by John DellaGiustina. -- First edition.
pages cm
Includes bibliographical references.
ISBN 978-1-55571-821-3
1. Smith, Elmer O., 1897-1968--Diaries. 2. World War, 1914-1918--Personal narratives, American. 3. World War, 1914-1918--Campaigns--Western Front. 4. United States. Army. Field Artillery, 119th. 5. United States. Army. American Expeditionary Forces--Biography. 6. Soldiers--United States--Diaries. 7. Lansing (Mich.)--Biography. I. DellaGiustina, John, editor. II. Title. III. Title: World War I diary and letters of Elmer O. Smith.
D570.9.S553 2015
940.4'1273092--dc23
[B]
2015018538

Printed and bound in the United States of America
First edition 10 9 8 7 6 5 4 3 2 1

AN AMERICAN SOLDIER IN THE GREAT WAR

THE WORLD WAR I DIARY AND LETTERS OF ELMER O. SMITH

Private First Class, 119th Field Artillery Regiment, 32nd Division

Edited by

John DellaGiustina

CONTENTS

To my

Mother Sharon, Aunt Margo, and Uncle Steve,

children of Elmer and Marjorie Smith

and their families

... It's what's left that matters.
Photographs, letters, empty clothes,
no, it's the stories behind them,
those are what matter.
Stories live forever,
but only if you tell them ...

From the 2012 movie *Memorial Day*

PREFACE

In August 2014, the world remembered the 100th anniversary of the start of one of the most ghastly conflicts in human history—"the Great War," "the War to End All Wars," and commonly referred to in recent times as World War I or the First World War. In 1917, the United States joined the Allied effort to defeat Germany, culminating with victory in November 1918.

Over the past decade the last survivors who fought in this major war have passed from this earth. Now the only sources of information from this conflict are the written records. These include the numerous personal accounts, unit files, newspaper articles, journals, and books that have documented the carnage and events of that now distant past. This book centers on one soldier's actions in that conflict and adds to the existing record of primary source material.

Elmer O. Smith was my grandfather. Enlisting in the U.S. Army in April 1917, he started a diary on New Year's Day 1918. Throughout that pivotal year he made short entries into this diary to document his activities and thoughts. These entries captured what he faced in his unit's training, their deployment overseas to France, battles with the German Army, his wounding, subsequent convalescence, return to the front lines and the armistice. It describes the rigorous day to day activities of a soldier training for and facing combat during World War I.

The unpublished diary's entries are supplemented throughout the book by many of the letters he wrote to his mother, Olive Smith and sister, Zelma Smith. The diary and letters were transcribed from the existing documents and incorporated in their original form, misspellings, punctuation errors, and all. Multiple primary and secondary sources have contributed to a more complete war record of this soldier and framed his war life within its historical context. As a soldier at the bottom of his chain of command, Private Smith did not have the luxury of the wider perspective that these additional sources can now provide. Thus, this book aims to show how Private Smith was just one part of a much larger, broader effort to bring American combat power to bear on the German Army and bring about the end of four years of devastating conflict in Europe and elsewhere.

I personally thank and acknowledge the extensive efforts over the years of my Aunt Margo to preserve the Smith family history, to include the transcribing of her father's handwritten diary and letters. As a trained historian and career U.S. Army officer, I accept responsibility for any errors or omissions contained in this book.

Tucson, Arizona
April, 2015

CHRONOLOGY

World War I Timeline of Elmer O. Smith

April 6, 1917: The United States declares war on Germany

April 30, 1917: Elmer O. Smith enlists in Battery B, First Michigan Field Artillery Battalion, Michigan National Guard, Lansing; Begins twice-a-week training, initially at Lansing Armory, then Camp Hoague in east Lansing

May/June, 1917: U.S. Draft established

July 3, 1917: Proclamation of President Wilson federalizes the National Guard units of Michigan, Wisconsin, and most other states

August 3, 1917: 32nd Division established and organized. Michigan National Guard units incorporated. Battery B becomes part of 119th Field Artillery (FA) Regiment, 57th FA Brigade, 32nd Division

August 5, 1917: All National Guard soldiers formally drafted into Regular Army

August 17, 1917: Battery B moves via train to mobilization site, Camp Grayling, Michigan

October 1, 1917: 119th FA Regiment moves via train to Camp MacArthur, Waco, Texas

January 1, 1918: Private Elmer Smith starts 1918 Diary

January 4, 1918: Private Smith transferred to Headquarters Company, 119th FA Regiment

February 6, 1918: 119th FA departs Camp MacArthur via train for New York City vicinity

February 11, 1918: 119th FA arrives at Camp Merritt, Tenafly, New Jersey

February 26, 1918: 119th FA departs New York harbor on British transport ship Olympic bound for Great Britain

March 6, 1918: 119th FA unloads ship in Liverpool, England

March 10, 1918: 119th FA crosses English Channel on ferry from Southhampton, England; arrives in Havre, France the next day

March 13, 1918: 119th FA arrives at Camp Coetquidan, France, artillery training post, via train

June 4, 1918: 119th FA departs Camp Coetquidan by train for the Western Front

June 7, 1918: 119th FA arrives Toul, France. Moves to French village 12 miles behind front lines

June 13, 1918: 119th FA moves to French village six miles behind lines

June 14, 1918: 119th FA moves to firing positions

June 16, 1918: Private Elmer Smith wounded in action in enemy artillery attack on position at approximately 3:30 PM. Evacuated to front line hospital

July 11, 1918: Private Smith departs hospital in vicinity of Toul; travels by train to hospital at Basiolles

July 16, 1918: Private Smith travels to convalescent camp 3 miles from Basiolles hospital

July 22, 1918: Private Smith declared fit for service; leaves convalescent camp, travels to Neuf Chateau and Chaumont via train; arrives St. Aignan the next day

July 29, 1918: Private Smith leaves St. Aignan for replacement camp via Tours and Bordeaux; arrives at Camp Corneau near Atlantic Ocean the next day

August 7, 1918: Private Smith departs Le Corneau replacement camp by train; travels via La Teste, Bordeaux, Tours, Orleans, Nancy Le Sec, Chateau Thierry

August 9, 1918: Private Smith arrives at 32nd Division Headquarters, Mezy

August 11, 1918: Private Smith arrives at 119th FA Regiment rear echelon headquarters

August 23, 1918: 119th FA moved to the rear around Chateau Thierry toward Soissons; 32nd Division is the only American division on this front

August 30, 1918: 32nd Division captures Juvigny

September 2, 1918: 119th FA moves forward to Juvigny area to support 1st Moroccan Division

September 4, 1918: Private Smith receives a little mustard gas from German artillery attack

September 5, 1918: 119th FA firing batteries move forward

September 6, 1918: 119th FA moves back from front, camps at Mortamont

September 9, 1918: 119th FA Regiment moves to Villers Cotteret; takes train to vicinity of Danmartin, arrives the next day, hikes to Danmartin

September 17, 1918: 119th FA moves again to Bienville

September 18, 1918: 119th FA continues to move forward

September 21, 1918: 119th FA camps in the vicinity of Vaubecort at Dombasle

September 24, 1918: 119th occupies positions near the frontline

September 26, 1918: 119th FA moves forward to support infantry advancing across "No Man's Land" on first day of the Meuse-Argonne Offensive

September 27, 1918: 119th FA continues to move forward

September 30, 1918: 119th FA moves toward advance position near Verdun while under fire

October 9, 1918: Major 32nd Division infantry brigade attack supported by artillery fire

October 10, 1918: 119th FA Moves to within machine-gun range of the front line

October 21, 1918: 119th FA moves up its Regimental command post three kilometers (km)

October 27, 1918: Private Elmer Smith promoted to Private First Class (PFC)

November 1, 1918: Massive 119th FA artillery barrage supports 15 km infantry brigade advance

November 2, 1918: 57th FA Brigade and subordinates including 119th FA Regiment pulled out of the line for first major rest since June 14, 1918

November 11, 1918: Germany agrees to armistice. The World War ends

November 14, 1918: 119th FA decotized/deloused at Villers sur Cousances

November 22, 1918: The 119th FA moves to Mussey, France

December 21, 1918: The 119th FA moves to Mauvages, France and is headquartered here until they depart for transport to the U.S. in April 1919

December 28–January 10, 1918: PFC Smith takes rest and recuperation furlough to Nice, France, including travel to and from

February 2, 1919: Catholic Church in Mauvages, France holds service to thank the 119th FA

May 3, 1919: 119th FA returns to U.S. via ship, U.S.S Frederick; shortly thereafter, travels via train from Camp Mills, Long Island, New York to Michigan

May 13, 1919: 119th FA participates in Victory parade in Lansing, Michigan

May 15-16, 1919: PFC Elmer Smith discharged from U.S. Army at Camp Custer, Michigan

ABBREVIATIONS AND TERMS

AEF: American Expeditionary Forces

Barrage: Various methods artillery units use to concentrate artillery fires to achieve specific effects in support of ground maneuver forces and the mission

Boche: A French term for the German Army and its soldiers, literally translated as "hard headed or stubborn ones". Other common terms used for the German enemy were Hun or Jerry. In one diary entry Elmer Smith called them Dutchmen, a derivation of Germany's name for itself—Deutschland. The Netherlands/Holland remained neutral during the war, so no true Dutch units or soldiers overtly participated in the fighting. In another entry he calls them George

Bois: The French word for woods or forest

Caisson: A two-wheeled cart meant to carry artillery ammunition

Decotize: To delouse, ridding a person or animal of lice

Doughboys: An informal term for American infantrymen that many used to refer to all of the soldiers of the AEF. The term originated during the Mexican-American War, conceivably due to the dust-covered marching U.S. infantrymen appearing like adobe bricks in color and formation

DS: Direct Support

FA: Field Artillery

Ferme: The French word for farm

Fourgon: A wagon for carrying baggage

Goldbricking: To loaf or avoid one's duties

GS: General Support

HQ: Headquarters

KIA: Killed-in-action

km: kilometers

Limber: A two-wheeled cart meant to be pulled in tandem with an artillery piece or a caisson for transport

MIA: Missing-in-action

mm: millimeters

NCO: Non-commissioned officer

PC: Post of Command, also known as CP for Command Post

Pincer movement: A *military maneuver* where the *flanks* of the opponent are attacked simultaneously in a pinching motion after the opponent has advanced towards the center of an army. Also called a double envelopment

Red leg: A nickname for a U.S. artilleryman. The primary branch color of the U.S. Army Artillery Corps is red

U.S.: United States

U.S.S.: United States Ship

WIA: Wounded-in-action

Introduction: Pre-War Life in Michigan

ELMER OSCAR SMITH was born on March 5, 1897, in Wheeler Township, Gratiot County, Michigan, to Wilfred F. and Olive I. Smith (Oakes). Like many American soldiers who entered the military during the war, he was raised on a farm. The Smith property was an 80 acre family-owned farm in Fairfield Township in the northwest corner of Shiawassee County. The family moved there about 1906. In 1910, a large barn was built on the property. The family received mail at Box 127 in the small, mid-Michigan farming community of Ovid, Clinton County, about three miles to the south. The small unincorporated town of Carland in Shiawassee County was also close to the farm.

Wilfred "Fred" and Olive Smith married in November 1892. Elmer was the second of five siblings—older sister Zelma (born 1893), younger brothers Clarence (1904) and Dee (1908), and younger sister Genevieve (1913). As a boy one of Elmer's favorite activities after a large rainstorm was to visit the creek that ran through the property and search for Native American arrowheads and artifacts exposed after the water receded. He frequently found artifacts after his father would ask him to dredge the creek as well. He graduated from the eighth grade in June 1912 and as the oldest son spent subsequent years helping his family on their farm.[1] His grandfather, Oscar Thomas Oakes, a Civil War veteran, died in February 1916 in Michigan. In the fall of 1916, at the age of 19, Elmer left his rural life to attend formal schooling at Lansing Business University and earn a living in Michigan's capital city of Lansing, 40 miles south.

The Great War

After a Serbian nationalist assassinated Austria's Arch Duke Franz Ferdinand in Sarajevo on June 28, 1914, peace in Europe quickly disintegrated. In August 1914, the geopolitical web of alliances established in the decades before drove the European nations to mobilize their militaries and precipitate the greatest conflict in human history to that point. By 1916, the World War had been raging in Europe for over two years. It had expanded elsewhere as the Central Powers of Germany, the Austro-Hungarian Empire, Bulgaria, and the Ottoman Turk Empire partnered to fight against France, Great Britain, Russia, Serbia, Italy and numerous other Allied countries with combat spanning three continents. The rapidly advancing technology of the industrializing world was now producing the deadliest weapons ever known. The devastating firepower of these weapons of war provided such significant advantage to the defender in dug-in positions that the main Western Front battle line in France became largely static with two opposing trench lines extending from the English Channel over 500 miles to Switzerland's border. Thousands of soldiers on both sides were killed or wounded every week as the future main area of U.S. operations became mired in stalemate. Once stabilized in 1914, the front lines shifted no more than ten miles in either direction for almost three years.[2]

The U.S. avoided the European-centric war for over two years. But as aid shipments to Great Britain and France increased, German U-boat submarines began to actively track and attack American maritime traffic in the Atlantic Ocean. By early 1917 these torpedo attacks escalated to the point that America had little option but to actively defend itself and its political and economic interests.[3]

Other events also drew the U.S. closer to war. In March 1916, Mexican revolutionary Pancho Villa raided U.S. territory at Columbus, New Mexico, killing eight soldiers and nine civilians. In response, U.S. President Woodrow Wilson sent the U.S. Army under Brigadier General (BG) John J. Pershing into Mexico to pursue Villa and reduce the threat along the border.[4] On March 1, 1917, President Wilson made public the famous Zimmermann telegram incensing Americans throughout the country. The telegram from German Foreign Secretary Alfred Zimmermann to his minister in Mexico proposed a defensive alliance with Mexico and at the war's conclusion promised to return former territory in Texas, New Mexico, and Arizona.[5]

Finally, as a result of continued German provocation, President Wilson acted. On April 2, 1917, in a joint address to Congress, he declared, "We will not choose the path of submission... but... exert all... power and employ all... resources to bring the Government of the German Empire to terms and end the war... The world must be made safe for democracy." After affirmative votes in the Senate and House of Representatives, President Wilson signed the U.S. declaration of war on April 6, 1917.[6]

As a young man who had recently moved to a moderate size, growing American city, Elmer Smith, sought to begin his adult life. Through the following letters it is possible to understand what a future American soldier typically experienced as a civilian in the months just prior to the start of America's entrance into the war. He sent these letters and postcards to his family at the Ovid post office, Box 127. Typical of the era's low cost of living, a postcard required a one cent stamp and a letter cost two cents. In November 1917 the rate for a letter increased to three cents.

Letter to Sister Zelma, November 8, 1916

817 Washtenaw St.

Dear Sister:

Well how are you now days. Am feeling fine myself. Am getting along in my school work just fine. It is a little hard but will be able to master it. I like my boarding place just dandy. Have anything I want to eat. Mother said you were going to have a social Thanksgiving. I calculate to come home then I think they will let me off at the restaurant. I am going to tell them I am going to come anyway. I have two tables to take care of and they keep me bobbing every second during the eating hours. They put up the best 25 cent meal in the city. Received the Ovid paper from home today. Are they having many dances around there now. Had a letter from Frank he is coming home Thanksgiving and wanted me to come home. And he would write to A Squiers and have him get the Hall and the music and we would put on a dance.

We had a Hollowen party up here last week. I didn't have a very good time as I didn't know many.

I sent grandma Oakes and grandma Smith each a card the other day and forgot to put any stamps on them so got them back yesterday. Have you heard from Harry. Send me his address if you will. Well I guess I will have to quit and go to bed as I am tired. I get tired working at the restaurant and then walking way up here, I don't feel a heck of a lot about studying. Am supposed to be on the job at 5:30 in the morning. I work from then until nearly school time, but don't have much to do after 6.45. Spend about an hour there at noon and go to work about 5 at night and work until 7 then I eat. So you see it is usually eight or after when I get up to my room. I am going to see if I can get a room nearer my work. Well my roommate is scribbling and probably will be half the night, but believe I will close.

Goodbye,
Elmer

Letter to Sister Zelma, November 21, 1916

526 W. Allegan St.

Dear Sister:

Well how are you getting along now days, and how is everybody. I am getting along with my studies all O.K.

Just received that box of good things to eat that mother sent me. Have just returned from supper so don't feel like eating it now, but it will taste pretty good a couple of hours from now. Will be glad when I come home so I can have something besides restaurant fare to eat.

Tell Ma that I thank her many times for the lunch.

I am coming thanksgiving, job or no job. But then I guess my job is safe. I spoke to them a week or two ago and told them I was coming home Thanksgiving. and they said all right. I am not worrying about my job for their is any amount of them here. I can arrange it so I get home the night before.

Hope you have a good crowd to your social. Would like to be there to attend it. Have gave that kid any more washboard rubs.

Hope their is a dance there while I am home. I haven't been to a dance since we were up to Elsie last. Don't get much chance to go any where here for every thing costs money. I take in a movie once in a while, but not very often.

There is quite a little expense here more than I imagined. I have to spend 40 to 50 cents a week for paper for school. I bought a few things in the line of wearing apparel that I could have gotten along without but as they calculate getting started the first two months is more expensive than any other two. I am figuring on saving enough from the rest to make up for it.

Was over to Slessman's Sunday, they wondered if the folks wouldn't bring me back and then come up to their place, Albert said to tell ma if they come, a dish of baked beans, seeing their were so high, would taste pretty good. They start their new house next month.

Tell Clarence & Dee they will have to let me come home and show them how to catch muskrats. I should say they were having pretty good luck catching skunks. Does Genevieve miss me yet I presume I will see some change in her when I come home. Tell her if she is a good girl I might bring her something. Is grandma Oakes coming out Thanksgiving would like to see her. I wrote her a card but haven't heard from her. Wrote a letter to Harry but haven't received any answer yet. Well it is getting late and I can't think of anymore to write about, and have some work to do besides so will close.

Goodbye,
E.O.S.

P.S. Write right back and tell me the news. Am about ready to make a raid on that box.

Letter to Mother, December 11, 1916

526 West Allegan St.

Dear Mother and all:

Well how are all the folks now. Was suprised to hear that pa was sick a bed. Hope that he will be out again. How did he get it. It was to bad about the cow. Hope that you don't have anymore bad luck.

Have fixed with my boarding job. I have to work mornings and noons and get my supper throwed in. That makes it a lot better I think. I am getting along in my studies all right. Staying out Thanksgiving put me behind a little but I am catching up. I didn't stand as good on my report card as I would of liked to. But expect to stand better this month.

You had better talk pa off the farm as quick as you can. Because he wouldn't last long if he stayed there. If you want me to come home, write and I will come at once. We may not have any room when we get back after Christmas as the landlady says we must pay for Christmas week wether we are here or not in order to hold our room. But we told her that we wouldn't do it. I won't be home until the sat. following Christmas. Saw the mailman over here today just to speak to him. Well there isn't much to write about so had better go to bed. I got out of bed to write this.

What's the matter Zelma she dosen't write. Write soon and let me know how pa and every thing else is. If you want me to come home don't be afraid to write and say so. Does Genevieve miss me. Well it's 10:30 and time I was to bed.

Good bye,
E.S.

Postcard to Mother, January 25, 1917

526 West Allegan St.

Dear Mother:

Will scribble a few lines this morning my eyes are some better but have had to give up studying nights. If i thought I could get a job for a week or so i would quit school until my eyes are better. Don't think I will stay at the restaurant very much longer. They keep putting it on to me more and more. I feel all dragged out when I get down here in the mornings. They give only 20 minutes to eat my dinner & get to school. Will write.

Good bye,
E.S.

Postcard from family friend Mrs. Curtis, February 9, 1917

Hello Elmer your Ma wanted me to let you no [know], they are all better and that your Mas [Ma's] Uncle George is dead he burnt up in his house your Ma said. Take good care of yourself Zelma is at school

Your friend,
Mrs. Curtis

Letter to Mother, February 11, 1917

Lansing Mich.

Dear Mother and all:

Well how are you getting along and how soon do you expect to be out.

I have been feeling pretty good of late an am getting along fine in school. Tell Mrs. Curtis I received her card, butt had some difficulty in placing that factory. I had to rake my brains to remember in such a city. That was to bad about uncle George. Did you hear any particulars about it. When do you expect to have your sale. Let me know and I will come home that week. I presume you haven't found a house to move into yet. When does Jap take. How is Genevieve did the vaccination make her sick? My roommate has quit Havens restaurant and has went to work at another restaurant. I don't know what he wanted it quit for he only had to work 3 hours a day. To the other place he has to work five he gets 2 dollars a week extra. But he has to be on the job at 5 o clock in the morning. Don' think he will stick to it long. Because he is always grunting around because he has to work for his board. Mrs Havens was glad to get rid of him. He sort of got the big head is making a darn fool of him self. All the help at the restaurant don't like him and have lots of fun about him. He is one of these kinds of fellows that think everything ought to come his way. He is going back to Owosso when he gets through. I told him I didn't think he could get a job. But I guess he thinks somebody is going to lay off his bookkeeper and give him the job. I don't think he will last long on any job. He has about 4 more weeks here. Will be glad when he goes too. One of the waitresses told me that Mrs Havens was going to make me a present. Some time or other. I didn't know when. She said that Mrs. Havens said that her and myself were the only ones she could depend on. Well I have written about enough for this time. So will close.

Goodbye,
Elmer

P.S. If you can find that piece in the Ford Times that you were going to send to me. Send it, I would show it to my roommate it would fit him to a T. Goodbye

Letter to Mother, March 14, 1917

514 West Allegan St.

Dear Mother and all:

Received your letter tonight and was glad to hear from you. How are you all? I am feeling fine. What are you going to do with your goods when you go up north. And how soon can you have McCreerys house. Have a new room, I am going to move Saturday. Have a roommate by the name of Fowler. Or will have when I move. It is the night chef's house. Think I will like it there, as they want you to be right at home and make use of the whole house. Why don't you if the roads are good come over here and out to Eaton Rapids while you haven't anything to do. I haven't been out to the Sleesmans since I have been back but I think I will go over next Sunday.

Well it is nearly supper time so I will have to close. My new address will be 504 S. Sycamore St. Tell Zelma to write.

Goodbye,
E.S.

Postcard to Mother, April 14, 1917

Lansing Mich.

Dear Mother and all:

How are all of you now. Haven't been feeling very well lately have had to work nearly all night at the restaurant. Frank came last fri. night and stayed until mon. noon. Am home before long. Well must close.

Good Bye,
E.S.

Postcard to Mother, April 20, 1917

407 S. Sycamore

Dear Mother and all:

How are all of you since left. Arrived here safe and sound. Did you get home without anymore blow outs.

Told Mrs. Havens tonight guess I would quit and get a day job. For I am getting sick of working nights. Can't go anywhere because it is so late when I get through work. She wants me to stay next week. I know where I can get a day job and a little a week besides. Will write a letter soon.

Goodbye,
E.S.

As the letters and postcards portray above, Elmer was a bit frustrated with the dual responsibilities of attending school while working to earn a living.

With the U.S. declaration of war in April 1917, Elmer's plans and life in Lansing would soon be placed on hold and his path changed forever. As April drew to a close he made the monumental decision to enlist in the U.S. Army and serve his country in a time of war.

NOTES

1. Michigan Public Schools, Shiawassee County, *Elmer O. Smith, Eighth Grade Graduation Diploma,* June 17, 1912.

2. Byron Farwell, *Over There: The United States in the Great War, 1917-1918* (New York: W.W. Norton and Company, 1999), 21-41.

3. Farwell, *Over There,* 31-32.

4. Thomas Boghardt, "Chasing Ghosts in Mexico: The Columbus Raid of 1916 and the Politicization of U.S. Intelligence during World War I," *Army History* (Fall 2013): 7-10.

5. Farwell, *Over There,* 33-34.

6. Farwell, *Over There,* 35-36

An American Soldier in the Great War

Chapter 1
Enlistment in Lansing, Michigan

After the U.S. declaration of war in early April 1917 and before a nationwide draft began in June 1917, many young American men felt a call to duty and enlisted in one of the branches of the Armed Services, either the U.S. Army, the U.S. Navy, or its naval land component the U.S. Marine Corps. Elmer O. Smith was one of these men. On Monday April 30, 1917, the 20 year old enlisted in Lansing into the state militia's field artillery unit, Battery B, First Battalion, Michigan Field Artillery. In letters home he provides rationale for joining this Army National Guard unit, explaining that he was better off enlisting than being drafted. He thought there was less likelihood of deploying to France and a shorter duration of service as a National Guard enlistee vice a Regular Army draftee.

The U.S. Congress passed the Selective Service Act or Selective Draft Act and on May 18, 1917, President Wilson signed it into law. Subsequently, during the war, there were three main draft registrations.[1]

- The first, on June 5, 1917, was for all men between the ages of 21 and 31.
- The second, on June 5, 1918, registered men who reached age 21 after June 5, 1917. A supplemental registration, included in this second registration, was held on August 24, 1918, for those becoming 21 years old after June 5, 1918.
- The third registration was held on September 12, 1918, for men ages 18 through 45.

In retrospect, since Elmer Smith was not yet 21 on June 5, 1917, he would not have been required to register for the draft until June of 1918 after turning 21 in March 1918. He would likely have never left the U.S. if drafted in the summer of 1918. But Elmer felt compelled to serve his country in April 1917.

This decision set him on a course to deploy to France as a U.S. Army soldier with the 119th Field Artillery Regiment, 32nd Division in early 1918.

In the first two letters below, Elmer states his reasons for enlisting vice waiting to be drafted. In the May 1st letter, he writes that by enlisting in the state National Guard he would be required to attend unit drill but otherwise be "free to do as you like in a time of peace." Perhaps this is how the Battery B recruiters or leadership helped convince him to enlist, but this was wishful thinking. This was not "a time of peace," as the U.S. had formally declared war three weeks earlier.

An increase in military preparedness throughout the U.S. started a year earlier. The National Guard Act of 1916 activated Battery B and most units of the Michigan National Guard following the Pancho Villa raid on Columbus, New Mexico in March, 1916. These units deployed to El Paso, Texas, starting in June 1916, and spent about six months performing training and garrison duties there before returning to Michigan.[2] Thus, the Michigan National Guard, headquartered in the state capital of Lansing, as well as Battery B's leadership had recent experience in recruiting and enlisting new soldiers into their ranks. In the spring of 1917 with war formally declared, Elmer Smith was one of the unit's first enlistees. Although never mentioned in his correspondence, Elmer was aware of the Lansing Battery's 1916 deployment to west Texas and as a young man was likely intrigued by their mission and activities. The Batteries A and B Michigan National Guard Drill Hall was located in downtown Lansing on the 301 block of South Capitol Avenue near its intersection with Washtenaw Avenue, quite close to where Elmer worked, lived, and went to school.[3]

Based on Elmer Smith's letters, postcards, and other documents this chapter provides a relatively accurate picture of how National Guard unit activation and mobilization proceeded until August 1917. Elmer seemed genuinely excited about being a part of his unit as it organized for war. The unit met several times a week at the Artillery Drill Hall downtown before moving to Camp Raymond Hoague in eastern Lansing, where initial drill, training, and equipping occurred when the unit was activated in July. Located on the Espanore farm, the camp was named for a Lansing soldier who had died during the Mexican border deployment.[4] A and B Batteries trained at Camp Hoague, while C Battery drilled on the grounds of the Michigan Agricultural College located a few miles further east. This school would later become Michigan State University in East Lansing.

In early July 1917, President Wilson signed an act federalizing state National Guard organizations and drafting its soldiers into the U.S. Army. Phased in over the next month, all National Guard combat units and their soldiers, henceforth, came under the formal command and control of the active Army.[5]

Letter to Mother, April 24, 1917

407 S. Sycamore St.
Lansing Mich

Dear Mother & all:

Thought I would drop you a few lines to let you know I am all right. How are all the folks. Have you had any more tire trouble.

I told you on my card that I was going to quit at Haven's. She dosen't want me to. She told Fred that she couldn't blame me for not wanting to work these warm nights. I was getting pretty sick of this night stuff. Never had a night for myself. She wants me to stay this week yet. Fred is going to his home for a couple of days and she wants me to work in his place.

Begins to look as if I would have to go to war. I hear that they are going to start drafting them, and I probably would get caught in that. I believe I would rather enlist than to be drafted in. I guess I will have to enlist or get some new clothes my coat has worn through on the elbow and my best shoes have started to come to pieces. Received a letter from Frank he expects to get that scholarship. One of the headmen of the college took him aside one day and told him that he wouldn't be surprised that he got it. So he is pretty sure of it. If he does. He will get his tuition and all his expenses paid for another year. Well it's time I was going to work. Write soon.

Goodbye,
E.S.

Letter to Mother, May 1, 1917

407 S Sycamore St.

Dear Mother and all:

How are all of you folks now days I am feeling good. Have some news for you it probably wont sound very good to any of you folks. It had to come sooner or later from the way draft system looks. I enlisted with battery B. yesterday. Took the exaimination & was sworn in last night. As for you worrying about me don't do that for I hardly think I will ever see service in France because it takes a couple of months to get the recruits in shape to send them. And besides you count on the U.S. in not sending all her men over their anyway. For they could do more by sending the Allies munitions and food. You see if I was drafted in I would have to serve 3 yrs in the regular army of continual service while in a battery you are free to do as you like in time of peace. I don't have to report only two nights a week and have the rest of the time to myself. Expect to go & drill a little tonight. But please don't worry about me.

I have a new job working in the Empress Cafe during the meal hours now. I get $2 a week besides. I got pretty sick working nights at Haven's. Mrs Havens hated to see me go she told Fred she didn't blame me for not wanting to work nights. She told me I could come back any time I wanted to.

I scrubbed a hole in the knee of my best pants last night. It was raining and I was running so as to get home. The sidewalk was slippery and I fell down on one knee. I guess I can get Mrs Harvey to fix it. Will try and come home next sat. if they will let me go at the restaurant.

Well it is getting near five o clock and must go to work. Come when you can and write soon.

Goodbye,
E.S.
Don't worry

Postcard to Mother, May 6, 1917

407 S. Sycamore St.

Dear Mother and all:

Received your card today. I am feeling pretty well. Yes I went to A.A. [Ann Arbor] and had a fine time. Frank has not enlisted. Have sent quite a little of my clothes such as handkerchiefs to laundry will send the rest home. I am planning on coming home in about 3 weeks & stay until we are called out. I wonder if I could have 5 or 6 dollars will try to make it due me through. If you haven't got it now perhaps I can make get along with out it. Well it is bed time and have got to shave. Still have to get up 4:45

Goodbye,
E.S.

Postcard to Mother, May 10, 1917

407 S. Sycamore St

Dear Mother & all:

Have a couple of minutes so will drop a line. I am feeling good for me. Don't know yet when I will be called out. Uncle Jim sent the glasses yesterday. How is all the other folks. Well its about school time so must stop write soon.

Goodbye,
E.S.

Postcard to Mother, May 14, 1917

407 S. Sycamore St

Dear Mother and all:

Will drop you a line or two this morning to let you know that I am all right. Was over to Sleesmans yesterday When are you coming over let me know.

Don't think I will be called out for a while yet. Expect my uniform this week. Bought me a new pair of shoes the other day had to give $7 for them. I couldn't get anything that looked durable for less.

Goodbye,
E.S.

Postcard to Mother, May 15, 1917

407 S. Sycamore St.

Dear Mother and all:

How are all of you. I have a hard cold don't know how I caught it. Let me know if you are coming over this week. If you don't come I may go to Ann Arbor. Come if you can.

You can send me the Ovid paper if you want to. I think I will take out a little life insurance in a little while. Write soon

Goodbye,
E.S.

Letter to Mother, May 27, 1917

407 S. Sycamore

Dear Mother & all:

Received your letter yesterday and will try to drop you a few lines.

I am feeling pretty good now days and hope you are all well.

No I am not in that section that comes to St. Johns. I have been transferred into the Battery C. until further notice. I have to report to the armory tomorrow for battery inspection. You see this new battery has to be inspected by a U.S. inspection officier before it will be accepted. If we get the battery that will make a battalion and we will be under a Major. From the way things look now I don't think we will be sent to [Camp] Grayling. From what we have been told by our captain and the way the paper we will be sent to El Paso Texas for training about the 15th of July.

Don't know when I can get home again. Say why can't Zelma come over here and stay for awhile. Sleesmans would be glad to have her come and stay with them. She could bring along a couple of quart of beans to pay for her board. Tell her to think it over.

Haven't had my second exam yet won't get that until I go into training camp. Think I will pull through it all OK. I am going to send you a sort of a picture you can pin on the wall in a few days. Well I guess I have written about all I can think of for this time. Every thing is going well at school. Write soon.

Goodbye,
E.S.

P.S. Saw H.R. Dunham a few minutes the other day. Mrs Havens has sold her feed barn.

Postcard to Mother, May 29, 1917

Dear Mother and all:

I am feeling fine and hope all of you are the same. Think I will go to Ann A this weekend. Did not go to school this after noon. Had to be a pallbearer to a funeral of a man who lived in Ovid a couple of yrs ago. Say have pa make me a sort of box about 30 x 20x 12 I will have to have one when I go away. Tell him to fix it so I can put a padlock on it. Think I can get a job doing clerical work & typewriting for our battery. I inquired last night and they said there was quite a demand for such people and I would stand a good chance.

Goodbye,
E.S.

Letter to Mother, May 29, 1917

407 S. Sycamore

Dear Mother & all:

Received your letter tonight I am feeling fine. To bad about Zelma she wants to take care of herself and not have to stay in bed too long. I dont know what that mans name is. Sheldons were not there just a few of the mourners. There was a Geo. Smith there from Ovid. Bucks had charge of the funeral and I had to ride out in their great big Owens limesouine. It is some car believe me. Nicest car I ever rode in.

Haven't sent the picture yet will try and send it tomorrow. Don't expect a picture of anything fine or of myself it isn't.

I want a sort of chest made. something like a trunk. You know how I mean. Don't care what color it is would rather have it dark I have got to have a box of some kind to put my stuff in or it will be stole. Just a box of any kind that will stand ruff use. Would like the cover lined with tin or something so if it was out in a rain it wouldn't leak through.

About the clerical job there is nothing sure about my getting it. I am going to try to see the captain tomorrow night and see what I can do. Lieut. Spencer [First Lieutenant Earl H. Spencer, Battalion Adjutant (Personnel Officer); he was promoted to Captain on June 12, 1917] told me the other night I could get in on it he thought. They got to have them. Don't know what pay I would get. The job would mean all the while the army was in service. You see I probably would not have much guard duty to do and real fighting if any. Wont know if I get it until we go into training camp.

I am going Ann Arbor Sat morning [June 2]. When are you folks coming over. I presume Sleesmans are looking for you ever Sat. How is Dee, Clarence & Genevieve. Well I must study a little and then go to bed.

Goodbye,
Elmer

Postcard to Mother, unknown date, on or about June 2, 1917

407 S. Sycamore Lansing

Dear Mother and all:

Received your letter a few minutes ago. I received my washing O.K. Did not go to Ann Arbor & don't know when I will. I get 90 some cents for every drill night.

Had to come to the room this noon to change my shoes. The rubber is all coming off of one and have got to have them half soled. I went in to see how much it would be and they $1.25. Don't know when I will be home again my job holds me down more than my other one. All that was why I didn't get to A.A. [Ann Arbor] What seems to be the trouble with Zelma. Tell Zelma I want another picture of Pete.

Goodbye,
E.S.

Postcard to Mother, June 12, 1917

407 S. Sycamore

Dear Mother & all:

Will drop you a few lines this morning. Received the money all right. Wouldn't be surprised then I would be home next week. If you folks want to come over here why don't you wait and come some Fri. You see I will have to be here every Fri. night & Sun for drills. Did not get the Battery job. Well I am going to eat my breakfast. Write soon.

Goodbye,
Elmer

Postcards to Mother, June 20, 1917

407 S. Sycamore St.

Dear Mother and all:

Will drop a few lines this morning to let you know I am well. Expected to be home in a day or to but they want me to stay at the restaurant until Sat. as I have drill Sun morn and Mon. night I might as well stay until Tues. A fellow can't quit at one of these d--m restaurants unless he gets fired. Why can't you folks come over Sat. then I can ship my trunk back by you. I am going to have my picture taken this morning.

Goodbye,
E.S.

P.S. Have just had my picture taken. Will have to have some money to settle for them.

Wed. P.M.

Dear Mother & all:

Will drop you a line to let you that I may be home tomorrow night. They have a waitress coming and if she is satisfactory will be there. Will get the pictures when I come over again.

Goodbye,
E.S.

Postcards from friend Frank Nethaway, July 5, 1917

Postmark July 5, 1917, 12:12PM

Greetings Bob [Elmer]:

Your last postcard at hand this afternoon. Its' rather late to pospone my trip out as I can't get away next week end before sat. night. Have written to the boys & Archie that I will be out tomorrow night. Would like to see you at Carland tomorrow night. Think it over. See if you can't be at home also on sat. & sunday. Well must hop out and mail this. Hope to see you tomorrow.

Frank

Postmark July 5, 1917, 3:00 PM

Dear Fuzzie [Elmer]

Am coming out friday night. I hope there is a dance. If there isn't, let's go cooning [raiding for] watermelons.

Yours,
Frank

Letter to Mother, July 9, 1917

Mon. eve. Camp Raymond Hoague
Lansing Mich.

Dear Mother & all:

Will drop you a few lines this evening. We aren't straightened out yet haven't done much today received my equipment but not my uniform. I presume we will begin tomorrow and it will begin to get a little stiffer each day. Say send an old blue shirt or some other dark colored shirt for this one will soon get dirty. I did not have to come out to camp last so stayed with Lamour Paraby. When you address my letter send it to Battery B First Mich. Field Art. Lansing.

Well can't think of anything more to write about so will close. Write soon.

Goodbye,
Elmer

Letter to Mother, July 12, 1917

Postmark July 16, 1917
Camp Hoague
Thurs. July12

Dear Mother and all:

Received my shirt OK but did not get any letter. I like it all right, get good grub to eat and have lots of fun. It seems more like going out on a camping party. We had drill today for the first time. It has been so wet we couldn't do anything. Set the tents up in the mud so went to bed in a pretty nasty place. We each have cots to sleep on. There is ten fellows in our tent I have been assigned as cannoneer. I don't know wether we will go to [Camp] Grayling or not. A lieutenant told us this afternoon we would go to Waco Tex.

We have our federal physical exaim's tomorrow, so will know wether I stay or go. Received my uniform but not a hat or any leggins so can't wear it. Well its getting dark so will close. Are you coming over Sunday you probably saw the visiting hrs. in the State Journal. Well will close.

Goodbye,
Elmer

Letter to Mother, July 23, 1917

Postmark July 24, 1917
Camp Hoague
July 23, 17

Hello everybody:

How are you all these hot days. Just received your card today. Looked for you yesterday. Glen & Ross and the girls were here yesterday. There was about two thousand here yesterday The Reo band gave a concert. Well will have to close for a little while as I have to go to do stables.

Well will finish as I didn't have to do stables because I go on Guard tonight. Passed the physical exaim. All right. Had my vaccination and a shot of typhus in my arm this morning. So expect to be a little sick.

Say I wonder if you would lend me $5 until pay day. Then take it out of what I send home I get $5 a mo. extra as I take care of the Lieut. horse. The visiting hrs. are 2 until 8 Sundays & two hrs. at night. Well come over when you can. Don't know when we leave here.

Goodbye,
Elmer

Postcard to Mother, August 8, 1917

Camp Hoague
Aug. 8, 17

Hello everyone:

Got here all right Sun night. And haven't broke camp yet I doubt if they do this week. We had the hardest rain I have ever seen this year here yesterday. I haven't seen grandma. If I knew where she was would go & see her. I am on guard tonight and tomorrow. Well this is all for this time.

Goodbye,
Elmer

Postcard to Mother, Aug 10, 1917

Camp Hoague

Hello everybody:

Received your card. Wouldn't wonder if we moved from here in a few days our clothes & equipment arrived today. I have been feeling good. Have you had much rain out there we have had a lot here. Well will close for this time.

Goodbye,
Elmer

Letter to Mother, August 13, 1917

Camp Hoague
Aug. 13, 17

Hello everybody:

How are you all. I am feeling fine. Did you go to South Lyons.

I think we will leave here sometime this week. We have received all our equipment so there is nothing holding us here. We had a large crowd here yesterday and had another review.

The Home Guards and the Industrial boys with their band & the Old soldiers also marched. There was an awful crowd. It started to rain so we got a little wet.

They have been drilling us hard and getting pretty strict. One fellow got a day of hard work for digging his ear in the ranks. Well I can't think of anything to write, a new fellow in our tent is talking like the devil, can't think of any thing. We has got another wind jammer in here and I guess they are trying to see if they can't compress enough wind to blow the tents off the stacks. Just heard we are not to go to Grayling to Texas instead I don't know wether there is anything in it or not. Well must close.

Goodbye,
Elmer

Letter to Mother, August 16, 1917

Typed on The Young Men's Christian Association (YMCA) Letterhead with notation:
CAMP RAYMOND HOAGUE
LANSING, MICHIGAN
Aug 16, 1917

Hello Everybody:

Received your letter yesterday was glad to hear from you. Glad you had a nice time on your trip to South Lyons. We received word tonight that we were to start loading in the morning, So we will get out of here tomorrow sometime. I don't know where we are going but probably to Grayling. The three batteries attended the funeral of the fellow that was shot at East Lansing. It made a hike for us of about seven miles so am a little tired. Well it isn't but a few minutes before retreat & am in a hurry so I can't think of much to write. I am going to take some clothes down & keep in my chest tonight that I don't want to take with me. Well must close as I must go, will write again as soon as I can.

Goodbye,
Elmer

Excerpt from "A Brief History of the 119th Field Artillery"

August 17, 1917, was a memorable day. The morning was spent in breaking camp and in cleaning and repairing equipment, the afternoon in saying "good-by" and that evening, amid cheers, sobs and salutations from over 20,000 men, women and children, the Lansing batteries departed from the city at 9:05 on a special train via the Michigan Central. They arrived at Camp Grayling on the morning of August 18th.

NOTES

1. Colonel Leonard P. Ayres, *The War With Germany: A Statistical Summary* (Washington: Government Printing Office, 1919), 17-19.
   Byron Farwell, *Over There: The United States in the Great War, 1917-1918* (New York: W.W. Norton and Company, 1999), 50-51.

2. Colonel Chester B. McCormick, "A Brief History of the 119th Field Artillery," *Honor Roll and Complete War History of Ingham County in the Great World War: 1914-1918* (Lansing MI: The State Journal Company, 1920), 219-220.
   Farwell, *Over There*, 27, 38.
   Captain Bruce Jacobs, "Three Centuries of Service: The National Guard in War and Peace," *The Dedication of the National Guard Memorial* (1959), 26-29.

3. Library of Michigan, Michigan Documents, *Downtown Lansing, Michigan Plot Map* includes location and layout of the Batteries A and B, Michigan National Guard Drill Hall, circa 1915.

4. McCormick, 219.

5. Woodrow Wilson, President of the United States of America, *Call into Federal Service and Draft of the National Guard* (Washington: July 3, 1917). McCormick, 219.

Chapter 2
Mobilization at Camp Grayling, Michigan

ON AUGUST 18, 1917, PRIVATE E.O. SMITH and Battery B along with several other federalized Michigan National Guard units arrived via train at Camp Grayling from Lansing for mobilization and training. Originally called Camp Ferris when it opened in 1915, Camp Grayling was a Michigan National Guard training post approximately 150 miles north of Lansing in the northern portion of the state's Lower Peninsula. It continues to be the state's primary field training reservation today.[1]

As part of the federalization process, Battery B, First Battalion, Michigan Field Artillery was officially mustered into the Regular Army on August 5, 1917. In mid-September it became part of the newly formed 119th Field Artillery (FA) Regiment. Other Michigan militia units, including the state's Cavalry Squadron, also were subsumed into the 119th FA.[2]

The 119th FA Regiment was organized into eight companies—a headquarters company, a supply company, and six firing batteries lettered A through F. The battery was the Field Artillery equivalent of a company-sized element. Throughout the rest of the Army, a unit this size was called a company. The Cavalry also differed, calling a company-sized unit a troop. The Regimental Band was part of the 119th FA's Supply Company[3]

B Battery consisted of the following key personnel. It was commanded by a Battery Commander, a Captain (CPT). Initially this was CPT Joseph H. Lewis. The remaining commissioned officers were two First Lieutenants and two Second Lieutenants. The senior Non-Commissioned Officer (NCO) was the First Sergeant (1SG), often called "Top," initially filled by Sergeant Joseph Redner. The Battery also had a Supply Sergeant, a Stable Sergeant, a Mess (Food) Sergeant, and a Chief Mechanic. Other specialty soldiers included buglers, saddlers, mechanics, and cooks. But the majority of B Battery soldiers were the men who manned the artillery sections and individual howitzers. Led by Sergeants, these sections included Corporals, Privates First Class, and Privates.[4]

Private Smith was initially assigned to B Battery. In January 1918, he transferred to Headquarters (HQs) Company which planned and supervised all operations within the regiment. The 119th FA was slated to be equipped with 75mm pack howitzers but did not receive these light artillery pieces until it arrived in France. Each firing battery had four howitzers—two sections with two howitzers each. Thus, a total of 24 howitzers were assigned to the 119th FA Regiment. The mission of the 75mm howitzer regiments was to provide direct support (DS) fires for infantry brigades and other ground maneuver units in direct contact with the enemy.[5]

The 119th FA was commanded by Colonel (COL) Chester B. McCormick of Lansing. At the start of the war he was a Major (MAJ) commanding First Battalion, Michigan Field Artillery, as it was mobilized. COL McCormick was a stellar commander leading the artillery unit throughout the war including its extensive training regimen and five months of sustained combat. In May 1919 he brought the unit back to Michigan. Because the majority of the unit's original soldiers came from the capital area, the 119th FA was termed "Lansing's Own." [6]

On the following page is a short primer on the ranks and organization of the U.S. Army during World War I.[7]

U.S. Army Ranks of World War I. From lowest to highest, the rank structure for the U.S. Army generally followed the below construct except for certain technical specialists in each of the Army branches/corps.

Enlisted Soldiers Ranks

(Corporals and above are Non-commissioned Officers)

PVT: Private

PFC: Private First Class

CPL: Corporal

SGT: Sergeant

1SG: First Sergeant

SM: Sergeant Major

Commissioned Officer Ranks

2LT: Second Lieutenant

1LT: First Lieutenant

CPT: Captain

MAJ: Major

LTC : Lieutenant Colonel

COL: Colonel

BG: Brigadier General

MG: Major General

LTG: Lieutenant General

GEN: General

U.S. Army Organizational Structure. Although slightly different within each functional branch, the general structure of the U.S. Army from the smallest echelon to the largest command headquarters employed to conduct combat operations is delineated below with applicable abbreviations.

Echelons
Lowest to Highest:

Team (TM)/Crew
Squad (SQD)/Section
Platoon (PLT)
Company (CO)/Battery (Btry)/Troop (TRP)
Battalion (BN)/Squadron (SQDN)
Regiment (RGT or Regt)
Brigade (BDE)
Division (DIV)
Corps
Army

The following letters portray the experiences of Private Smith and his unit at Camp Grayling conducting field training activities in preparation for combat operations.

Letter to Mother, August 19, 1917

Mobilization Camp Grayling
Aug. 19, 17

Hello everybody:

Well how are you all. I am feeling fine altho am quite tired as have been rastling with boxes and baggage since yesterday morning. We got here all right about seven thirty mon. We haven't got straightened around yet. It is a hilly sand country up here with lots of pine trees stumps and brush. I like it first rate for a change. We are situated just a little ways from Portage Lake. It is a nice lake they say it is 60 miles around the beach. It dosen't look it altho it is quite a big lake. There is an animal reserve park right across the road from us. Saw 5 deer and two large elk when going swimming last night. Didn't rest good when coming up here we had a couch to ride on. We tore up the cushions and made beds of them. I don't think we will be here much over two weeks if that. Battery C goes this week to Waco.

Well will close for this time. Have some clothes to wash today if have time. Write soon.

Goodbye, Elmer

P.S. My address is
Battery B. 1st Mich. F.A. Grayling, Mich.

Letter to Mother, August 24, 1917

Mobilization Camp Grayling
Aug. 24

Hello everybody:

I received your card yesterday & it is funny you didn't get my letter for I wrote you one & sent mon. morning. I am feeling fine. We had hard rainstorms yesterday & is drizzling away this morning. The nights are pretty chilly. Don't think we will go south for awhile. We are going to put our stove in this morning. Well write soon.

Goodbye,
Elmer

Letter to Mother, August 26, 1917

Mobilization Camp

Dear Mother & all:

Well how are you all now days. I am feeling good. Received my apples and papers all right. Was tickled to get them. The apples didn't last long in this place. They were a treat to everybody.

Have received my pay for July. We get payed again the first of next month. Am going to try to send most of it home. Won a saftey razor on a raffle the other day. Am going to send it home to pa. It is supposed to be a pretty good razor it is a Gillete. Only put 15 cents into it.

Received a card from Ross yesterday. He says his girl has left him and he was feeling pretty bad. He said he would come up if he had a

Ford. His cousin from Jackson was over the other night. He seems like a nice fellow. Expect the Governor to be in camp this afternoon so expect to have a review. Was over to the signal tower the other night it sits on a high hill you can see all over the lake and country. You can't see anything but high hills. It has been pretty cold and has been raining for the last three days. We had a few snow flakes yesterday morning, I don't know what we will do if it wasn't for our stoves. Well I must close. Hope to hear from you soon.

Goodbye,
Elmer

Letter to Mother, September 5, 1917

War Work Council
Army and Navy Young Men's Christian Association
"With The Colors"
Grayling, Mich.

Dear Mother & all:

Will drop you a few lines tonight. Started a letter the other day but didn't finish it. Have a cold in my head don't know I caught it.

We haven't had any drill since sat. We never have any sat. & sun and not any today because it is Labor Day. We had drill this morning to see which was the best Battery. This afternoon we had swimming, wrestling on horse back, tug of war and a number of events. Our Battery was in last place after the points were all summed up. Received my apples and was glad to receive them. Was glad to hear that Zelma got her job. I think she will like bookkeeping. I think pa should give up working on the machines. Don't know what kind of stuff there is in that razor, but don't think it cost more than $6.

Would like to have you folks come up if you could. It would be best if you started so as to be here sun. morning. If you could come a week from sun. it would be most convenient for me. Expect to be on guard next sun. It probably would take a day and a half of good driving to get here. One of the fellow's brothers in this tent came by auto today. He said the road was awful sandy.

Was out exercising horses this morning. Rode one and led the other. Went on a ride way back in the hills. Didn't have a saddle or any blanket so am lame and have two nice little sores.

We received some nice sweaters from the Red Cross of Lansing. They are hand knitted without sleeves or collars. They are made the same as a jersey otherwise, put them under our shirts and keeps us warm as can be. Well must close & go to bed as it is getting late. Come up if you can.

Goodbye,
Elmer

Postcard to Mother, September 10, 1917

Grayling, Mich.

Hello everybody:

Received the apples and your card O.K. The apples were fine but didn't last long in this crowd. It's funny you didn't get my letter sent you one week ago today. Still have a cold. I think we will leave sometime the first of next week. Most of the other camps have had orders to leave this week. Are you folks coming up. Expect payday any time. Well must quit.

Goodbye,
Elmer

Letter to Sister, September 12, 1917

Grayling, Mich.

Dear Sister:

Received your letter yesterday. and was glad to hear from you. I am kind of stiff and sore tonight have been on a fifteen mile hike. We started out 9 this morning. About eleven we pitched our pup tents. You see each man has half a tent which he uses to roll his blankets in, while on the march. When we pitch two men have a half tent and they are stiched together. They are open on one end and just large enough for two. Well when we got them pitched the two of us made a small fire place to cook our meat and potatoes. We were given two raw potatoes three onions three pieces of bacon and three slices of bread and also some coffee and sugar.

First we got a cup of water and put coffee and sugar in it and put it on to boil. Next we put our bacon in our meat pan to fry. We sliced our potatoes & onions and when the bacon was done we put the potatoes in and fried them. When they were done we had dinner. believe it tasted the best of any meal I have eaten since I have been in camp. We camped about two hours & then struck our tents & started on. We camped near a old house that three years ago they fired on with a shrapnal shell. The distance was 4400 yds. It tore it up some.

Was out on Equitation yesterday. Am learning more about horses sinse I have been in the army than I ever knew before.

Well must close & go to supper. Will resume after eating boiled potatoes, tough steak, sweet corn bread & gravy. Don't think we will leave this week. You see we are the First M.F.A. [still stating he is part of the First Michigan Field Artillery not yet the 119th FA Regiment] and are not in any regiment like the 31st & 32nd [Infantry Regiments].

I am glad you like your work. I don't know wether any my books would help you out a lot if you think they will help yourself.

Well it's almost time for Retreat so must close. If the folks come and you get the letter in time send your camera and some films, will write soon.

Goodbye,
Elmer

Letter to Mother, September 16, 1917

Grayling Camp

Hello everybody:

Received the card & the box yesterday. Was disappointed to hear that you people couldn't come. The plums were fine and went like fire.

Am sending some pictures & five dollars home. Intended to send more money home but owed ten dollars to the canteen & had to pay for the pictures. Also had to send Frank four& one half dollars for my share in the camera we got together and thought I would keep a little to have on the way down south. That will make five dollars more I owe you & and probably will be able to send a quite a little more home next pay day. We spent quite a little at the canteen for candy and & ice cream &etc. For we don't get as much sweet stuff in our meals here as we do in civil life & seem to have more of crave for sweets. Hour meals here are fair. Sometimes we get a good feed & sometimes a rotten one. For breakfast we generally get 2 slices bread 1 spoonful of potatoes some oatmeal without milk& and not much sugar & a cup of coffee. For dinner we get as a rule bread some sort of cheap pudding potato gravey & some kind of meat. For supper we get about the same as for dinner.

Frank is in Calumet working as a common laborer. Shoveling mud & doing all sorts of work. These pictures are of our section altho they aren't all there. The four are of a ball game between the batteries. Two are of guard mount which takes place everyday. One is of inspection of the guard & the other is after inspection & marching guard up to the guardhouse to relieve the old guard. The other one is of the camp. The two big ones are of the battery & the entire camp.

Don't know when we leave, But probably some time this week. It was rumored a few days ago we were to pack up tomorrow but know we won't. We don't until after the 32nd.

One of the fellows came in and said the 32nd [Infantry Regiment] had just left. So we probably will go as soon as we get cars to carry us.

[Not Signed]

Letter to Mother, September 21, 1917

Grayling, Mich.

Dear Mother and all:

Received your letter yesterday & was glad to hear from you. How is the weather down there. The days here are fine but the nights are cold. We haven't had any rain for a long time.

Received them plums on Sun. They were certainly fine. Don't get much fruit. Our meat isn't of the best or anything else for that matter. Have put in application for a pass to Grayling tomorrow night. Am going to try & have something real to eat. Am on kitchen police today. Have to wash dirty dishes and up around the kitchen.

Frank didn't come up this way he took the boat from Detroit. He is coming back this way so will probably see him if we are here a week or more. We had made plans on buying a camera before I was called out. I expect him to send it most any day. He is to let me have it where ever I go to get views. So probably will have it till I get out of the army.

Don't know when we will go. I hear sorts of rumors. But don't any them come true. Well it is nearly mess time & must get back to the kitchen. Well will try and finish altho this Sat. morning. Have just had our weekly inspection. We have to move our cots out & line them up in the streets. Our blankets, haversacks, overcoats, slickers, mess kit, & clean clothing have to be arranged just so. If there is anything dirty found we have to clean it up and get confined to camp for ten days, Have escaped so far.

We have quite a few prisoners in the guard house. Some went to sleep on post, some were caught with booze, some went without leave of absence. They don't have any privilages & have all the hard work to do. At no time are they allowed to rest during working hours. Every night when they go to the guard house, every thing is taken away from them, including matches & tobacco. They are worse off than slaves.

Have just heard that we are to move Mon. or Tues. I wouldn't wonder but what we will.

There is a pretty good bunch of fellows in our tent. We have some great times. Have lots of chewing matches & call each other all kinds of names we can think of. Haven't had a fight yet. Well have wrote about all I can think of so will quit for this time.

Goodbye,
Elmer

Letter to Mother, September 26, 1917

Grayling, Mich.

Dear Mother:

I received your letter this forenoon & was glad to hear from you. Have been on guard every since last night. Guarded the officiers mess hall last night & prisoners this forenoon and so have this afternoon off.

The wind has been blowing awful hard all day. Probably will get a hard rain. We will leave for Waco sometime Fri. forenoon. We have most every thing loaded and are waiting for the coaches. We will probably pull through Owosso late fri. afternoon or early Fri. night. But won't stop. If we did we wouldn't be allowed to get off the train. I think I will enjoy the trip all O.K.

Their is seven other fellows in my tent. Is supposed to ten.

I don't know if there is anything you can send me unless it is a small old pillow when I get south. Something that isn't any good. I am sorry to hear that things on the farm isn't turning out good. What are you thinking of doing another year. How is Zelma getting along with her job. And how much salary does she get. I was surprised to hear that Vern has a girl. Gee! I'll bet she looks like the wrath of gods. Was up to Grayling last Sun. afternoon to ballgame between a battery and the ambulance corp.

Well don't know what to write about, can probably write a longer letter when I get south. Well will quit I guess and write more next time to make up for this time.

Goodbye,
Elmer

NOTES

1. *Welcome to Camp Grayling: 1949 Field Training* (Lansing MI: Adjutant Generals Office, Michigan National Guard, 1949).
   Michigan National Guard, Field Training Sites, Camp Grayling (Lansing MI: Library of Michigan Archives, 1958).

2. Colonel Chester B. McCormick, "A Brief History of the 119th Field Artillery," *Honor Roll and Complete War History of Ingham County in the Great World War: 1914-1918* (Lansing MI: The State Journal Company, 1920), 219.
   The Thirty Second Division, American Expeditionary Forces, 1917-1919 (Coblenz Germany: YMCA, 1919), 5-6.

3. McCormick, 219.

4. Captain Joseph H. Lewis, *Roster, Battery "B," 119th U.S. F.A., 57th Brigade, 32nd Division* (Waco TX: 1917)

5. McCormick, 219.

6. McCormick, 219-221.

7. "History of U.S. Army Ranks," The Institute of Heraldry, U.S. Army, accessed December 29, 2013, http://www.tioh.hqda.pentagon.mil/Catalog/HeraldryMulti.aspx.
   Paul J. Schultz, Hayes Otoupalik, Dennis Gordon, *World War One Collectors Handbook, Volumes 1 and 2* (GOS Publishing, January 1, 1988), 11.

Chapter 3
Training at Camp MacArthur, Texas

At the end of September 1917, the 119th FA Regiment, along with the rest of the 32nd Division units still at Camp Grayling, loaded their equipment and belongings on trains bound for Camp MacArthur, Texas. The camp located outside the city of Waco, was named for General Arthur MacArthur, a Civil War, Indian Wars, and Philippine-American War veteran and the father of General Douglas MacArthur.[1]

The first phase of the artillery unit's training for war was completed and another more intense and focused regimen of field training was about to begin. Elmer Smith observed the countryside during his three-day journey south across the U.S. heartland and kept a map of the railroad route to Texas.[2] It was likely the first time Elmer Smith had been outside of Michigan.

Training at Camp MacArthur was realistic and often difficult. Long foot marches with full packs of equipment were the norm to harden the men for the austere conditions they would encounter in combat. Since the majority of the 32nd Division units were at Camp MacArthur, collective training and planning as a team commenced.

The 32nd Division and its subordinate units trained at Camp MacArthur for nearly five months. The Division was organized with two infantry brigades, an artillery brigade, and divisional troops, as follows: [3]

The 63rd Infantry Brigade, consisting of the:

- 125th Infantry Regiment
- 126th Infantry Regiment
- 120th Machine-Gun Battalion

The 64th Infantry Brigade, consisting of the:

- 127th Infantry Regiment
- 128th Infantry Regiment
- 121st Machine-Gun Battalion

One Artillery Brigade, the 57th Field Artillery Brigade, consisting of the:

- 119th Field Artillery Regiment (Twenty four 75-mm guns)
- 120th Field Artillery Regiment (Twenty four 75-mm guns)
- 121st Field Artillery Regiment (Twenty four 155-mm howitzers)
- 107th Trench Mortar Battery (Twelve 6-inch trench mortars)

Divisional Troops, consisting of the:

- 119th Machine-Gun Battalion
- 107th Engineer Regiment
- 107th Field Signal Battalion
- Headquarters Troop
- Trains (Logistics support)

The division organization reflected the major changes the U.S. Army made to its structure at the outset of the war. Entering an ongoing war caused the Army to quickly adapt its structure to Allied lessons and the emerging impacts of 20th Century technology. The U.S. Army rapidly evolved into a modern military with two main characteristics distinguishing it from its previous state—the significant increase in combat support organizations and the instituting of staffs at tactical levels.[3]

U.S. Army Branches, Corps, and Related Functional Organizations of World War I

The below organizations were the primary elements responsible for the complex functional requirements essential to operate and sustain the AEF in France. Many had long been part of the U.S Army but several were new functions based on the exigencies of modern warfare.[4]

Adjutant General's Corps: Personnel and administration support

Antiaircraft Service: AEF unit formed to protect ground forces from air attack and observation

Army Air Service: Aviation to support ground operations and counter enemy air activity

Cavalry: Horse-mounted maneuver operations including reconnaissance

Chaplain Corps: Religious services, counseling, and moral support

Chemical Warfare Service: Support to defensive and offensive gas operations

Coastal Artillery Corps: Responsible for coastal and harbor defense

Corps of Engineers: Military construction and mobility/counter-mobility support to operations

Corps of Intelligence Police: Counterintelligence (CI) and counter-espionage activities

Corps of Interpreters: Language translation functions for all Army requirements

Field Artillery: Fire support to ground maneuver operations and counterfire missions

Infantry: Dismounted ground maneuver operations

Inspector General: Inspections and audit of unit missions

Judge Advocate General: Military legal actions

Medical Corps: Medical support from field and fixed site hospitals

Military Intelligence Division: Intelligence collection, analysis, and CI activities

Motor Transport Corps: Truck mounted movement of soldiers and supplies

Ordnance Department: Arms, ammunition, and weaponry-related equipment

Provost Marshal: Military law enforcement and police functions

Quartermaster Corps: Logistics and supply support

Services of Supply: The primary AEF logistics organization that fed, clothed, moved, equipped, and maintained the combat forces at the front

Signal Corps: Communications equipment and support

Tank Service: Tank-mounted support to ground maneuver operations

General Staff

Based on French and British Army models, the U.S. Army for the first time in its history instituted formal staff organizations at tactical levels during World War I. The purpose of the new staff organization was to support unit commander requirements in key functional areas. Modern warfare had evolved to the point where subject matter experts were necessary to manage the substantial amount of information and specific actions required to operate and sustain dynamic military operations in combat.

Each U.S. Army headquarters at battalion and above assigned staff officers to lead the functional requirements of the unit. At the battalion, regimental, and brigade level the sections supporting these functions were termed "S" for staff with the S-1 (Personnel and Administration), S-2 (Intelligence), S-3 (Operations and Plans), and S-4 (Logistics) known as the primary staff. These staff sections were led by the unit's second-in-command termed either the Executive Officer or Deputy Commander.

At the Division and above level the functional elements were known collectively as the General Staff under the direction of the Chief of Staff. G-1, G-2, G-3, and G-4 sections were responsible for the same functional areas as those in lower echelon "S" Staff counterparts. This facilitated improved inter-staff coordination and collaboration with lower, higher, and adjacent headquarters to address commander and unit mission requirements.

The U.S. military staff model has continued to evolve over the past century to support Service, Joint Services, and Coalition commanders.[5]

This chapter captures the significant amount of tactical training the artillery units underwent as part of the 32nd Division team training at Camp MacArthur prior to deploying to France. It includes the letters Private Smith wrote during the months of October through December 1917.

Letter to Mother, October 1, 1917

[On YMCA letterhead]
Sat. P.M. 1917

Dear Mother & all:

Will try to drop you a few lines. The train jiggles so I can hardly do anything at all. That sack was certaintly a treat & we ate out of it all the way to Lansing. Stoped in Lansing for about 15 minutes. Saw several

I knew. After we left Lansing went to sleep and woke in Michigan City Ind. We had breakfast at Hammond just outside of Chicago. pulled into Chicago about 10 o'clock. We were there until about 3 this afternoon. We are now on the Santa Fe heading southwest out of Chicago. The crops look here about the same as they do in Mich, only every thing looks greener. We are now in some city taking on water. One of the fellows just said it was Springfield. Will write another letter later. Don't know I will get this mailed as we aren't allowed off the train.

Goodbye,
E.S.

Postcard to Sister Zelma, October 1, 1917

[Postcard picture with caption—Santa Fe Passenger Station, Emporia, Kansas]

Hello:

I am feeling fine & enjoying trip great. We have just crossed the boundry Olkaholma & Texas. Expect to arrive at Waco some time tonight.We stoped at this city for exercise & eats.

Goodbye,
E.S.

Letter to Family, October 2, 1917

Postmark Oct. 4, 1917 12:00 P.M.
Camp McArthur Waco, Tex.

Hello everybody:

Well we all arrived here this morning about five o'clock. Enjoyed my journey fine. Most all the country was nice farming country and also saw a few cattle ranches in southern Oklahoma and northern Texas. most of the land in Illnois, Missouri & Kansas is devoted to corn raising. Oklahoma & Texas it is all cotton, they plant some corn but it never amounts to much.

We passed through the coal fields in southern Illnois & the oil fields in southern Kansas. We stopped at several places on the way for eats and exercise. Stopped in Claburn, Tex. last night for about five hours and was allowed to go up into town. The people seem to be about the same as the northern people but talk a lot different. The country around here is slightly rolling. Altho some of the land I saw is so flat you can see twelve & fifteen miles. Our camp is situated in sort of a grove. So you see we will have some shade. We have our own shower baths which are certainly fine. The water is something we have to learn to like. There is quite a little alkali in it. In pitching our tents we had to grub a hole before we could get our stakes in. The first 5 or 6 inches is a thin black dirt, below that it is rock. The days are not sultry but just warm enough to make you sweat good. There is always a breeze blowing. If get real hot and get in the shade you will soon cool off & comence to get cold. We have to guard against one thing and that is catching cold and letting it turn into pneumonia. A person that gets that in this country must make his will in short order.

We are now in a regiment of artillery. Three comps of Mich. cavalery have been made into Artillery. I think they are from Grand Rapids. Expect we will get the six inch howitzer in the course of months, so that will make us heavy artillery.

I am enclosing a map of our route. All the crosses are where we made stops. Well I am so tired I can't think of much to write. I have been working hard all day. It's kind of hard to realize that I am in Texas. My address is, Bat. B. 119th F.A., Camp McArthur, Waco, Tex.

Will write soon.

Goodbye,
Elmer Smith

Letter to Mother, October 10, 1917

Waco, Tex.

Dear Mother & all:

Will drop you a few lines tonight. I am feeling fine. Have been looking for your letter but haven't heard from you yet.

We are kept busy drilling & are made to buckle into it hard. The only time we get to ourselves are the nights. It is pretty hot during the middle of the day around about ninety five & a hundred in the shade. Last Sun. noon it stood about ninety five & mon. noon about ninety.

Mon. night was the coldest night at this time of year they had had for twenty seven years. I signed up for two fifty dollar liberty bonds tonight. We are to pay five dollars for each every month. Thats about the only way you can save up anything here. I was down town last night. The first time since I came. We are allowed to go down any night as long as we are in camp by eleven o clock. There has been a case of diptheria in A battery. So they were quarantined in. They shut the whole battalion up at first, but we were allowed to go later.

They have started a French Class at the Y.M.C.A. and I am going to take it up. We have band concerts three nights a week.

How is Genevieve and the boys. How are things on the farm & what are you thinking of doing another year. I may come bak on the farm until Clarence gets big enough to work it. When I get out of the army. Well I am going to the french class and will finish afterwards.

Well I will finish. I have been to the French class & also to the picture show. They show some just as good pictures that you would want to see. Well its pretty hard for me to think of anything to write. I was out on quite a long horseback ride this morning. I like that part of it. Will be glad when I get the camera for I can take some interesting pictures around here. Tell Zelma I will write to her if I get time but would like to have a letter from her.

Well must close as it is getting late and must go to bed. Write soon.

Goodbye,
E.S.

Letter to Sister, October 14, 1917

Waco, Tex.

Dear Sister:

I received your letter the other day & was glad to hear from you. Am glad you like your job. Is it hard work for you and how is your health.

Yes I can remember most of the sights coming down here. Especially the Miss. river. We crossed it about midnight, as their was a full moon I had a good view. It was about a mile wide where we crossed it.

It is hot here some days and cool others. It is about the same on sea level as Mich. Yes you can notice the heat here altho I don't think so much as in Mich.

That was a Perry boy that was in the car window with me that night we came through Owosso.

Tell mother that she needn't worry about me, for I am attending to my business. I hope they catch them fellows that deserted from Camp Custer and give them all they deserve. A bawling out is something we get a dozen times a day. I have been lucky so far and have had nothing above a corporal & a sergerent bawl me out. Also have been able to keep out of the akward squad. We have a new set of officiers to drill us for a while and they don't as much as any of our serganents do. I guess they are some from the officiers training school, any way their isn't any body any use for them. Frank did not get to Grayling. He came through there the same day we left.

Got another shot in the arm this afternoon that that make about five all together. Consquently it is swollen and pretty sore tonight.

Received a letter from Frank today & also from Lulu Sepior. Well must close as I want to take in the movie at the Y. I don't know what we would do if it wasn't for the Y.M.C.A. Write soon.

Goodbye,
Elmer

Letter to Mother, October 20, 1917

[Y.M.C.A. Letterhead]
Waco, Tex.

Dear Mother & all:

I received your letter the other day and haven't had time to answer it. I don't have anytime to write except nights and so far when I have been at the Y. every writing bench has been filled up. Will try to write a little tonite altho I have quite a painful arm. The batry. received another shot of para-typhoid today.

I received the pillow and papers alright. I was glad to receive the pillow but didn't dream that it would cost so much to send it. What did you put that letter in the paper for. If I knew you were going to do that I would of used my grammer a little more. If I knew you were going to do it I would of arranged it so it would of sounded a little better. Let me know when you want to put another one in.

How is pa and what is he working at. I hope Clarence likes his job delivering papers as it will help him learn what business is. I received a letter from Frank today. He is back to Ann Arbor buckling to it again. I also received a card from V. Easlick.

That paper that I am sending to you, I subscribed for. I get it for three months for a dollar. They are giving us a hard schedule of drill here. We have an hour and a half for class and five classes a day. We get up at 5:30 and stand reveille, have mess at 6:00 and go to drill at seven. We have from 11:30 to 1:00 for mess and rest, and then drill until four. At five mess and at 5:30 Retreat. So as you see we are busy all day. We probably will be here until Feb. first.

Well I can't think of much more to write now and they are going to have a movie here in a few minutes so will close and try to write again in a couple of days. Let me know how everybody are around there and tell them to drop me a line when they have time. I always feel disappointed when the mail comes in and I don't get any. Write soon.

With Love,
Elmer

Letter to Sister, October 24, 1917

Waco Tex.

Dear Sister & all:

Will drop you a line or two to let you know that I am feeling good except for a bad cold. How are all the folks.

We are having some pretty cool weather here. Especially nights. We sleep with two folds of blankets and a shelter half over us and we are cold at that. We had overcoats issued to us tonight and were glad to get them. What kind of weather are you having up there?

We haven't had any drill today. Had athletics this forenoon and attended a football game between a Mich. Co. and a Wis. Co. this afternoon. The entire Division was there. Their were about thirty thousand of us.

I don't know if I told you but we have a band now. The old 31st. of Det. was broken up and our Reg. got the band and supply Co. so we get up every morning to the tune of The Victors [University of Michigan Fight Song].

Well I don't know what to write about. We have been having the same old thing every day. I think it will be quite a little bit more interesting next mo. as we will then have all our horses and will have mounted drill with the carriages.

Do they have any dances around there this fall. I would like to back there to take one in.

I haven't been to a dance since we left Lansing.

I see by the paper that the Germans have been dealt quite a blow by the French and Russians. I hope they don't clean them all up for I would like to get a crack at them. Well I guess I will quit for this time. Write soon.

Your brother,
Elmer

Letter to Mother, October 30, 1917

Camp MacArthur

Dear Mother & all:

I received your letter today. I have a hard cold but it is getting better now. I have a little cough caused by the dust. It is quite windy here lately and causes quite a dirt storm. It isn't very good on anybody lungs.

We had a shot in the arm this morning. That makes about seven or eight. We are supposed to have at least eighteen hours off after each shot. But have been working hard all day digging trenches in the rock along the stables and building walks with stone. My arm was so sore that I couldn't get above my head but I had to swing a pick just the same.

Tomorrow is fields day for the whole camp. We have athletic events with the other regiments. Everybody has to take part. I am put down for the 100 yard dash.

I like my pillow fine and couldn't get along without. We have had some pretty cold nights lately. I was on guard night before last when I came off at ten it was clear and so warm you didn't want any covers over you. When I went on again at two oclock. It was raining & so cold I couldn't keep warm no matter how fast I walked. and I had my overcoat on too.

I get lots of reading matter at the Y.M.C.A. but don't have much time to read.

I received the camera from Frank the other day. Its a nice one a Premo 2A and like it real well. Haven't taken any pictures yet because I have got to wait to pay day to get some film.

I can't say I like it around here altho I think I would in other parts of Texas. I was over to Lover's Leap on the Brozos river Sunday. It is a cliff about two hundred feet high rising straight up from the river. I can't hardly wait until I get some film and take some pictures of it. They claim that the Birth Of A Nation was laid out around this cliff.

Well I guess I will close as I have another letter to write too Frank.

Goodbye,
Elmer

P.S. What kind of a teacher is there in our district. I received a letter from E. Miner and she wanted to know if I wanted a introduction to her. I told her sure.

Letter to Sister, November 1, 1917

Camp MacArthur

Dear Sister:

I received your card last night and was glad to receive it.

I am feeling pretty well and nearly over my cold. I still have a little cough. I have been digging and pecking stumps out in around the stables So I am a little tired tonight. We had a big fields day last wed. During the forenoon we had athletics in the afternoon we laid around slept and signed the pay roll. Expect we will get paid about sat. Yes we had a touch of that sand storm a week ago Wed. It drove us all to our tents but the dirt came through cracks and made our faces look as though we were negroes.

How are you getting along with your job. Do you think they will raise your pay any. Hope you are still working there when I get home perhaps I can get in and review on my bookeeping. I probably will forget a lot.

There has been a bunch of drafted men coming in in the last few days. I don't know any of them. Their are yet a few more to come.

Received a letter from Frank today. He is having a good time but has to study hard. He generally sends some pictures he took up to Calumet each time. Well I can't think of any thing to write and it is getting near bedtime.

Goodbye,
Elmer

Letter to Mother, November 11, 1917 (One year prior to the Armistice of 1918)

Camp MacArthur

Dear Mother & all:

I received your letter the other day and have just had time to answer it. I have been feeling fine the last few days. Most of my cold has dissappeared.

The weather has been fine the last few days. We haven't had any rain since we have been here. I never received a letter from E Curtis. It probably got lost in the mail as there is a lot of it lost that way. I have quite a little lady correspondence more than I have time to answer.

Went out and took some pictures today until I broke the camera. I broke the little clamp you turn the film with.

I was down to the Cotton Palace Exposition last wed. night. Their was competition drills between the Mich. and Wis. troops. The Mich. troops put it all over the Wis. troops and made them look like two cents. A section from each Bat. of the reg. [Regiment] took part and certainly showed up the Wisconsin battery as our maneuvers were faultless and wis. made so mistakes until they were hooted. I would like to have you seen our bunch. It is fun. and if you had never had an adventureous thrill you can get them in the artillery when the horses are running on a dead run hitched to the carriages doing artillery manuavers. Its getting to be more fun and interesting every day here. Don't know when we will go to France probably in about ten weeks as we aren't supposed to be only sixteen and we have already been here six. I don't dread the trip and am crazy to go. As to coming back that is something that never worries any of us. and each one thinks that he is lucky and the other fellow isn't.

I received those papers from Mrs. Dunham call her and tell her I thank her very much. Well I must close as I have a number of other letters to write.

Your Son,
Elmer

Letter to Mother, November 15, 1917

Camp MacArthur

Dear Mother & all:

I received your letter this forenoon and was glad to hear from you. I am feeling good and my cold has all left me.

I have been on guard since last night and have to go in again at four o clock. We have been having some great weather. The days are warm and sun shining. I haven't got my winter underwear yet. Don't need them for a while. Never mind the socks I can get them from the quartermaster. We are getting good food. Have pie and ice cream Sundays. I don't expect anything for X-mas because it cost to much to send anything down here and you haven't money enough to buy presents. Say is there any of those large pictures I had taken in Lansing left. If their is send one to Helen Dunsmore, Mason Mich. I had some postcards taken down town the other night. They aren't very good I shoved my hat on the back on my head before I was taken and I forgot to put it down again. Did you drive the machine to Lansing. Did Mrs Barnaby say any thing because the box was there so long.

Don't be surprised if you don't hear from me so often from now on because we go out on the firing range next week. It is twelve miles out there and we will probably be out there for a month. The Captian said we would be ready to go by Christmas. Well I guess I have written about all I can think of for this time. We had a review before Governor Sleeper [A.E. Sleeper, Governor of Michigan] yesterday. Hope to hear from you soon.

Goodbye
Elmer

Letter to Sister, November 20, 1917

Camp MacArthur

Dear Sister & all;

I am feeling fine these days. How are you folks. I received the candy and apples O.K. and they certainly did taste good. They were in good shape when they got here considering the distance they came.

We had a hard rain last Saturday night the first since we've been here.

I took out $5000 dollars of life & accident insurance today. It is the Soldiers & Sailors Insurance Co. and is run by the government so you see it is the safest insurance you can find for the government will never go broke and they assume all risks. Of course it will take quite a little hunk out of my pay day but that is the best plan to do it. I named mother my beneficiary so I am killed in France she will get the full amount. If I am disabled I get a pension off it. Otherwise I wouldn't. I would of like to take the full amount $10,000 if I could of stood it.

I was at the football game at the Cotton Palace Sat. afternoon between our divisional team and the Second Texas from Camp Bowie Tex. We won 21–0. The Camp Bowie Team had the best team from the army camps in the south and hadn't been beaten in two years. Sunday afternoon our Regimental team was beaten 26-0.

I don't know when we are to go out on the range. I heard it was this week but don't think the barracks are completed for us out there.

The weather has turned chilly since the rain. We have drawed our heavy underwear. I now have six suits of underwear, two cotton and one wool uniforms and an extra pair of cotton pants.

We haven't had to pay for any benefits of the Y.M.C.A. & Red Cross Not unless it is something out of the ordinary. That fellow in the picture isn't me. He looks to me like a (infantry) dow boy [doughboy] as we call them. Well I must close for this time. write soon.

Goodbye,
Elmer

Letter to Mother, November 25, 1917

Camp MacArthur
Dear Mother & all:

I received your letter today. I suppose you are having some quite cool weather up ther now. The nights get quite cold here but the days are fine. Its clouding up tonight and looks as if we were going to get another rain. Its about time for the rainy season to commence.

I was out on a long horseback ride into the country this afternoon. I am a little tired as I haven't rode a horse for about a month. I thot that there was more than three of those pictures left. Send one of the poorest. To my knowledge she is nothing more than a good friend to me. I met her in Lansing last summer. As to getting married that is to many years from now for me to think about. I am planning on having some good pictures taken anyday.

I would like to get a furlough & come home for Christmas but seeing I have my Liberty Bonds and insurance to keep up I don't feel like burrowing it. It would cost me about $50 round trip as soldiers get a cent a mile. I don't want you to send me anything for X-mas as it cost to much and I don't expect anything. Roswell Smith was over the other night. He likes it pretty well down here.

We see lots of aeroplanes here. Saw a fellow looping the loop the other day. If I ever get enough money ahead I am going over someday and go up in one. I see lots of negroes and mexicans but not much cotton as we have had a little frost and a lot of rain. We are getting fine grub. Had fried potatoes, cornflakes, coffee, fried cakes and fried bananas & milk for breakfst. For dinner we had bread& jam, boiled ham, dressing, celery, potatoes, leomonade, juice, cream and pie. We don't get such dinners only on Sunday.

Well I must close as I have another letter to write.

Goodbye,
Elmer

Letter to Sister, December 2, 1917

Camp MacArthur

Dear Sister:

Received your letter of the 25th and will try to answer it altho I can't think of much to write about. I am feeling fine. I suppose it is cold and snowy up there now. It doesn't seem like Dec. 2nd here it is quite warm and clear. The temperature is about 75 today. That box of stationary would come in handy if you want to send it.

We had a big feed Thanksgiving. I will mail the menu of it tonight. I was on kitchen police that day and thot I would die of misery of eating so much. What do you want for Christmas.

I won't be able to keep up the insurance after the war. I have about three and a half dollars a month to pay on it.

It wouldn't surprise me if the war ended in ten to twelve weeks. From the way the papers read. Some of us fellows got the Bible the other night and figured it that the war would end Jan. 27, 1918. I don't put confidence in that tho. Altho it has followed it up to the present conditions. If you want to look it up I think you will find it in the 13th chapter of revelations.

I am glad you have a permanent job. I hope I can succeed in getting a good job when I get out. Do you think it more intresting than teaching school. Is grandma Oakes [Emma] married yet. What does she intend to do after she is married. I received a card from N. Squiers the other day. Well I can't think of any think more to write about.

Goodbye,
Elmer

P.S. Ever so much obliged for the stamps, am sending one of the pictures. E.S.

The above letter contained a newspaper poem called *"Hell In Texas."* It read as follows:

Hell in Texas

The Devil we are told, in Hell was chained.
And a thousand years, he there remained;
He neither complained, nor did he groan
But determined to start a Hell of his own.

Where he could torment the souls of men,
Without being chained in a prison pen,
So he asked the Lord if he had on hand,
Anything left when he made this land.

The Lord said yes I had plenty on hand.
But I left it down on the Rio Grande,
The fact is Old Boy, the stuff is so poor,
I don't think you could use it in Hell anymore

The Devil went down to examine the truck,
He said if he took it as a gift he was stuck,
But after examining it, carefully and well,
He decided the place was too dry for a Hell

So the Lord in order to get it off his hands,
He promised the Devil he'd water the lands,
For he had some water, or rather some dregs,
A regular cathartic, and smelled like bad eggs.

Hense the trade was closed, and the deed was given,
And the Lord went back to his home in Heaven,
The Devil said "I have all that's needed,
To make a good Hell, hence he succeeded.

He began by putting thorns all over the trees,
And mixed up the sand with millions of flees,
He scattered tarantulas along the road,
Put thorns on the cactus and horns on the toads.

He lengthened the horns of the Texas steer,
And put an addition to the rabbit's ear,
He put a little devil in the broncho steed,
And poisoned the feet of the centipede.

The rattle snake bites, and the scorpion stings,
And the mesquito delights with his buzzing wing,
The sand burs prevail, and so does the ants,
And those who sit down need half soles on their pants.

The Devil said that through out the land,
He'd made arrangements to keep up the Devil's own brand,
And all should be mavericks, unless they bore
Marks of scratches and bites and thorns by the score.

The heat in the summer is one hundred and ten,
Too hot for the Devil and too hot for Men,
The wild boar roams through the black shapperal
Tis Hell of a place he has for a Hell.

Letter to Mother, December 5, 1917

[Letter on camp stationery]
Camp MacArthur
Postmark Dec. 6, 1917

Dear Mother:

I received your letter and am feeling fine. How are all you folks now days. I suppose by this time you have enough snow for sleighing. We are having some chilly nights here so we keep fire in the evening.

I took part in a review before General Hoan [BG William G. Haan, Commander, 57th FA Brigade, later promoted to MG and served as 32nd Division Commander in France] this afternoon. Our battery went out mounted. We had a little accident just as we got past the reviewing stand. When we get past the reviewing stand a little ways we have to double time in order to get out of the way of the next formation coming behind us. Well just as were given double time one of the horses on the lead team of the cassion I was riding commence to plunge and kick. The result was he got one leg twisted in the traces. We had to stop and get him straightened out. But before we got him straightened out another battery and supply train had went past us on the run. When we got fixed up our battery was halfway to camp. Of course we got a bawling out from our captain and he probably will get one from the general tomorrow. We are getting a lot of mounted drill. I presume we will go out on the range for a few days next week. It wouldn't surprise me if we packed up within a day for Long Island. We probably will get paid tomorrow. Don't think their will be any furloughs granted for X-mas. I have gloves that were issued me. We were all issued a new suit of woolens today. I have so much clothes that I hardly know where to keep them. Have about seven suits of underwear. I guess I have to send pa a suit for a X-mas present. Well will close. Write soon.

Your son,
Elmer

Letter to Sister, December 12, 1917

Camp MacArthur

Dear Sister:

Received your letter the other day but haven't had time to answer it. I am feeling fine. It has been pretty cold down to fifteen above zero. It has commenced to warm up a little today.

We go out to the range tomorrow for a couple of days target practice. A & D battery are out there today. We can hear their guns way into camp. and they are 16 miles away. Some noise. I expect I'll be almost deaf when I get back. Well I expect to be in France in two months. They are getting ready to move out of here. I think we will be here for X-mass but won't be here much after X-mass. I hear they are going to hold up our mail next week so won't anybody know when we move. We probably will go to Long Island from here.

I did not get a bible from the Red Cross. Received a letter from grandma Smith the other day. I guess I never told you that I had a new nickname did I. They fellows call me Grace. I was on guard yesterday but didn't have to stand today. We haven't been doing much drilling lately just tinkering around. We have drawed our horses (162) from the remount station. Well it is nearly drill call so must quit. Write soon.

E Smith

Letter to Mother, December 16, 1917

[Crossed Cannons Stationery]
Camp MacArthur from artillery camp paper

Dear Mother:

How are you feeling now days. I have caught a little cold and have quite a cough.

We hiked out to the range last thursday. We fired until Friday afternoon and then hiked back.

I dreaded the first shot a little but didn't mind after I got used to it. My ears still ring altho I had my ears packed full of waste. We started back about five oclock fri. afternoon. F battery got started out ahead of us and got about an half hour start. We made a brag to them that we would catch them before they got to camp. Well when we got started we walked believe me. F battery was determined that we wouldn't catch them. It was the most killing pace I ever was in. I was lame when we started and thot I wouldn't ever be able to stand it the whole distance. The was a truck behind us to pick up the stragglers and their was quite a few of them too. I came very close to going down a number of times but I made up my mind I would go until I dropped. But we caught F battery about a mile out of camp. We covered the distance (16 miles) in four hours and fifteen minutes and only had one rest of fifteen minutes. I was staggering when I came into the tent and my eyes were blurred until I could hardly see. Am still lame. Our battery showed up best of any on the range.

Wish you people could of come down on that special train that is to leave Lansing. Why don't you and pa come down here. It wouldn't cost so very much. I don't know as I will be here but I believe you would like the country. If you could sell the farm and buy a little land down here, land is cheap out from the city. Have seen them drill barley and oats the last two weeks.

We probably will be here X-mas but will pack up soon after. I received a day book from Mr. & Mrs. Dunham today will have to drop them a letter and thank them. [the day book could likely be the diary titled "Day by Day" on its front cover]

Well am going to try and dig up two bits and go down to the end of the street and get me a supper. Write soon.

Goodbye,
Your Son Elmer

P.S. Have Zelma send me some of her pictures if she has any extra ones. Did you get those I sent you.

Letter to Mother, December 23, 1917

Camp MacArthur

Dear Mother & all:

I have received the box and it was some box. Everything you sent just suited me and was what I needed. I won't you to thank all the folks that helped to contributed to it. Did Zelma get the pillow top I sent her. And did you get the pictures.

Their was a train load of Lansing people arrived last night. It sure has been warm all day today. and it is a peach of a moonlight night out tonight. You can't imagine what nice nights we have here. They are some nights believe me. Nothing like them in Michigan. We turn in some of our horses tomorrow. Don't know anymore about movin.

We were over to the gas school the other day. If you ever saw a gasmask you can imagine how handsome I am with one on. We were put in the gas chamber with the masks on and then taken out and made to walk through without them. We are to hold our breathe and take two or three sniffs. I took one and that was enough. A couple of lungs of that would kill a guy.

I had a letter from grandma Oakes the other day and one from Lila Pearse. V. Easlick sent me a couple of hankerchiefs and a letter. I wish people would send me stamps if they want me to write to them. I guess I'll quit for now as I can't any thing to write. Tell uncle Jim I 'll write him a letter just as soon as I get time. I wanted to thank you again for the box.

Goodbye—

Letter to Sister, December 28, 1917

Waco Texas

Dear Sister

How are you tonight. I am Feeling fine. I have just got thru two hours of guard duty. Have to go on again at twelve and come off at two. I was lucky to get on street guard and do not have to stand tomorrow.

Did you get the pillow top. It isn't much. But I won't to use and put it out where people can see it. I received a box from Mrs. Barnaby. She sent me a cigarette case a safety razor a large towel, a pipe, a box of candy, tobacco, cigarettes and some handkerchiefs. A pretty nice box, don't you think?

Don't know when we will pull out but probably will be within a couple of weeks.

Are you getting the same wages at the Roller Mills? Are you busy there? I suppose it is cold as the dickens up there now. It is going to be cold as the deuce here tonight. How is Genevieve. I suppose she is full of mischeif as ever.

Tell Clarence I said thanks for that candy. It certainly tasted good. Your paper came just in time as I was nearly out.

I can't think of any thing to write.

Oh yes: We are getting used to the sound of bullets. The Rifle range is situated back behind a large hill about a mile from camp, So their are quite a few stray ones that whiz over this way every day. The other day one came down thru the tent and just missed one of the fellows and buried itself in the floor. Their has been two or three fellows hit by them but they have never proved fatal. Well guess I will quit as I must get a little sleep before I have to go on post again. Write soon.

Goodbye,
Your Brother,
Elmer

End of Letter Home (first page is missing), Unknown Date, likely December 1917 or January 1918

Don't know how long we will be in the south.

Think we will see France but think we will come home all right as they calculate we will have to have three months training there before going into action. Hell! The war will be over by that time. Well don't know what else there is to write. Write for our mail will be forwarded to Waco if we are shipped out of here.

Goodbye,
Elmer

P.S. Have had number hard frosts. One night it froze water quite hard. It isn't so cold but that I went swimming yesterday.

Elmer

NOTES

1. *Pictorial Souvenir of Camp MacArthur, Waco, Texas* (Waco TX: D.E. Hirshfield, 1917).
2. *The Atchison, Topeka & Santa Fe Railway Transcontinental Line* (1917). On one side of the paper is a U.S. map west and south of Chicago to California with major rail lines, cities, and routes. On the other side are three sections: General Information; Altitudes of Principal Stations; and the Chicago and Kansas City Local Schedules.
3. American Battle Monuments Commission, *32D Division Summary of Operations in the World War* (Washington, D.C., U.S. Government Printing Office, 1943), 1. U.S. Army Center of Military History, *Order of Battle of the United States Land Forces in the World War, American Expeditionary Forces: Division, Volume 2* (Washington: U.S. Government Printing Office, 1988 (Reprint originally published 1931-1949), 176. Robert J. Dalessandro and Michael G. Knapp, *Organization and Insignia of the American Expeditionary Force, 1917-1923* (Atglen PA: Schiffer Publishing Ltd., 2008), 165
4. "U.S. Army Branch Insignia and Plaques," The Institute of Heraldry, U.S. Army, accessed December 29, 2013, http://www.tioh.hqda.pentagon.mil/Catalog/HeraldryMulti.aspx.
5. Byron Farwell, *Over There: The United States in the Great War, 1917-1918* (New York: W.W. Norton and Company, 1999), 103.

Chapter 4
"Day by Day"
The 1918 Diary

On New Year's Day, Tuesday, January 1st, 1918, Private Elmer Smith began his diary. In doing so the 20 year old displayed the maturity to record the events of his life as a soldier in the U.S. Army. It was recorded in a small booklet, entitled "Day by Day," which devoted a page to each day of the year. The booklet measures approximately 5 ¾ by 3 ½ inches. He may have purchased this pre-formatted diary from a soldier exchange store at Camp MacArthur or in nearby Waco. However, the diary is likely the "day book" Elmer received from Mr. and Mrs. Dunham (see the December 16th letter to his mother in previous chapter).

Inside the diary is still a loose calendar with the year 1917 on one side and 1918 on the other. On the inside cover is a deployed soldier star sticker with "Pvt. Elmer O. Smith, Battery B, 119th Reg. Camp MacArthur Waco, Texas," written on the opposite page of the inside cover.

On the next set of pages, prior to the start of the diary, Elmer summarized additional information, noting the camps at which he served in the U.S. and his home address as follows:

Service in Camps.
Camp Hoague. Lansing. Mich.
Camp Mobilization. Grayling.
Camp MacArthur. Waco. Texas
Camp Merritt. Tenafly. N.J.

Home address. Ovid, Michigan.
Father—W.F. Smith,
Ovid, Mich.
Box 127

Although Elmer made short entries mostly about routine duties and actions, the diary allows one to gain a sense of his unit's major focus as they trained for war and later executed combat operations. It provides a significant window of understanding on what their unit was experiencing, allowing a more complete view of the 119th FA Regiment's daily operations. The entries, expressed freely by a young American man, also provide the reader a glimpse of what the individual soldier went through and was thinking in the wartime environment of that era.

In his letters, he rarely discusses names of soldiers or officers, perhaps due to censorship guidelines. But in his diary he often does provide names. In this book the person's full names are annotated in brackets when they correspond with soldiers identified from other sources. These sources include the unofficial poster, *Roster, Battery "B," 119th U.S. F.A., 57th Brigade, 32nd Division*[1], and the book, *Honor Roll and Complete War History of Ingham County in the Great World War, 1914 to 1918.*[2] Officers serving in the Michigan National Guard at the time of mobilization are listed in the document *Officers of Michigan National Guard, Call of the President, July 15, 1917.*[3] Elmer also had a small notebook with the names and home addresses of 64 enlisted soldiers he served with. Another major source was a May, 1919, Detroit Free Press newspaper article that listed the names of many of the 119th FA Regiment officers and soldiers returning to the U.S. from France via ship.[4] Lastly, the casualty reports that the unit compiled in September and November 1918 list all soldiers wounded or killed in action.[5]

On January 4th 1918, Private Elmer Smith was transferred from B Battery to the Headquarters Company of the 119th FA Regiment. This change was a bit of a shock for him since he had enlisted into and served with Battery B for the past nine months.

Since he only kept the diary during 1918, the year is not annotated after each entry. However, the appropriate year continues to be reflected for letters, newspaper clippings, and other sources.

Diary Entry Tues. January 1

Stationed at Camp MacArthur

New Years. Were all given a holiday. Had a fine dinner with oyster stew, ice cream and pie.

Spent most of the forenoon doing stables. D--m the stables. When I get out of the army I am going to buy a horse so I can get up every morning and do stables. Bill [Bill Jarm], Pete [Private Peter Tiedjens] and myself took pictures this afternoon. Corporal Cook [Corporal Frank L. Cook] came home dead drunk.

Diary Entry Wed. January 2

Thank god, the horses were all turned in today. We now can rest in peace with no top cutler's whistle blowing; "Fall in for stables."

Pete T. [Private Peter Tietjens, B Battery] was over to the base hospital for an examination for his knee. The result turned out to be rheumatism of his knee caused by his teeth.

Diary Entry Thur. January 3

Took a part in a ten mile road hike this morning. We done squads east and west all the afternoon. The horses are gone so we can't d--m them so dam the foot drill.

Diary Entry Fri. January 4

Another long road hike this forenoon. Was given the welcome news this noon that I was to be transferred to Headquarters Co. of this Regiment. My cursed luck again. I moved over this afternoon. Was assigned to Corporal Ogdon's tent. I would like to get my hands on the guy that got me over here.

Letter to Sister, January 4, 1918

Waco, Texas

Dear Sister:

I received your letter and was glad to hear from you. I am not feeling in a very good humor tonight. I was transferred from the battery to Headquarters Co. of this regiment. It made me very mad but that was all the good it done. Their was six of us sent out of the battery. Some of them went to the captian [captain, the battery commander] about it. But he couldn't help us. It made him pretty mad he didn't know anything about it until a couple of sergerants [sergeants] went to him and complained that they were taking some of the best men in their sections You see when we first came down here their was some of the crummiest of the battery sent to hdqts [headquarters company]. They didn't prove to be any good so the captian of hdqts sent a man over to our battery to inquire for some efficient men he got us six. So the captian of hdqtrs took the name of the men from our bat. And said they prove inefficient to coloneral [Colonel McCormick, the Regimental Commander] and wanted to trade them for us. So you see how it happened.

I received the stamps and wish to thank you for them. They came in handy as I was nearly all out. You had better coax pa to take that trip to Florida. It would do him more good than anything I know of. I would be glad to get the Ovid paper anytime you want to send it. Yes you can send most anything across.

I dare say we will be here at least two weeks yet. I guess I didn't tell you what our work was going to be like over here. We wont have any guns, it is most all detail work such as signaling, telephoney wireless and etc. Well I can't think of any thing more to write so I guess I will quit. address my mail to the Hdqts Co. instead of Bat. B. Write soon

Goodbye,
Elmer

Diary Entry Sat. January 5

Slept well last night considering the bad humor I went to bed in. An inspection of all our issued stuff took place this morning. All our junk was checked up to see what we had. Was issued a pistol belt and succeed in bribing them into giving me an extra shirt. Getting ready to go to Europe

Diary Entry Sun. January 6

We had an inspection of quarters this morning. Nobody confined. Something very unusual for this crumy Co.

Laid around and wrote letters this afternoon. Borrowed a dollar. Took Bill [Bill Jarm of Niles, Michigan] and C. Harper [Private Charles Harper, B Battery] down to the board walk and treated them to flapjacks and coffee.

Diary Entry Mon. January 7

Went out on a seven mile road march this morning. Stoped over by the aviation field and watched the aeroplanes. Drilled this afternoon.

Diary Entry Tues. January 8

Lost our old captain, Captain Lewis [Joseph H. Lewis of Lansing] and got Captain Bow [Warren E. Bow]. Don't like him very well to much of a boy.

Went on another hike over to Cameron Park at N. Waco. Slept an hour there. Pretty soft officers.

Washed some clothes and tried to learn a sergeant semaphore. Some bunch of non com's here that has to have a buck private learn them semaphore.

Diary Entry Wed. January 9

Another hike. We will soon be bullet proof if we take many more of them. We had athletics this afternoon. I boxed a couple rounds with Scott Noble [Private Scott Noble, B Battery].

Letter to Mother, January 9, 1918

Waco, Texas

Dear Mother & all:

I received your letter and was glad to hear from you. I am glad [pa] has gone to Florida. If he dosen't do any worrying while he is down there it will do him more good than any medicine under the sun. He probably will begin to worry after he has been there a couple of weeks. You want to write to him two or three time a week at least.

I am feeling fine. Have begun to like it a little better here at Hdq's. We don't get as good a feed as we did in the battery. I guess thats because the mess sargant here is under quarantine. And the cooks wont do anymore than they have to when their isn't any body around to make them. We been having eight and nine mile hikes every morning.

You tell Genevieve to save her candy for me. For I know she likes it better than I do. Is she growing much. So Clarence thinks he's quite a man does he. Tell him he'd better get that idea out of his head or some one will liable to come along and give him a couple of black lamps sometime. Thats the way some of them get them in the army. I suppose that Dee can take him down by this time can't he. I have been boxing a little this afternoon and the result one eye is a little sore. I am sending my discharge paper from the Mich. Nat. Guard into the regular army. Save it I may need it some day. [This document is unlocated] How are you people making it on the food proposition this winter? What do you do for food? Gee I wish you could sell the farm and come down south and buy a small place. It doesn't seem much like Jan. here now. But we do get a little cold weather once and a while. I don't know any more than I did about moving. It wouldn't surprise me if we didn't get out of here this month. Well I can't think of anything more to write about so I guess I will quit for this time.

Goodbye,
Your Son,
Elmer

Diary Entry Thur. January 10

We went out on another hike with the 2nd battalion under Major Lewis [Joseph H. Lewis]. Went thru Cameron Park into North Waco.

We got hell for a dirty tent and had to stay in this afternoon and clean house.

Went to a band concert at the "Y" tonight. A full pack hike scheduled for tomorrow morning. A hard sleet and thunder storm has set in. Was called over for a fire at the officers mess.

Diary Entry Fri. January 11

Its cold as the devil. Snowed and blowed all night. Three inches of snow. Hike called off. Hurray! We are getting paid. Don't know what the devil good it will do me. I owe 40 cents more than my pay comes to now. Oh! This is the life. Like hell.

On guard tonight. Cold as the deuce.

Diary Entry Sat. January 12

Show down inspection.

We were told this noon that we would move in a few days. Worked, getting ready to leave.

Diary Entry Sun. January 13

Inspection of quarters. Made up our surplus kit. Went down to the end of the street to a show.

By doing some brainey headwork I succeeded in getting out of paying for a supper for three of us. Leave it to "Grace" for that.

Diary Entry Mon. January 14

It was so muddy we did not do much but help pack up the Q. M. [Quartermaster, the Regimental logistics officer] Corporal Warren [Carl L. Warren of Adams, New York] is back from the hospital.

Diary Entry Tues. January 15

Went out on a hike this morning.

Drawed clothing and had one of Major Kerr's [Major Murdock M. Kerr of Larium, Michigan, the 119th FA's medical doctor and commander of the Medical Detachment] old stand by inspection this afternoon.

I went to the "Y" tonight to a band concert by the 121st Art. Band.

Letter to Sister, January 15, 1918

Waco, Texas

Dear Sister:

I received your letter the other day and have just got around to answer it. I am feeling fine except a little cold in my head. I like it a little better now at Hdqts. than I did but I would rather be back with the battery.

We have been having some nasty weather here for the last week. It turned cold and rained one of the hardest sleet storms I ever saw and then it commenced to snow. It snowed about three inches. When I got up the next morning I was covered with snow. And then it got warm the other night and rained all night. The result is our feet are the biggest part of us when we stir out. You have probably heard of gumbo. Well thats what we have to put up with here.

Well we will probably pull out of here the last of this week or the first of next. We have every thing packed and are waiting for the word. Reg's are pulling out every day. As near as I know now we will go to Hoboken N. J. Undoubtly we will be there six or eight weeks.

Have you heard from pa since he got to Florida. Gee I am glad he went. I received a letter from Frank. He said he saw him when he was home Xmas and said he looked considerly better than when he saw him last. Well I guess I must close as I can't think of any thing more to write. And the band has just started up. The 121st Artillery band gives a concert here tonight at the "Y". I wish you were here to hear them as we have some of the finest bands I ever heard down here. I don't know about the stamps yet but will let you know. I am enclosing a letter to let you know what some of the girls think of me. Well Goodbye.

Your Brother,
Elmer

Diary Entry Wed. January 16

Hiked.
Went to the show at the end of the street.

Diary Entry Thur. January 17

Hiked out to the infantry trenches this morning.
Worked over to officers mess cleaning up this afternoon.

Diary Entry Fri. January 18

Worked over to the officers mess all day. We are all getting ready for a practice move of troops in the morning.

Diary Entry Sat. January 19

We had reveille at 5'oclock. Went right to work on our packs and equipment. Had every thing packed ready to move at ten a.m. Had an inspection of every thing by the general and colonal. Didn't get anything to eat until 1:00 oclock. Hungry? Hell no! Laid around all the afternoon. We were complimented on our showing. Received a loving little letter from Helen.

Letter to Mother, January 19, 1918

Waco Texas

Dear Mother & all:

I received your letter today and I was glad to hear from home. I am feeling fine.

I have begun to like my transfer a little better as I get acquainted with more of the fellows. I wasn't sent over because I did not make good in the battery. I just happened to be the one to go. All of us were supposed to be good men because their was a number a men that was no good. I suppose pa is down where it is nice and warm now. I hope when we leave we go by the way New Orleans and straight east and then up along the coast. I don't think you will have to worry much about my coming back because it will be six or seven months before we get into actual service and I doubt if we ever do.

Well I must close as I have a couple more letters to write. I dare say that any mail sent here will be sent on to any place we go.

Goodbye
Your Son,
Elmer

Diary Entry Sun. January 20

We had a nice long snooze this morning as their was no reveille. Gosh! I envy these "er" civilians. I laid around all day long. It seem rather queer. Of course we never work in this army.

Diary Entry Mon. January 21

Hiked to beat the devil.

Diary Entry Tues. January 22

Hiked some more. To hell with it. Sent a telegram to Zelma for money. Gee I hated to do it but I had to.

Diary Entry Wed. January 23

Another hike of fourteen miles. Oh, baby, what a cute big blister I have. Received an answer to my telegram. Was excused from drill this afternoon to go down and get my money.

I kept my date with Miss Woltman and had a very fine time.

Diary Entry Thur. January 24

Did not go on the hike this morning. Reported to the infirmary with my sore blisters.

I can walk to see my girl but be darned if I can hike with the Co.

Diary Entry Fri. January 25

Another full pack hike. Did I go? Not me. Whats the use of going when you can get out of them. W. Greene [PFC Walter R. Greene] and myself took the girls to the Hipprodome tonight.

Diary Entry Sat. January 26

I worked like a son of a gun all the forenoon shoveling dirt. We were given a lecture by Maj. Kerr, Lieut. Shaw [1LT Milton Shaw, Medical Detachment of Lansing], Lieut. Wilson [1LT William E. Wilson, Medical Detachment] on personal care of the body.

Diary Entry Sun. January 27

Laid around all day. Got ready and went to church with Olga. Can you imagine it. Me going to a real church.

Diary Entry Mon. January 28

Took a hike over in Cameron Park. We were giving a lecture by Lieut. Stillwell [1LT William G. Stillwell of Pellston, Michigan] on censorship of the mail.

Letter to Mother, January 29, 1918

[YMCA letterhead "With The Colors"]

Dear Mother:

I received your letter today. My cold seems to be sticking with me.
It is to bad pa doesn't like it in Florida. It seems to be a cold winter all over. Some people write me wishing they were here where it is warm. But I am afraid its far from the weather they imagine it to be. We have had to wear overcoats to keep warm most of the time. This morning when we got up the ground was covered with ice and sleet. But in almost no time it began to warm down here as well in Florida. So perhaps pa will enjoy his two months of stay there. I wrote him a good long letter yesterday. I never told as it slipped my mind every time I wrote. But I took out $5000 more in insurance in pa's name. So if anything ever happened to me it would mean about $28 each to the both of you. You see they don't pay the full amt. out if I should get killed But pay it by pension for about twenty years.

My work at headquarters will be scouting, signaling, telephony & range finding and a lot of other stuff I don't even understand.

So you think Helen is to be something more than a friend. Do you? Well it's news to me. I haven't any intention of getting married for quite a while. I was to church with my little girl down here last night. It had been so long since I had gone to church I did not hardly know how to act. Well I haven't heard anymore about moving. So i'm not sure when we will go. Well I must close for this time. Will write again soon.

Goodbye,
From Elmer

Diary Entry Tues. January 29

The first battalion detail went over in the woods and established telephone communications. We were then given a lecture by Lieut. Oliver.

We drilled and had instruction in blanket rolling this afternoon.

Diary Entry Wed. January 30

Oh hell! The same old routine. Signed the pay roll. I payed a visit down on Gorman St. <u>Son of a gun!</u>

Diary Entry Thur. January 31

We mustered for pay this morning. We were given lectures the rest of the day.

Diary Entry Fri. February 1

Oh god! That full pack hike we took this morning. Oh! We are motorized on legs.

Ahem! Went down to the Hipprodome with the charming young lady down on Gorman St.

Diary Entry Sat. February 2

We had an inspection of quarters and of personnal this morning.

Went down to Waco this afternoon. I also was at 2226 promp 4:30.

Diary Entry Sun. February 3

Took up my new duties of one weeks kitchen police this morning. Some job believe me. It makes me feel as tho I wanted to hand in my resignation.

Diary Entry Tues. February 5

We were paid this morning. Went down and paid my last respects to Miss Woltman. We leave tomorrow.

NOTES

1. Captain Joseph H. Lewis, *Roster, Battery "B," 119th U.S. F.A., 57th Brigade, 32nd Division.*

2. *Honor Roll and Complete War History of Ingham County in the Great World War, 1914 to 1918* (Lansing MI: The State Journal Press, 1920), 219-250. Pictures of 22 commissioned officers and 316 enlisted soldiers of the 119th FA Regiment from the Lansing area.

3. *Officers of Michigan National Guard, Call of the President, July 15, 1917* (Lansing MI: Michigan National Guard, July 15, 1917), 8.

4. William N. Hard, "119th to Land This Morning," *Detroit Free Press,* May 3, 1919.

5. *General Orders 19: Officers and Men Entitled to Wear the Wound Chevron* (Headquarters, 119th Field Artillery, American Expeditionary Forces, France, 14 September 1918).
   Casualty Report (Headquarters, 119th Field Artillery, American Expeditionary Forces, France, 14 November 1918).

Chapter 5
Movement to France

THE 119TH FA REGIMENT'S MOVEMENT from Texas to the Atlantic Coast, and then onward to England, and finally to France took just over a month. This journey would be repeated by hundreds of mobilized units throughout 1918.

According to Private Smith's diary and letters the deployment to France was relatively uneventful. The month long transition showed that the Army had a relatively well-organized process to ensure effective movement of units to the Western Front in France.

Private Elmer O. Smith was on his way to war in France. It was the largest war in human history to that point. Some of his specific personnel data as a soldier are delineated below.

FULL NAME: Elmer Oscar Smith
HOMETOWN: Ovid, Michigan
RANK: Private (PVT) (April 1917–October 1918); Private First Class (PFC) (October 1918–May 1919)
SOLDIER'S NUMBER[1]: 297070
PAY[2]: $36.60 per month (minus $6.50 for War Risk Insurance coverage of $10,000)
ASSIGNED UNITS: Battery B, First Battalion, Michigan Field Artillery:
April–September 1917
Battery B, 119th Field Artillery Regiment: September 1917–January 1918
Headquarters Company, 119th FA Regiment: January 1918–May 1919

The 119th FA Regiment was subordinate to the 57th FA Brigade, the primary FA organization assigned to and supporting the 32nd Division. The 32nd was the fifth American division to arrive in France and the second National Guard division.

According to his enlistment record, Elmer Smith was five feet nine inches tall, had blue eyes, a fair complexion, and light brown hair.[3]

Uniforms and Accoutrements

Elmer Smith kept many of the uniform items he wore during the war. These included a steel helmet, a wool overseas cap, a wool shirt or tunic, a wool overcoat, canvas leggings, and a gas mask. He did not keep his wool trousers or boots after the war since they were likely well-worn and needed to be disposed of. Other than the wool overcoat he did not keep any of his cold weather uniform items. If he had, most of them may have been used and worn out in the subsequent cold Michigan winters. His large canvas campaign hat was not among the uniform items he kept and may have been thoroughly worn out after two years of constant use.

On his wool tunic Private Smith wore the following accoutrements. At the top of his left sleeve was the 32nd Division "Red Arrow" unit patch. Below that was his Private/Private First Class rank in red to signify he was part of the U.S. Army Artillery Corps. On the cuff of that left sleeve he had two Overseas Service Chevrons signifying two six month periods of combat service in France. On his right sleeve cuff was a Wound Chevron for his being wounded in action. On the left side of his neck collar he wore a Corps device, a round metal insignia with the symbol of two crossed artillery cannons signifying his assignment to an Artillery Corps unit. On the right side of his collar was a round metal insignia with "U.S." emblazoned specifying the United States Army. All but the collar insignia were also sewn onto his wool overcoat. The wool tunic and overcoat had the standard U.S. Army insignia on the metal buttons. On his overseas cap, the front left side had a round metal insignia similar to those on the collar. This insignia had "MICH" inscribed on it specifying his unit of origin as the Michigan National Guard. On the back of Elmer's helmet was painted the 32nd Division "Red Arrow" symbol. This was probably done so a soldier's specific unit could be readily identified in combat.

The major campaigns PVT Smith participated in and the decorations he received are described in Chapters 7 through 14. But during the overseas voyage, Elmer expressed confidence, effusively writing, "Lookout all ye Germans. The 119th is nearly ready."

Diary Entry Wed. February 6

Worked like a son of a gun this morning in getting the kitchen cleaned up. Put on the finishing touches this afternoon. We were all loaded at 3:30 [P.M.]. Pulled out of camp at 4:00 on the train. I am booked to do K. P. [kitchen police] all the way on the trip.

No knowledge to where we are going.

Diary Entry Thur. February 7

I woke up this morning in Louisiana. Some country too believe me. I wouldn't live in that country for love or money. We reached New Orleans at 6:00 p.m. Laid there for three hours. Were ferried across the Mississippi.

Diary Entry Fri. February 8

Slept all the way thru the state of Mississippi. Woke up in Mobile. Got a good look at Mobile Bay. We traveled all day in Alabama. It is very interesting country. Made a 3 hour stop in Montgomery. This is 7:00 p.m. and we just crossed the line into Georgia.

Diary Entry Sat. February 9

Had to wait until the train stopped before I could get to the kitchen as the car next was under quarrantine. Stopped in N. Carolina about 4:00 p.m. Our next stop is Raleigh, N.C. Goodnight.

Letter to Father in Florida, February 9, 1918; Subsequently sent to Mother in Michigan

Dear Father,

How are you. I am feeling fine. We are on our way at last. Left camp last wed. p.m. We came by the way of New Orleans. We are now somewhere in Georgia

Address My mail as
Pvt. E. Smith
Hdqs Co. 119 F.A.
America Ex. Forces
Via New York.

Will write again soon.

Goodbye,
Elmer

Diary Entry Sun. February 10

I woke up in Richmond Va. Made a stop in Wash. D. C. and we were given a lunch served by the Red Cross. Pulled thru Baltimore with out stopping. Pulled into Philadelphia and were treated by the Red Cross. Expect to arrive in the morning.

Diary Entry Mon. February 11

I woke up in New York. Pulled out early for camp. Arrived there about 9:00 a.m.

I found Camp Merrit an up to date camp. With fine barracks and electric lights. We are about 15 miles from N. York.

Letter to Mother, February 11, 1918

Dear Mother & All:

I will drop you a few lines to let you know I arrived safely. I am feeling fine and enjoyed the trip fine. We came by the way of New Orleans, Montgomery, Atlanta Geo., Raleigh N. C. Richmond Va. Wash. D.C. Baltimore, Philadelphia and then here. We have a fine place here. Can't tell you how long we are going to be here. The place here is Camp Merrit.

Address my mail as Hdqs. Co 119 F.A. A.E.F. Via New York

How is every thing at home. It is no where near as cold here as I expected it would be. They must be having a warm spell. That insurance I took out is paid in the case of death as a pension for a period of years. It is paid monthly. Some where near $58 on a 10,000. It costs me about $8 per month. Their has been a mix up on my Liberty Bond and their wasn't any money taken out on it the last pay day. It got mixed up some way when I transferred. Well I must close and go to bed for I am tired. Write soon.

Goodbye,
From Your Son

Diary Entry Tue. February 12

Slept fine last night. Why? Because we had real spring beds and mattresses. Had an inspection this forenoon.

We have commenced to clean up camp. Gee its a dirty place.

Diary Entry Wed. February 13

Got up with a beautiful little ear ache. It turned out to be an abcess. Went to bed with hot applications on it. It broke tonight. Its nice and comfortable, that stuff running out of my ear all the while.

Diary Entry Thur. February 14

Went on sick report this morning. My ear is better but still runs. We were given a lecture this afternoon.

Diary Entry Fri. February 15

Gosh! Took a long hike clear to Englewood and back this morning. Pretty hard on a guy that hasn't been feeling well and who didnt have any breakfast.

Diary Entry Sat. February 16

We had an inspection by Captain Bow [Warren E. Bow] this morning. Laid around all the afternoon. An order was put up that their was to be no more passes granted to New York. Gee Whiz? And I was going Monday.

Diary Entry Sun. February 17

As today has been Sunday I laid around and slept all day long. I also answered a few letters. It is getting quite cold.

Diary Entry Mon. February 18

Well this Monday we have laid around all day. Some snap here.

We are all confined to Co. street. Those in barracks No. 1 are confined to barracks because of Scarlet Fever.

Letter to Mother, February 18, 1918

Camp Merritt

Dear Mother:

Received your letter yesterday. Will try and write you a few lines this morning. How is the weather in Michigan now? It has turned quite cold here. The snow is almost all off the ground but their is still a lot of ice.

How are all the people around home? Do you have much to live on?

I received a letter from father yesterday. He seems to be improving quite a little doesn't he? I don't see why you can't sell the farm and buy a little place in Florida. I am sure it would add quite a few more years to his life if you would.

Don't figure on getting anything on my birthday I won't be in the U.S. then and I don't expect anything. And would rather you wouldn't try to give me anything.

The band is quartered beneath us and are now having a rehearsal. They drive us nearly crazy sometimes.

What time does pa expect to be home? How is Jap making it on the farm? Are you getting any returns from it?

Gee I wanted to see a little New York while I was here. But I can't now. I waited to long before applying for a pass. I should of went today. But that order from Divisional hdqs. knocked it all in the head.

How is Genevieve? Does she grow any. I presume she will forget me before I get back.

I'll tell you something you can send me if you want to. Some pictures that Zelma has taken. Some olds ones if she has them. She needn't mind about printing any for me. Well I guess I will quit for this time.

Goodbye,
Elmer

P.S. The tempture drop about 48 degrees in 24 hrs Some change & I guess we are going to have colds out of it

Diary Entry Tue. February 19

We took a nice long hike to the Hudson this forenoon. I got a very good glimpse of the Palasides [Palisades, the cliffs along the Hudson River].

We were entertained at the "Y" this afternoon. Learned to sing many new artillery songs there.

Diary Entry Wed. February 20

We took a long hike into Englewood this forenoon.

We had school this afternoon. Were issued overshoes.

Diary Entry Thur. February 21

Was on guard last night and today in the bath house. Caught "-ell" from the "Top" [Company First Sergeant] for letting the fires go out.

We make a practice move for embarkation in the morning.

Diary Entry Fri. February 22

Well today is Washington's birthday. Did we celebrate? Yes. By packing up everything and scrubbing out all of the barracks and doing a full pack hike. We also packed and loaded our barrack bags. France for us soon.

Diary Entry Sat. February 23

We scrubbed out everything in general. I was put on a delightful spud pealing detail which lasted the forenoon.

We were all made to take a bath and wash our dirty clothes.

Lookout all ye Germans. The 119th is nearly ready.

Diary Entry Sun. February 24

We had two physical inspections this morning. Policed up the camp.

We were lined up and were giving places as we are to go aboard. Hurrah! Reveille is at 1:00 tomorrow morning. Goodnight.

Going to bed. Hell they just come to get me for a detail. Cursed luck.

Diary Entry Mon. February 25

Reveille woke us at 1:00. I was not sleepy considering I worked until 11:00 last night. Breakfasted at 1:30. Packed up all our stuff. Scrubbed out the barracks and had everything ready to leave at 4:00. Left at 6:00. Took the train to Jersey City and the ferry to Hoboken.

We went aboard the British Liner Transport Olympic. You ought to see our sleeping room. 100 men in a 25 by 20 room. Our hammocks are delightful to sleep in.

Diary Entry Tue. February 26

Gee! Slept rotten last night. Dont think much of these hammocks. Pulled out of the dock at 7:00 o'clock. Saw the Statue of Liberty.

I begin to feel sick and we have been out of sight of land only two hrs. We had boat drill this afternoon. The band gave a concert. Done pretty well, only heaved up four times today. Oh I am so sick.

Diary Entry Wed. February 27

These hammocks are some beds believe me. Woke with a light head and a dizzy stomach. Was put on guard. I eat a big dinner. Am feeling considerable better. We passed 3 ships this afternoon. We were given a drill which is to take place in case we are torpedoed.

The waters are quite smooth. But the boat keeps rolling from side to side. That is what makes us heave.

Diary Entry Thur. February 28

Woke up feeling fine. Went on guard at 8:00 oclock.

Had another drill the same as yesterday. Mustered for pay. It has been a fine day. The waters being very smooth. It looks stormy tonight.

Diary Entry Fri. March 1

We all slept late this morning and so of course a bawling out was due. I am put on sanitary guard. You will know me from now on as I have a white band around my left arm.

Saw a school of Dolophins. The ocean has been remarkably calm today. A wireless was received saying our convoys are on their way to meet us.

Diary Entry Sat. March 2

D--m these hammocks. I'll be a skeleton when I get off this ship if I dont rest better than I did last night.

Took up my duties as sanitary guard again. Sweeping, mopping and cleaning. Some hell of a job, believe me.

Ran into a gale this afternoon. It is quite rough tonight and the white horses show very plainly.

Diary Entry Sun. March 3

I woke up with a headache. The ship is rolling heavily. Their is quite a hard gale out. I was seasick again all day. I am feeling better tonight after eating a large supper. We are about 300 miles from the coast of Ireland. We are in midst of the danger zone. Watch out for the subs.

Diary Entry Mon. March 4

Feeling fine. Picked up four convoys last night. One of them shot at a supposed sub.

Diary Entry Tue. March 5

I was born 21 years ago today. Its a hell of away to celebrate a birthday with a mop and broom. Sighted the coast of Wales. One convoy shot for a sub. It looks as tho we got one as the water was covered with oil afterwards.

The ship fired with one of the big guns at a piece of driftwood that was taken for a periscope. Reached the docks at Seaport at 3:00 oclock. Unload tomorrow.

Diary Entry Wed. March 6

We unloaded at ten o'clock. Marched to the London and North Western railway. Loaded on and left for somewhere. Passed thru some of the most beautiful farming country I ever saw. The buildings are all built of brick and tile. Passed thru the cities of Wolverhampton, Birmingham and Oxford. Arrived at Winchester at 10:00 oclock. Marched out to a camp. After a hard tramp reached our barracks. Our bed consists of boards and straw ticks.

Diary Entry Thur. March 7

Everybody slept until ten o clock this A.M. Had a breakfast of rye bread and butter, beef and coffee.

Laid around all day. Had dinner at four o'clock. It consisted of rye bread and butter, cheese potatoes, beef, jam and coffee. Good what their was of it but not enough per man for a person with a to healthy appetite. Start in with regular routines tomorrow.

Diary Entry Fri. March 8

We took a hike to Winchester this morning. Marched over an old road made by the Romans in their conquest on England in 52 B.C. Saw several old historic places.

The streets of Winchester are very narrow, just room enough for two carriages to pass each other. The houses are built together out of brick and reach out to the sidewalk.

Diary Entry Sat. March 9

I was appointed table orderly. So was excused from the hike to Winchester. A bunch of fellows went down this P.M. to go thru the castle and cathedral. I preferred to wait and go tomorrow. But I am out of luck as we leave camp for good tomorrow. This camp is Winnalldown.

Diary Entry Sun. March 10

Cleaned up the huts and left for Winchester at 11:00 oclock. Took the train for Southhamton a distance of fourteen miles.

Loaded on the transport St. George. Sailed away about 4:30 P.M. Crossed the channel and docked at Havre about midnight.

NOTES

1. Lieutenant Colonel Richard S. Johnson and Debra Johnson Knox, How to Locate Anyone Who Is or Has Been in the Military (Eighth edition, 1999). In February 1918, the U.S. Army established Service numbers to track and index the approximately five million enlisted soldiers who joined the Army. After World War I, commissioned Army officers and the other U.S. military branches established Service numbers. On July 1, 1969, the U.S. military ceased using Service numbers in favor of Social Security numbers as the method to document individual service members. Beginning in 2011, the Department of Defense (DOD) started to phase out use of Social Security numbers in favor of a 10 digit DOD identification number.

2. General Orders Number 126, Soldier's Individual Pay Record Book (France: General Headquarters, American Expeditionary Forces, August 1, 1918). The instructions mandated pay book use was to start October 1, 1918.

3. Private First Class Elmer O. Smith, U.S. Army Enlistment Record, signed by Captain Corwin J. Schneider, Captain, Field Artillery (FA) , Commander, Headquarters Company, 119th FA Regiment, May 15, 1919.

Chapter 6
Coetquidan, Artillery Training in France

In March 1918, the 119th FA Regiment including Private Elmer Smith finally arrived in France. After landing at the port of Le Havre, the unit proceeded to Camp Coetquidan, an artillery training camp on the Brittany peninsula in western France. The unit received their French-made 75 mm howitzers here and underwent their first detailed training as an artillery unit in support of ground infantry elements.

Through repetitive training the unit soon mastered the intricacies of their artillery equipment. The "French 75," considered the first modern artillery piece, was the first field gun to include a hydro-pneumatic recoil mechanism. This feature kept the gun's trail and wheels perfectly still during the firing sequence. Since the artillery piece did not need to be re-aimed after each shot, the crew of six could fire as soon as the barrel returned to its resting position. By affixing a stool to the frame the gunner could open the breech during recoil making the weapon ready for immediate reloading. In typical use, the French 75 could deliver fifteen rounds per minute on its target, using either a high explosive or shrapnel shell with a maximum range of about 5 miles (8,500 meters). Its firing rate could reach close to 30 rounds per minute but only for a very short time and with a highly experienced crew which most in the 119th soon became.[1]

Private Smith was assigned duties as a telephone operator. He continued to receive more detailed training and instruction on how to establish field telephone operations to support the batteries as they dispersed on the battlefield. His job was to operate the regimental switchboard as well as run the communications wire to link the Regimental Headquarters with the two battalions and the six firing batteries.

Training for combat was intense at Camp Coetquidan. In addition to specialty training, physical fitness and mental toughness were built through numerous foot and mounted marches.

After arrival in France, a unit Censorship Officer reviewed all outgoing soldier mail to ensure that no operational details of the unit's mission were described in case the enemy captured the mail. Only in one of Elmer's letters was a portion clipped out. Thus, mail censoring largely served as a routine but necessary requirement. The Censorship Officer normally signed the lower left hand of the envelope certifying that it had been reviewed. This is captured for the letters that still had corresponding envelopes.

Just prior to moving to the front in early June, Private Smith was threatened with a court-martial. The commander of the 120th FA Regiment, Colonel Carl Penner, allegedly observed him severely whipping a horse. Given Elmer's previously expressed frustration about dealing with horses, it is likely he did inflict some form of punishment on the creature. But the issue was quickly resolved. After an hour and a half in the guardhouse, Private Smith's unit leadership determined that the "balky" horse required the necessary discipline. The matter was likely soon forgotten. The very next day the 119th FA boarded trains bound for combat.[2]

Diary Entry Mon. March 11

Unloaded 7:00 this A.M. Marched thru Havre to camp about five miles. Havre seems to be a large and progressive city. Everything in the line of foodstuffs seem to be more plentiful than in England.

Our camp consists of small tents. It is only a rest camp. And here is hoping to god we aren't here long.

Diary Entry Tues. March 12

We were ordered to move this morning.

Marched thru Havre to the railroad station. We were loaded into cattle cars. The cars are marked Hommes 40 or Cheavux 8 [40 men or 8 horses]. Their are 36 men in the car I am in. Pulled out of their about noon. Such a train. It is worse than riding in a limber wagon. Passed thru some interesting cities and country. All we have to eat on the trip is hardtack, red horse [~ beef jerky] and water. We were told we would be at camp nine o clock tonight.

Diary Entry Wed. March 13

My god such a night we put in last night. We never reached camp but kept a going on the trains. Last night was by far the worst night I ever put in, in all my life. We all sat huddled up and nearly froze to death. We certainly welcomed daylight. It was so cold that nobody slept much. If these d--m engineers put as much energy in travel as they do in blowing their whistle we might of reached camp last night. As it was we arrived in the city about two P.M. Marched out camp a distance of about four miles. We found nice steel cots and ticks awaiting us. Oh boy!

Diary Entry Thur. March 14

Ah! We slept until 8 o'clock this morning. It seems good to get back to regular meals once more.

We cleaned up the barracks and washed our clothes.

This is an entirely artillery camp. We woke by the noise of the big guns out on the range.

Diary Entry Fri. March 15

Finished cleaning my clothes. We had an inspection of personnel by Capt. Lewis [Joseph H. Lewis].

I went to the "Y" tonight and saw the movies. Apples were passed around there.

Letter to Mother, March 15, 1918

YMCA letterhead

Dear Mother:

Well this is the early evening and I am wondering what you folks are doing this minute.

I have just had supper and I suppose you are about eating dinner.

I am feeling fine outside of a little soreness and lameness. You wouldn't doubt my word if you could see some of the cattle cars we have rode in. We were packed in so tight we were not able to move around much. We had to put up in them one night and it was by far the most miserable night I ever spent in my life. It was so cold nobody could sleep. All we could do was huddle up in a corner and let our teeth chatter. I was so stiff from the cold when morning came I found it hard to walk. The cars here are marked, Hommes 40 or Chevoux 8. Meaning forty men or eight horses. You can imagine how comfortable it was.

I think I am going to like it here where we are. It is a little hard to make the natives understand but I am beginning to pick up a few French words and hope to speak it well enough to be understood while we are here.

I haven't had any mail in so long that I would give ten dollars for a letter from Ovid or there abouts.

I am anxious to hear how father's health is. I suppose he will be back from Florida by the time you receive this. I am trying to get my Liberty Bond and insurance straightened out. I think I will have it fixed up in a few days.

Well I can't write much of anything because the censor doesn't like to read interesting news. I hope this letter will find you all well. Write often.

Goodbye
Your son, Elmer

Postcard to Father in Florida, Date Unknown, March 1918

Dear Father:

I have arrived safely.

Elmer

[Know this was sent from France as it was marked "Censored"]

Diary Entry Sat. March 16

We did not do anything all day long. Went to the concert given by the 119th band at the "Y".

Diary Entry Sun. March 17

We had a showdown inspection in the morning. Quite a few of the fellows were confined to camp because of dirty pistol belts.

I went down and had a belly full of beer. Ah! Hot Dog!

Diary Entry Mon. March 18

We started our training today. We took a hike this forenoon. Started to going to telephone school this P.M. We worked with picks and shovels digging communication trenches for the telephone wire.

The worlds all wrong. I thot we were thru useing picks and shovels.

Diary Entry Tues. March 19

We started on a hike but it commence to rain so we came back. After getting on dry clothes we were sent over to the stables to feed horses. It looks very much as tho we would get horses again.

Went to telephone school this P.M. We pumped water out of the trenches and tore down the telephone communications out. The whole regiment were put in under quarantine tonight because of scarlet fever.

Diary Entry Wed. March 20

Warm and sunny. On account of the quarrantine we did not have reveille until 6:40. We had setting up exercises with music by the band.

This afternoon we picked up stones and sticks from a tract of open ground.

Diary Entry Thur. March 21

It was very warm and clear.

We done exercises and close order drill. This afternoon we went out in the woods and strung up telephone communications.

Diary Entry Fri. March 22

We had exercises and did laundry.

Had a regimental field meet this afternoon. Hdqs. finished first.

Diary Entry Sat. March 23

We were given telephone school this forenoon.
This afternoon the entire Co. done nothing but bunk fatigue.

Diary Entry Sun. March 24

We stood and early morning inspection. After that I attended the regimental services conducted by Chaplain Atkinson [Chaplain William A. Atkinson of Detroit].

Saw the first battalion ball team take a good walloping by a 9–4 score this afternoon.

Diary Entry Mon. March 25

We begin reveille again at 5:45.

We had telephone and close order drill this forenoon.

General Chamberlain [MG John L. Chamberlain, Inspector General of the U.S. Army] of this made an inspection of the Regiment this afternoon.

Received my first letter since I have been in France.

Diary Entry Tues. March 26

Footdrill, exercises and telephone school this forenoon. Telephone school all the afternoon.

Letter to Sister, March 26, 1918

France

Dear Sister:

I haven't received any letters from home yet but I am going to keep on writing. I received a letter from Helen yesterday. It was the first letter I had received since we left Camp Merritt.

I am feeling fine. And I never remember of having such an appetite like I have now. I eat & eat and it seems as tho I can never get enough. I am waiting for pay day. Three of us happen to know where we can buy a whole roast chicken & everything with it but the wine for about fifty cents apiece. Where can you buy a feed like that in Michigan.

How are things around Ovid? I suppose you are plodding around in the mud about this date. The spring rains seem to be all over here. We have been having warm sunny days most the time we have been here.

What is father going to do this summer? Does he say anything more about selling the farm and moving to Florida? I certainly wish he would if his health is much better by staying the winter there. I think you ought to do your part in trying to coax him to do it.

I will try and square up that debt I owe this pay day. I have finally gotten my Liberty Bond straightened out. I will not have any but my insurance coming out of my pay this pay day. I signed the pay roll before getting the bond straightened out. That is the why nothing will be payed on it this pay day. I made an allotment of fifteen dollars a month on it. I have sixty eight dollars more to pay on it. It will come to mother when it is payed for.

I would appreciate the home paper if you want to send them. We do not get many papers to read here. Their is a little one paged paper we get from Paris once a day. But it hasen't much of interest in it.

I suppose you have all ready read of the long range gun the Germans are shelling Paris with. I think they say the shell travels seventy five miles and at a highth of twenty miles.

How are you getting at the office. I some times wonder what in the deuce I will do when I get out of the Army. I will probably forget everything I knew by that time. I'll probably make a good tramp if I don't anything else.

How is Genevieve and the boys? I suppose Dee is as rough and ready as ever. Well I must quit writing as I want to write to Frank yet tonight. Write often.

From, Your Brother,
Elmer

Censor Review 1LT Corwin J. Schneider

Diary Entry Wednesday March 27

It is quite a little colder. We went thru the same classes as we did on the 26th.

Except at telephone school we commenced on the service code.

Diary Entry Thur. March 28

It rained so we had telephone school inside.

Our barracks was placed under quarantine. We were given two shots under the shoulder blade of diptheria serum. Bennack [Private Fred Bannack, B Battery] is in the hospital with diptheria.

Letter to Sister, March 28, 1918

Location censored from this letter.

Dear Sister:

I received your letter of Feb.27 today. You may be sure I was glad to receive it as it was the first I had heard from home since we left Camp Merritt.

I also received a letter from Helen and one from Waco. So I am feeling quite happy.

I am glad to hear that father is gaining. You didn't write anything about yourselves. Are you having a rather hard time this winter.

I never received the candy you sent me. Perhaps it hasn't had time to reach me yet. I dare say the package burst open and somebody else has eaten it. Anything sent to us now days wants to be done up pretty well.

[Sentence torn off by censor] We have lost three men since we left Camp MacArthur. One from B. Battery and two from Hdqs.

It is rather dismal out today. A cold drizzly rain has been falling most of the day. We have had some fine warm weather tho.

You shouldn't worry about not do anything to help out. Your time will come someday. And then perhaps you will see as much as I have. I am getting a good education out of it in some ways. Perhaps I will be home to tell you about it some day. I can't think of much to write as I just wrote a couple of days ago. We can't write anything interesting anyway as the censors does not like to read anything of interest. Well write often. Goodbye.

Your Brother,
Elmer

Newspaper Article, The State Journal, March 1918

Ovid Guardsman Has Arrived in France
Special to The State Journal, March 1918.

Ovid, March 28—Mrs. W.F. Smith has received word of the safe arrival in France of her son, Elmer O. Smith. He enlisted in the National Guard at Lansing last summer and was located at Waco, Texas for several months. Previous to leaving the United States he was promoted to the headquarters company.

Diary Entry Fri. March 29

The captain gave us orders to lie still today as we were affected by the serum.

We were paid. Hell of a lot of good it will do us being under quarantine.

Diary Entry Sat. March 30

Ah! Ha! Bunk fatigue the entire day.

Diary Entry Sun. March 31

Inspection. Easter services conducted by the Chaplin. We were taken down to the hot showers for a bath this afternoon.

Diary Entry Mon. April 1

We had gun drill on the 75s and telephone school.

Diary Entry Tues. April 2

We had close order drill and telephone school.

Diary Entry Wed. April 3

We were given gun drill and telephone instructions.

Letter to Mother, April 3, 1918

France

Dear Mother:

I will try and write a few lines to let you know I am feeling fine. I am eating all I can and am getting fat as a pig. I have grown quite a little and am getting quite broad shouldered.

It has been raining all day long. We have some quite disagreeable weather here. But when it is nice and warm it is fine. The scenery here is quite beautiful.

I don't hardly know what to write about. About all I can tell you is that I am feeling well.

I have never received the box of candy you sent me. I had a letter from Frank, he said he sent me a box but I have never received it.

If I were you I would sell your interest in the place to grandmother. If thats the way she feels about it. Besides I presume the money would come in pretty handy to you folks anyway.

Well this is a short letter but will write in a day or two.

I am glad to hear father is better. Write often.

Your Son,
Elmer

Diary Entry Thur. April 4

We were out observing gun drill by the batteries this A.M. Telephone and sketching work this afternoon.

Succeed in running the guard safely and in getting a little wine and other articles tonight.

Diary Entry Fri. April 5

Were given telephone school.

Diary Entry Sat. April 6

We had an inspection this forenoon. Went out with the first battalion detail under Major Ashley [Amos H. Ashley] for instruction on sketching, telephone, and the use of the French B.C. Scope.

Diary Entry Sun. April 7

Took a good hot bath at the camp bath house this morning. We were out with Major Ashley on the range for instruction.

Took a little trip down to the White Way tonight. A fine bunch of guards we have here.

Diary Entry Mon. April 8

We left for the range early this morning. A and D battery took up the firing. They fired only one half day.

Went to telephone school this afternoon. Had a lecture on the telephone system.

Sneaked out and down on Broadway again tonight.

Diary Entry Tues. April 9

We were out on the range early this morning. Their was no firing done on account of a heavy fog.

We had heilograph signaling this afternoon at telephone school.

Letter to Sister, April 9, 1918

France

Dear Sister:

I received your letter of Feb. 20th. I don't see what made it so late as I have received letters written by you dated in March. Their must of been a mistake for their was a lot of mail that came in late.

I am feeling little rheumatism in my knees. It has been so rainy lately and their is no floor in our barracks so I think that is how I got it.

I received the papers and also the pictures. The pictures were fine and I was glad to get them. I haven't received the candy yet.

I am sending you and mother each a handkerchief. Please let me know if you receive them O.K. Their is quite a little danger in sending anything in an envelope as we can't seal them. But I guess I will risk it. I didn't send the money as I said I was going to do for fear you wouldn't ever receive it.

I don't know what to write about hardly. All I can say about what we are doing is that we are busy as the dickens from daylight to dark. Well I think I will quit for now and write again when I feel a little more like writing.

Goodbye,
Your Brother,
Elmer

Censor Review: James P. Boland 2nd Lieut. F.A.O.R.C. [Field Artillery Officer Reserve Corps]

Diary Entry Wed. April 10

I fell in with the "Gold Brick" detail to go to the range. We observed the fire until about 9:30. We came in to take a bath but were disappointed as the bath house was not in working order.

Went to telephone school. Learned the method of splicing wire.

Diary Entry Thur. April 11

Fell in with the "gold brick" crowd again this morning. Washed some clothes and were again fooled on the baths. Worked on the three point problem the rest of the fore-noon.

Diary Entry Fri. April 12

Went to telephone school this forenoon and afternoon.

Diary Entry Sat. April 13

Went to telephone school this A.M. We were having an inspection this P.M. when word came that their was a forest fire on the range. We were armed with picks and shovels and marched about 4 miles to the fire. It took three regiments and a lot of hot hard work to check the fire. Some of the fellows caught a couple of wild young hogs. The fire was caused by an artillery shell bursted on a wooden building. We were late getting back and were very tired.

Diary Entry Sun. April 14

Got up for breakfast and reveille and then went back to bed. I was just intrested in a nice quiet snooze. But alas, was awakened to go on kitchen police. Drat the luck.

Diary Entry Mon. April 15

Was transferred to the Regimental detail. The detail was taken out by Capt. Bow. We strung telephone wires and communicated to different stations.

Went to telephone school as usual this afternoon.

Letter to Sister, April 15, 1918

France

Dear Sister:

I received two letters from you today one dated Mar. 15th and one Mar. 25th. It is the first letters I have had for nearly two weeks. You may be sure I appreciated them.

Those pictures were fine and you all looked natural. Those other pictures you sent some time ago were fine too. You don't how well I appreciate your kindness for taken the trouble to make them and sending them to me. I have not received the box of candy you sent. I received a nice one from Frank a little while back. Gee! They certainly tasted good too.

You will probably receive some form of paper from the government on my insurance later. They are very slow on anything like that.

I suppose father is back home by this time enjoying himself. I hope the weather continues good so he won't get worse.

We had a little excitement Sat. in fighting a small forest fire on the hill side about four miles away. It was caused by range practice. A number of the fellows run on to a litter of young wild hogs and caught a number of them. They are very queer looking animals and are stripped on the back like a chipmunk.

Gee the newspapers like to make a good story of the German losses. If they would divide that number by 8 I think they would strike nearer the truth.

I suppose most of all the young fellows around home are about all thinned out. Is their ever any more parties around Ovid.

What did you mean about Archies entrance into military service. Is he drafted or is he going to get his commission.

Well it is time for tattoo so I will quit for tonight. Write often.

Your Brother,
Elmer

P.S. I received the Ovid papers

Diary Entry Tue. April 16

We were taken out under the new ork (U.S.A.) [?] for the same work of yesterday A.M.

Telephone school this P.M.

Diary Entry Wed. April 17

The same old routine as that of yesterday.

Diary Entry Thur. April 18

Check April 17th.

Diary Entry Fri. April 19

We drew horses for the 119th this A.M. Telephone school this P.M.

Diary Entry Sat. April 20

We drew 86 horses this forenoon. Darn em!

We had a show down inspection and gas mask drill this afternoon.

Stables once more.

Diary Entry Sun. April 21

Took a hike way over to the stables before breakfast this morning in the rain to feed a few measly horses. We worked like a son of a gun all day long. No more Sundays off in this darn outfit anymore.

I went on stable guard tonight.

Diary Entry Mon. April 22

Feel rather crabby this morning after last nights tour of guard. Worked like a devil all day long. Here's wishing they take me up on the firing line as soon as possible.

Diary Entry Tue. April 23

Worked like the deuce all day. The same d-m old guard as that in Waco.

Diary Entry Wed. April 24

Feed, watered & groomed all forenoon. Telephone school this afternoon.

Diary Entry Thur. April 25

Damn the horses. Went on guard again tonight. This is the darnest regiment I ever heard of. Some of these damed officers brains would not make a dot on a piece of paper.

Diary Entry Fri. April 26

Worked like the devil all this forenoon. Was excused to go to telephone school this afternoon.

Diary Entry Sat. April 27

A full pack mounted hike for today. As usual my horse was taken away from me and I was told I could walk. Curse the sergeants. Heres hoping I will be able to get even with some of these birds if I ever get in civil life.

Everything went off fairly well on the hike. I was full packed (blanket roll, pack, belt, holster, canteen, 2 gas masks, steel derbys, flag kit. Oh its light as _____.

Diary Entry Sun. April 28

I believe their is no more Sundays. We worked at the stables nearly all the forenoon. Stables nowdays from daylight to dark.

Worked on a kitchen detail the entire afternoon. No rest for the wicked.

Diary Entry Mon. April 29

The same old work today.

Diary Entry Tue. April 30

Telephone school and stables.

Diary Entry Wed. May 1

Stables, telephone and gold bricking was all I did today.

Diary Entry Thur. May 2

Was on guard.

Diary Entry Fri. May 3

Nothing worth telling.

Diary Entry Sat. May 4

Stables and wash day.

Diary Entry Sun. May 5

We did stables, took a bath and went to church conducted by Chaplain Atkinson. Laid around this afternoon. Guard tonight.

Letter to Mother May 5, 1918

France

Dear Mother:

I received your letter of Feb. 3 a few days ago and have got around to answer it. We busy from daylight to dark and don't have much time to ourselves only a few hours on Sun. afternoons. We are sure getting a strenuous period of training. Everybody is being pushed to their limit. I am a telephone operator.

I am in good condition except for a cold. I am glad to here that father is looking so good this spring. I hope he will continue to improve. He will have to go to Florida again this coming winter.

Never mind about sending me anything. You can't anyway unless an order comes from me signed by our captain. We can buy most anything we want here when we have money. It costs quite a little to send a package over here too. Did you ever receive those handkerchiefs I sent in a letter?

I received a letter from Mrs. Barnaby yesterday. She said she had been wanting to write you but did not know your correct address. She has a service flag for me that will hang, she says until I come back. She had quite a little to say about Helen. It looks as tho she wanted to make a match. I told Helen in a recent letter I couldn't see anything like that for quite awhile in the future if ever. Her letters sounded a little to much in that manner, She is valedictorian of her class this year. I told her what I thot and told her to think it over.

So Vern has an automobile has he. I wonder what he will do with Pete now. I suppose he will be getting married next.

I wish you could see me in my new steel hat. It certainly is a clumsy looking thing and we have to wear them all the time. They are a very uncomfortable thing. Well is nearly time for stables so will quit. Tell Zelma I will write her in a few days. Hope this will find you all well.

Your son,
Elmer

O.K. Matt Battelle, 2nd Lieut. F.A.R.C.

Diary Entry Mon. May 6

Was excused this morning for telephone school.
Goldbricked this afternoon.

Diary Entry Tue. May 7

Telephone school this forenoon.
We took a horse back ride this afternoon.

Diary Entry Wed. May 8

I went to telephone school this forenoon.

Diary Entry Thur. May 9

We were given lecture at telephone school this forenoon. We were given equitation this afternoon.

Diary Entry Fri. May 10

We were out to the communication trenches this forenoon.
We study under our telephone officer afternoons.

Diary Entry Sat. May 11

We did equitation this forenoon. We were given this afternoon to clean up in.

Diary Entry Sun. May 12

Hooray, we were allowed to sleep in until 7 o clock.
I did nothing but lay around all day. Guard tonight.

Letter to Mother May 12, 1918

Somewhere in France

Dear Mother:

I wrote to you a few days ago but I am going to write again as this is Mothers Day.

Nearly all the soldiers over here are writing to their mothers today. I suppose all these letters will be sent straight thru.

I am feeling fine. My cold being quite a little bit better. This part of France is certainly a good place for colds. It rains nearly every day now. I understand the summers here are cool.

I received some mail today. The first in quite a few days. One was from grandmother Smith. I wrote to her when I was in [censored/crossed out location] and I guess it made it her lonesome.

Say if you folks want to send me anything send magazines or anything to read. I think you can send them so they wont come in under parcel post. We don't have much spare time here but when we do we like to have something to read.

Did you ever get those handkerchiefs I sent. If you receive them all right, I will try sending something else.

I enjoyed the best sleep this morning for some time. Nobody was up until 7:00 o clock. We are not supposed to do any thing more than we have to on Sundays from now on.

I am sorry you couldn't send that maple sugar. For it would of tasted good. Well it is nearly time for church call and I will quit for this time.

Your Son,
Elmer

O.K. Matt Battelle 2nd Lieut. F.A.R.C.

Diary Entry Mon. May 13

Worked out to the range all day.

Diary Entry Wed. May 15

Worked out on the range putting up telephone lines and installed a switch board.

Diary Entry Thur. May 16

Finished the work on the station.

Diary Entry Fri. May 17

I was made a driver. So stuck around the stables all day. Guard tonight.

Diary Entry Sat. May 18

Stood guard all day. The brigade fired today.

Diary Entry Sun. May 19

Slept until 7:00 o'clock this morning. Wrote letters all day at the "Y".

Diary Entry Mon. May 20

Started to telephone school this afternoon. We were allowed to clean up this afternoon.

Diary Entry Tue. May 21

We went down to telephone school this afternoon. Capt. Bow [Warren E. Bow] is no more. Lieut. Kolb is in command.

Diary Entry Wed. May 22

After we did stables we came back to barracks and went to the woods. Had buzzer practice all A.M. We were under Lieut Stillwell's [1LT William G. Stillwell] instruction this afternoon.

Diary Entry Thur. May 23

Commenced work on the lines and station for the 2nd brigade problem.

Diary Entry Fri. May 24

Finished work on lines and station.

Diary Entry Sat. May 25

The problem was fired. Time 55 minutes. Took up all lines and station this afternoon.

Letter to Sister May 25, 1918

France

Dear Sister:

I received your letter all O.K. and was glad to hear from you. I am feeling fine. I also received the box with the maple sugar. It certainly was good. Don't worry if you don't hear from me so often in the near future. For I may be so busy and in such conditions so I could not write as often.

I presume by the time you get this you will be taking your vacation from the office. It would be nice if father & mother would take that trip north about that time and you go with them.

I had a fine supper last night. Their were seven of us. We got away with 22 bottels of beer, one bottel of champagne and say nothing of the egg ommelettes and french fried potatoes. The people here have the Americans skinned when it comes to making ommelettes & french fried. The supper only cost eight Francs.

Say never publish any letters in the paper as somebody might get a court martial out of it. That is the instructions we have had. I meant to tell you before. I received a little apology from Mason the other day. I wonder what grandmother O. [Oakes] had under her hat. I have more trouble with the <u>durn women</u> now than I know how to handle. Ask Frank if I don't. I guess I will have to quit writing to some of them. Well this is a short letter and I don't know as you can read it I wrote it in such a hurry. Write again soon.

Your Brother,
Elmer

O.K. W.B. Caldwell, 2nd Lt.

Diary Entry Sun. May 26

Stood guard and worked like the devil all day.

Diary Entry Mon. May 27

I was made a driver. Worked all day.

Diary Entry Tue. May 28

Took part in a mounted hike.

Diary Entry Wed. May 29

Another full pack mounted hike.

Diary Entry Thur. May 30

Worked.

Diary Entry Fri. May 31

We were given another hike this forenoon.

Diary Entry Sat. June 1

Inspection followed by a full pack mounted hike. Stables in P.M.

Diary Entry Sun. June 2

Worked all day on harness. Picked my team.

Diary Entry Mon. June 3

Drove team wagon all day.

Was put into the guard house by Colonel Penner [COL Carl Penner, Commander of the 120th FA Regiment] of the 120th for whipping a balky horse. Was in an hour and a half. Was not given a court martial as they decided it was what the horse needed. Picked a new team. Loaded my wagon.

Fortunately, Private Smith's only encounter with the military justice system throughout his service was short-lived. Occurring on the eve of his unit's movement to the front was also fortuitous. Every trained soldier would be necessary to accomplish the unit's combat missions over the next five months.

The extensive and detailed training program was over. The 119th FA Regiment was relatively well-trained and hardened as they proceeded to the front as part of the AEF. The 32nd Division was the second National Guard Division to be committed to the front lines. A French officer who trained the Regiment praised its abilities and discipline as they departed Coetquidan.

Newspaper Article, Detroit News, June 1918

"Michigan's Own" is Praised by Officer

Instructor on Eve of Battle Commends 119th Field Artillery Regiment

Boston, June 18—On the eve of going into battle, the One Hundred and Nineteenth field artillery, under command of Colonel Chester B. McCormick, Lansing has won the special commendation of Captain Risler, a French officer in charge of instruction of the Michigan batteries since they landed in France.

"You are fit," said the French officer, "and I am sure you will maintain on the battlefield the reputation you have established in your schools."

According to a letter received from one of the officers of the regiment, the following are extracts from a talk given by Captain Risler when he had finished his course of instruction for the entire 57th Brigade, of which the 119th is a part.

"Today is very likely the last time I shall have the pleasure and honor of speaking in front of you. It is not without purpose that I use these two words, pleasure and honor. Pleasure, because to deal with young men like you, clever, energetic, good, willing, understanding quickly, executing well. Honor, because you belong to the great and noble American nation whose high moral standard shines over the world."

"Gentlemen, I am very proud of you ... I am sure you will maintain this reputation on the battlefield. I have full confidence in you and if I am proud of the student officers of today I shall be prouder of the fighting men of tomorrow."

"Gentlemen, I wish you good luck and fine success to the world's glory and to the common honor of both France and America."

NOTES

1. Byron Farwell, *Over There: The United States in the Great War, 1917-1918* (New York: W.W. Norton and Company, 1999), 44-45.
   David T. Zabecki, "French 75 Gun," *World War I: A Student Encyclopedia* (Santa Barbara CA: ABC-CLIO, 2005), 726-727.

2. Carl Penner, Frederic Sammond, and H.M. Appel, *The 120th Field Artillery Diary: 1880-1919* (Milwaukee WI: Hammersmith-Kortmeyer Company, 1928). PVT Elmer Smith's run-in with COL Penner did not merit an entry in the daily record of the 120th FA's activities.

Chapter 7
Wounded In Action

AT THE END OF MAY 1918, the 119th FA Regiment received combat orders and on June 4 began its movement towards the front lines. The official order detailing the movement plan was found intact in the Michigan State archives.[1]

From June 6 to June 24 the 119th was attached to the 101st FA Regiment of the 26th Division. The 101st men were primarily from the Massachusetts Army National Guard and the 26th Division was known as the "Yankee Division" as most of its soldiers were from the New England states.[2]

The 119th FA mission was to receive live combat training in support of operations in their sector near the city of Toul, France. The 101st FA Regiment was situated about four to seven kilometers behind the main trench lines in this area of operations.

The 26th Division took command of the Toul-Boucq "Defensive" Sector of the Western Front from the 1st (U.S.) Division on April 3, 1918. Significant 26th Division combat operations occurred from April 10-13 in Bois Brule, on April 20-21 at Seicheprey, and on June 16 in the vicinity of Xivray-Marvoisin. During the June operation, German Army units supported by artillery fires throughout the sector attacked the U.S. front line infantry positions and the Americans "Doughboys" effectively repulsed the attack. It was during this operation where the 119th FA saw its first major action and Private Elmer Smith was wounded.[3]

The primary 101st FA account of the war specifically mentions the arrival and employment of the 119th to train and support their mission. A 101st map depicts how their firing batteries and posts of command (P.C.) were arrayed during this period.[4] The 119th batteries likely occupied the same firing positions in order to train and learn from their more experienced artillery brethren.

Battery F of the 119th wrote a war operations summary and described this period in it. These accounts are incorporated into the diary and letter entries later in this and subsequent chapters.[5]

The 119th moved into its initial firing positions on June 14. On June 16 at about 3:30 p.m. near the village of Noviant, Private Smith was working in a fortified dugout bunker installing communications wire when his position received incoming German artillery fire. The shell hit approximately 150 yards away. As this was the first time they had been bombarded, Elmer and several soldiers rushed out of the dugout to see the effects from the explosion. Soon they heard another incoming artillery round and rushed to get back inside their dugout. Just as they were about to enter the bunker the shell exploded about 15 feet behind them. Shell fragments tore through the air and wounded Private Smith and another soldier in the back. In the letter to his mother on June 22, Elmer states several soldiers were wounded. The wounds to these other soldiers must have been superficial as they were not noted in the unit's list of wounded. Elmer was rapidly evacuated after being severely wounded, so he may not have understood the extent of the exact casualties at the time.

Private Elmer O. Smith and Private First Class Louis K. Hice, of Three Rivers, Michigan, were the first two soldiers wounded in action (WIA) from the 119th FA Regiment. They were also some of the first wounded in the 32nd Division which had yet to commit its subordinate infantry forces into major combat operations.

The wound cards of PVT Smith and PFC Hice were found in the Michigan State archives.[6] Interestingly, Elmer Smith's card lists him as seriously wounded. After eight weeks in several hospitals and convalescent camps, Elmer recovered from his wounds and returned to his unit. PFC Hice's card lists him as slightly wounded. However, he died of his wounds the next day and thus, became the first soldier killed in action (KIA) from the 119th FA Regiment.[7]

The Regimental Chaplain, MAJ William Atkinson, in a letter home, likely written the night of the attack, stated a PVT Arthur or Archie Norris from Detroit was also wounded. Again PVT Norris' wounds might have been superficial since he is not listed in any of the rollup of soldiers wounded or killed in action the 119th FA published in September and November.

PVT Elmer Smith was initially evacuated to a front-line support hospital near Toul. Shell fragments had penetrated the left side of his back, entered his chest cavity, and lodged near his heart and lungs. Luckily one small iron fragment, approximately four by five millimeters, had not seriously harmed his vital organs. Due to the likely risk involved, the U.S. Army doctors caring for Elmer decided not to operate and extract the small shrapnel piece lodged in this delicate area. He lived the rest of his life with the small piece of iron embedded in his chest. Occasionally, throughout the remainder of his life Elmer coughed up blood. This could have been due to movement of the shrapnel piece or perhaps the mustard gas he was exposed to several times after returning to the front from August through November 1918. About 25 years after the war, another small shell fragment worked its way to the surface of the skin on his back.

News of PVT Smith's being wounded took eight days to reach his parents outside Ovid. They received an official War Department telegram on Monday, June 24.[8] It stated he had been severely wounded. His mother, Olive Smith, was upset but could only express hope for her boy so far away from rural Michigan. In her letter, she encouraged him to remain positive.

Elmer expressed embarrassment in his diary and letters that he had only been on the front lines for three days when he was wounded. In reality he had nothing to be ashamed of. He had simply been an honorable American soldier doing his duty while his unit was engaged in combat against the German enemy along the front lines.

Local newspapers quickly reported PVT Elmer Smith as wounded in action. Since U.S. forces had not been significantly engaged in front-line combat up to this point, this was likely one of the first times newspapers in central Michigan brought the sad report of local men being wounded or killed. But the true cost of war—the loss and wounding of sons, grandsons, brothers, husbands, and fathers—would substantially increase as the American Expeditionary Forces (AEF) including the 32nd Division became totally committed to direct combat with German Army units.

Initially, Elmer was in quite a bit of pain and had difficulty breathing. Over a month these symptoms subsided and he was transferred to convalescence camps far from the front. On July 22, doctors declared him fit for duty and he began the two week journey back to the 119th FA Regiment and the front lines.

119th FA Regiment Memorandum Detailing Movement to the Western Front

Headquarters, 119th Field Artillery
American Expeditionary Forces
FRANCE

May 31, 1918.
Memorandum:

1. This regiment will move from Guer on 7 trains, one train for each battery and one train for the regimental sections, including sections from Hq. Co., Sanitary detachment, Supply Company and Ordnance Detachment.

A train will comprise:
1 First Class Passenger Coach,
17 Flat cars,
30 Box cars,
2 Cabooses.
Each train commander will drop off at Guer any cars which are not used.

2. Train commanders may allot seats in cabooses and other unused sections in passenger coach to non-commissioned officers.

Harness in sacks, saddles and forage should be stacked in the center of each car.

Two men will ride in each horse car. Unit commanders should see that the horse cars are supplied with buckets for watering. No smoking must be allowed in horse cars. Sand may be placed in horse cars if available.

3. Units should have tools ready for blocking vehicles on flat cars. The load on escort wagons should not rise higher than nine feet ten inches above the ground.

If possible, one lantern should be provided for each troop car.

4. The Quartermaster of each train will sign a report at the end of the journey as provided in G.O. 66 AEF cs.

5. Equipment of officers and men that is not to be taken on the train should be transported to warehouse, Camp Quartermaster. All equipment thus stored should be in boxes, crates, bundles, or sacks, plainly marked thus: "Btry. A, 119th F.A. bed sacks".

Field officers are limited to one bedding roll, one trunk, one satchel, (or clothing roll, or suit case". All other officers, to one bedding roll and one satchel or clothing roll or or suit case). Where officers desire, the regimental entraining officer is arranging to ship personal property of officers for storage with American Express Co., at Paris.

6. The forage and ration per Par. 302, F.S.R is:

RESERVE

(a) On each man at least two days reserve rations, on escort wagon, 1 day's reserve per man.

(b) On vehicle for draft animals, 1 day's reserve grain ration, the same for riding animals carried either on vehicle or mount.

FIELD:

(c) On escort wagon, 1 day's field ration per man and 2 day's grain ration per animal.
(d) In rolling kitchen, 1 day's field ration per man is carried.

Two day's reserve grain has been issued in this camp. Travel grain and hay will be drawn by batteries at railway dock.

Each battery should take enough prepared fire wood for cooking at least three meals.

7. All ordnance equipment will be taken. Harness and saddles will be carried in the cars with horses. Men's personal equipment will be carried in the cars with the men. Fire control and signal equipment will be carried in fourgons. All other equipment will be carried in escort or ordnance wagons.

The field range, etc. are not part of equipment "A", but will be taken with the troops and carried on escort wagons.

8. It is planned to load vehicles as follows:
1 gun and 2 limbers—1 flat car
3 caissons—1 flat car
1 Fourgon and 1 ration cart—1 flat car
1 rolling kitchen and 1 water cart—1 flat car
2 medical carts,—1 flat car
1 motor car—1 flat car
1 escort wagon—1 flat car
1 chariot de parc—1flat car.

By order of Colonel McCormick,
Warren E. Bow, Captain, 119th F.A.
Adjutant.

Diary Entry Tue. June 4

Left camp Coltquidan at 11:00 A.M. for good. Pulled out of Guer at 5:00 P.M. Passed thru Rennes at 8:00 P.M.

Diary Entry Wed. June 5

Slept like hell in that box car last night. Passed thru Tours, Nevers, Bourges.

Diary Entry Thur. June 6

Another beautiful night of sleep.
Played poker most of the day.

Diary Entry Fri. June 7

Arrived at Toul at 3:00 A.M. Unloaded. We took every thing to a french village [Trondes] where we are billeted. We are 12 miles from the front. Can hear the big guns very plainly.

The sky is full of planes. Some so high you can not see them.

War Record of Battery F excerpt

...arriving in the Toul Sector June 8th, and going into billets in Trondes.

Diary Entry Sat. June 8

Worked at odd jobs all day long. Put on guard tonight. Could see the signals of projectors and flashes of the gun after dark.

Diary Entry Sun. June 9

Worked at driving and guard all day long. Some tired baby I am tonight.

No Diary Entries Mon. June 10, Tue. June 11, Wed. June 12

War Record of Battery F excerpt

On the night of June 11th two sections, those of Sgts. May and Rowland with Sgt. Wilder and the B.C. [Battery Commander] Detail left Trondes to take up a position northeast of Novia[n]t in support of the 101st Infantry of the Yankee Division and were fired on by the boche the same evening while on the road. This was the first Battery of the Regiment to be under fire. At 2 a.m. [June 12], the battery laid down its initial barrage on the enemy lines, which brought down some counter battery work [return fire], none of which was effective. On the night of June 16th the sections of Sgts. Brown and McAlonan took their place in the lines.

Diary Entry Thur. June 13

Slept nearly all the forenoon. We received orders to be ready to move at 4:00 P.M. Packed up and moved to a village about 6 miles behind the lines. Rolled in to get a little sleep at 11:00 bells P.M.

The 101st Field Artillery excerpt

...it had become the practice that if either side fired on a P.C., a reprisal would follow on a specified P.C. across the line. The reciprocal relation existed between the Chateau Ferme, the [101st FA] Regimental P.C. and a chateau in Essey, a German P.C. of some kind... On June 13, however, after supper, while the Regimental Staff was in the room used as an office, conferring with Colonel Chester B. McCormick, of the 119th F.A., about plans to bring that regiment into line for instruction, the French...

Diary Entry Fri. June 14

We hung around until four o clock. This afternoon we moved up to our position. Worked until late getting telephone communication.

Diary Entry Sat. June 15

Thank god no reveille up here. Unwound some wire this morning. Policed up this afternoon. Their are gun positions on all sides of us.

The village we are in [Noviant] has been shelled before. So I expect we will get ours as soon as they find out we are here.

Saw an aerial battle tonight.

The 101st Field Artillery excerpt

German activity had been growing more intense; new batteries had been coming in, and it looked as if something might happen. On the night of June 16, preceded by an artillery preparation of great volume, the Germans made an attack in force on Xivry. The 103rd Infantry [Regiment, U.S. 26th Division] completely repulsed it, and the enemy left many dead

Diary Entry Sun. June 16

We started work in putting the telephone central into a bombproof. Received my first baptism of fire at 3:30 this P.M. Their were about 8 shells thrown into the village. Received a wound from a shell that exploded in front of our bomb proof just as I was entering. Received the wound in the left side of my back. The shrapnel lodging near my heart. Took me to the hospital near Toul but would not operate on me.

Newspaper Article on the 119th FA's first Major Action and its first soldiers wounded

MICHIGAN BOYS PRIZE WOUNDS

113th [119th] Artillery Turns Every Gun on Enemy Trenches, Coming Off Victorious.

Chaplain W.A. Atkinson Writes of Men's Action Under Fire; Behave Like Veterans.

Because the Boche insisted on bombarding the villages in which they were quartered the One Hundred and Nineteenth Field artillery, in retaliation, turned every gun in the unit on the enemy trenches on the night of June 16th, and came off victorious, with only three wounded and no deaths.

According to a letter from Chaplain William A. Atkinson the three wounded feel highly honored at the distinction of being the first to receive the brand of enemy bullets. They are Louis Hise [Hice] and Arthur Norris of Detroit, and Elmer Smith, of Ovid, Michigan. All will recover. [PFC Hice died the next day] The letter in full says:

All Guns Active.

"Friends of the One Hundred and Nineteenth field artillery will be satisfied to know that all guns of the regiment will pay their compliments to the Hun tonight. Four of the guns have been in action since June 11, but tonight all will be doing their bit to end the war.

The immediate occasion for this is due to a bombardment we have been getting from the Hun. Four of the French villages in this neighborhood were shelled last night and this morning, killing some and wounding others. All of the casualties were members of the One Hundred and Fourth Massachusetts [104th Infantry Regiment, U.S. 26th Division] excepting three men from our unit. They are Louis Hise and Archie Norris of Detroit, and Elmer Smith of Ovid. These boys feel very much honored to be the first of our regiment to be wounded.

We all feel there is no cause for worry, but if the fact that we are 'doing' that for which we have been preparing for nearly a year will help to stimulate others to do likewise, we want Michigan men and women to know the fact."

Joyous and Eager.

"I never saw anyone go at their task with such joy and eagerness as does the American soldier. There is none of that 'awfulness' that at home we associate with the word war. He goes into position and comes out, quietly and with an air of finality. It's the thing to do and he does it with the same elasticity of action and spirit that he goes to a ball game or work.

Our regiment is firing now in conjunction with the One Hundred and First Massachusetts [101st FA Regiment, U.S. 26th Division], who have been here four months. Whether the boy comes from the east, west, north, or south he acts the same. I asked two infantrymen who just came out of the front trenches after a month's stay, how they liked it. Both replied as if in one voice; "I'd rather be there, sir, than back here resting."

Letter to Private Elmer Smith from Zelma Smith (sister), June 16, 1918

Ovid, Mich.

Dear Brother,

Mother intended to write you today but she won't have time. Mr. Pearce came about noon and said that grandma Oakes was sick with inflammatory rheumatism and wanted mother to come. He is visiting for the day near Carland and father is going to take her there so she can go back with him (Mr. Pearce). She has had to hustle to get ready. We didn't know she was sick. Mr. Eggleston might have let us known, but I suppose he was too busy.

I am still gaining but can't do much yet. I am going to go to the Toast Club Banquet Thursday night if I feel well enough.

So the "durn women" give you lots of trouble, do they? How? I will ask Frank when I see him but don't know when that will be. I have thought I would like to write to him but maybe it wouldn't be wise as he might not care to hear from me, and I don't know his address. I understand he took Ila to Nina's Red Cross social. I imagined they would go to-gether again. I think she would like to, but I imagine he is just the same as he used to be. He went to Battle Creek last week to see Lois and I have heard they were engaged. I don't know. Maud's mother told mother last night that she (Lois) is an adventuress.

Father is washing the dinner dishes. I suppose he will be the "chief cook and bottle washer" for the next few days. Clarence begins working on the seed farm in the morning. He earned $2.00 mowing lawns friday and saturday, and Dee mowed one small one for which he gets 25c..

Clayton Nethaway has the measles. I am sending you another American Mag. with the Ovid Paper. If you would rather have one with more pictures and less reading say so, for I want to send you what you will most enjoy.

Will Finch one of father's boy friends, was here last monday and said he was coming the next day to look at the farm as he wants to buy one. He didn't show up but I hope he will. We would all hate to see the farm go back but I believe it will be best if it can be sold.

There isn't much to write. The thoughts and prayers of our hearts are with you and I know that our boys over there are doing their part in bringing this awful horror to an end. Write when you have time and when it is so you can and we will write often without waiting (over) to hear from you.

Love and Best Wishes
From Zelma

P.S. I hope by this time you have gotten your women straightened out. I have never written to Helen. What does she intend to do after she graduates? What is Mrs. Barnaby's address and mother can write to her.

Diary Entry Mon. June 17

Laid in misery all night on a stretcher. Was x rayed in the early morning. After a consultation the doctors thot it best not to operate on me. I was in great pain.

Must be a hell of a soldier to be up to the front only three days and then get wounded.

Diary Entry Tue. June 18

Sleep a little under a hypodermic but did not rest. Felt about the same as I did yesterday. I am getting the best of care.

Diary Entry Wed. June 19

Another night about the same as last. Eat a little for first since I have been here. The pain is not quite as great. I am not able to move myself. Can stand it only to lie on my back.

Diary Entry Thur. June 20

Rested a little, very little. Tonight was the first night I did not need a hypo.

Diary Entry Fri. June 21

I am feeling quite a little better, do not feel much pain when I am still. I wish the d__m doctors would warm their hands before they come around prodding me.

Diary Entry Sat. June 22

Slept fine last night. I am still short of wind. Was propped up some today. I have quite a pain in my side.

Letter to Mother, June 22, 1918; Received July 12, 1918

France

Dear Mother:

I presume you have been wondering why I haven't written. I don't know as you have been notified of my being wounded. As I am able to write now I will tell you about it. I am gaining and am feeling better every day. I was hurt last Sun. afternoon. I feel kind ashamed of myself to think I was up at the front only three days and then to be sent back wounded.

We were working on a bomb proof with telephone lines when it happened. The first shell struck about 150 yds away a course everybody rushed out of the dug out to see what was happening. We hadn't been out but a few seconds when we heard another shell coming. We beat it for the dug out but the shell beat some of us to it. I was just at the door when it exploded about 15 ft. in front of the dug out. I got a piece of shrap in the left side of my back. It went in and up into my chest not far from my heart. It is still in their as they made up their minds not to operate on me. Their was one man killed and several others wounded by the same shell including one of our own men. I am not suffering from much pain now but was at first. All that bothers me much is my breathing. I am getting the best of care. I will say one thing for Uncle Sam's doctors over here they are certaintly great. They are saving many lives of the wounded.

Well mother I can't think of any thing more to write about. I will write often. It will probably a long while before I will be fit enough to go on the front again. Write often, Goodbye

Your Son,
Elmer

Diary Entry Sun. June 23

Woke up feeling fine. And it is certainly a fine morning outdoors. Much of the pain has left me.

War Department Telegram to Wilfred F. Smith (father), June 23, 1918; Received June 24

Western Union Telegram, June 23, 1918
W.D. [War Department] Washington D.C.

Wilfred F. Smith, Ovid Mich.

Deeply regret to inform you that it is officially reported that Private Elmer O. Smith Field Artillery was severely wounded in action June sixteenth.

McCain, The Adjutant General
[MG Henry P. McCain]

Letter from Mother, June 23, 1918

Ovid Mich.

My dear boy,

It has been quite a while since I wrote you a letter. But I let Zelma do the writing for she could do that better than she could do other things. I hope this will find you feeling fine and having some pleasures along with your work. We are feeling pretty good Zelma is gaining but will not go back to work the first of July as she planned to do at first. They sent word to come to Grandma Oakes last Sunday she was sick. I went and stayed until Wed. She had a trained nurse from Saginaw and a woman to do the work so I came home. She is better but I guess quite sick yet, has sent for me twice since but I cant stay up there all the time. Irene and Howard have been here today. Well yesterday was the first day of summer and we had a hard frost last night, killed lots corn beans & potatoes. We have to have rain soon or everything will be a failure.

How I wish I might know where you are & what you are doing today and all about it.

Haven't had a letter from you for about 2 wks. Archie is shining around with Ila Clark again. Clarence Tubbs is home for his last forlough. Theres not very many boys left but will be less as they are going all the time. Do you ever have any auto rides over there. Robert Hoffmyer is married.

Monday morning [June 24]: Well my dear boy a telegram came this morning saying you were wounded and thats all we know. We are so anxious for you and to know in what way your hurt—would gladly do for you if I only could. But keep up your good courage and look on the sun shiney side of life all you can and we will trust that all will be for the best. Hope that you have good care and I know that the good old U.S. will do the best it can for our boys. And am praying that the Germans will get their just deserts in the end.

Now I will close wishing you your health again in the near future with lots of love,

Mother

Diary Entry Mon. June 24

Was out of bed long enough for the nurse to make my bed. I guess I'll be a man yet. In spite of the fact that piece of shrap hurts a little at spells.

Diary Entry Tue. June 25

Had a good night of sleep and rest. I am feeling better every day.

Newspaper Article, The State Journal, June 25, 1918

Battery Boy from Ovid Reported as Wounded in Action in France

[Photo of Private Elmer Smith]

Private Elmer Smith, who enlisted in Battery B last year, was severely wounded June 16 while fighting in France. His mother, Mrs. W.F. Smith, Ovid, has just received word to that effect. Smith was employed by G.A. Barnaby, 304 North Washington ave., this city, previous to his enlistment. While at Waco he was transferred to headquarters company, 119th field artillery.

Private Smith is the first casualty reported in action among local batterymen and the report indicates the Lansing battalion is sending its shells at the Hun. No details have been received as to what his detachment was doing at the time the young soldier received his wounds but undoubtedly he was engaged in scout or signal work that being the particular duty of the members of the headquarters company.

*Another edition of The State Journal had an article with a verbatim first paragraph of the one above. But its title was different—***BATTERY BOY IS AMONG WOUNDED, Elmer Smith of Ovid, Member of Headquarters Company, Named.** *This article had no picture with it.*

Newspaper Article, Ovid Newspaper, June 25, 1918

SEVERELY WOUNDED

[Photo of Private Elmer O. Smith]

Ovid, June 25 –

Private Elmer O. Smith of this village, who was severely wounded in action June16, is the son of Mr. and Mrs. W.F. Smith. He enlisted in Battery B of the National Guard in Lansing April 30, 1917. He was called to service in July and mobilized with the battery at Grayling, going to Camp McArthur, Waco, Tex. March 5, his twenty-first birthday anniversary, he landed in England and after a few days rest was moved to France. On May 24 [actually June 4] he went into action and on June 16 was wounded having been in action less than a month. He is the first Ovid man to fall in active service.

Letter from Frank Nethaway to Mrs. Olive Smith, June 25, 1918

423 N. Craig St.
Pittsburgh, Pa.

Dear Mrs. Smith:

It was with a great deal of pain that I saw Elmer's name in the list of wounded tonight. It was the name I dreaded most to see there, for as you know, he is my very dearest chum in the world and any injury to him means so much sorrow to me as well as to you and the rest of the folks.

There are two comforting thoughts, however. We can be thankful that it was no worse, and we can feel pretty sure that he will be shipped to a hospital on this side of the ocean as soon as he can stand the journey.

Of course, you will be kept informed as to how he is getting along probably through Red Cross sources.

Would it be asking too much if you Mrs. Smith, to ask you to let me know anything you may hear as to his injuries and how he is getting along? A line or two to keep me in touch with him will be deeply appreciated as I can hardly hope to hear directly from him for some time to come.

With sympathy and best regards to you all. I am very sincerely your friend,

Frank N.

P.S. Any letter will reach me either at the address above or directly to the General Laboratories, Bureau of Aircraft Production, 7th & Bedford Aves.

Diary Entry Wed. June 26

I am feeling fine. I would certainly like to get up and get out doors.

Diary Entry Thur. June 27

I am feeling better every day. I get up every morning to have my bed made. I am still so weak I dare not try walking alone.

Diary Entry Fri. June 28

Last night the German airmen crossed the lines and tryed to bomb the aviation fields on each side of the hospital. They dropped several near enough to the hospital to jar us considerably. Our anti aircraft guns on nearby hills drove them off before they did any damage. Am feeling fine.

Diary Entry Sat. June 29

Walked over to the window and sit for awhile this morning. Am to weak to walk much.

Letter to Sister, June 29, 1918

On Active Service
WITH THE AMERICAN EXPEDITIONARY FORCE
France

Dear Sister:

Will drop you a few lines to let you know I am getting along fine. I am not in any pain now except a little in my chest when I move around. I get up long enough in the mornings to have my bed made. But of course I am very weak and dare not exercise to much. I couldn't ask for any better care than I am now getting. My breathing is not normal yet but it is getting better every day. It probably will be a month or more before I get back to my regiment. Gee I will be tickled to get back. I have had all the laying in bed I want for a while.

The Boche pulled off a little air raid night before last on the aviation fields on each side of the hospital. Their were a few bombs dropped near enough to the hospital to jar us considerable but no damage was done as they were soon driven off by our antiaircraft guns. One of those bombs leave a hole about the size of an elephant.

I expect to be sent back to a base hospital within a few days. Well write as usual.

Your Brother Elmer

Diary Entry Sun. June 30

I am feeling tip top.

Diary Entry Mon. July 1

Was out in the wheel chair this morning.

Diary Entry Tue. July 2

Was up and walked around the ward some. Am still to weak to do much.

Diary Entry Wed. July 3

Exercised my legs some more today. Getting along fine.

Letter to PVT Elmer Smith from Chas. E. Ebersol, Lansing Business University, July 3, 1918

Lansing Business University
Lansing, Michigan

Elmer Smith, Battery B.
Michigan Field Artillery
Some Hospital in France

My dear Mr. Smith:

Your picture has been in the *State Journal* [Lansing's primary newspaper] and also in the Ovid Paper, announcing that you were severely wounded.

I believe you were the first boy to volunteer from our school. We are proud of you. It was for you that the first star was placed in our Service Flag, which shows the number of boys who are representing us on the field of battle. This flag now has seventeen stars. Many other boys who have recently been connected with our school have enlisted or been drafted.

We certainly regret very much to hear that you have been wounded, and hope soon you will be able to return to the front or to us, to tell us of your experience. We think of you very often and of how you are fighting for us and trying to make the world safe for all the world to live in.

We are backing you up as is shown from the fact that Ingham County was the First County in the United States to go over the Top in its "Quota" for War Savings Stamps, this past week.

I have written to Lawrence Durre but have received no reply. I have heard from Lynn Reed and have written him, but he owes me a letter. If you see these fellows who are in Company A, or Lloyd Boyd or any other the L.B.U. boys, just remember me to them. We are anxiously hoping that our brave boys at the front will capture the Kaiser and put an end to this terrible War. You are all doing your part.

Nelia Babcock from Ovid, is a student in our school. She mentioned having gone to school with you in earlier days.

Our school is going on about the same as usual but with about ten girls to one boy.

J.A. proved very disloyal and was dismissed. I cannot understand how his wife can stand up for Germany at this time. She seems to think that Germany will win. She says that we started the war, and we are going to find out the Germans are stronger than the Americans, and if her brothers have to go to fight against Germany, she would shoot them first. I think she ought to be dropped from an aeroplane in the midst of Germany, right now.

We certainly would be glad to hear from you at any time and to know how you are getting along, and you may feel assured we will write you as soon as we receive any word from you or any of the boys.

With best wishes to you, and all of our dear L.B.U.boys

Your old friend,
Chas E. Ebersol

Diary Entry Thur. July 4

The nurses gave an entertainment to the enlisted men at the "Y". They served refreshments of ice cream, cake, lemonade and fried cakes.

I eat very heartily and was in misery a good share of the night.

Diary Entry Fri. July 5

I am feeling good. Expect to be shipped out soon.

Diary Entry Sat. July 6

Was out and around all day.

Diary Entry Sun. July 7

Feeling O.K.

Diary Entry Mon. July 8

Did not sleep much last night. Was given my clothes and put out into the convalescent tent this afternoon.

Diary Entry Tue. July 9

Laid around the tent all day.

Letter to Mrs. Dunham, family friend, July 9, 1918

ON ACTIVE SERVICE WITH THE AMERICAN EXPEDITIONARY FORCE YMCA

Dear Mrs. Dunham:

I received your letter and was very glad to hear from you.

I presume that you have heard thru the folks about the wound I received. I got along fine after the first three days. I am now back in my soldier clothes and expect to be shipped out tomorrow or next day to a base hospital or a replacement camp. They left the piece of shell in my chest. The doctor said it would never cause me any trouble. The wound does not pain me now unless I sneeze. I have a slight pain yet way down low in my side caused by some blood clots. But it is getting less noticable every day. I will be glad when I get back to the regiment. I have had all I want of hospitals. I will take the front every time for mine. I can't complain of the treatment I get here for we get the best of care and we get all we care to eat but I guess I get so restless is the trouble. I was up to the graveyard to the grave of the fellow that was wounded with me [Louis Hice] this afternoon. It was to bad it had to be for he was a prince of a fellow, an exception.

Tell the folks never to worry about me for I am having a good time and am happy. I never worry any about getting killed than I do about getting a little drunk. We all get so used to it that it does not seem much to us.

Well this is a very short letter but as it is bedtime I will have to quit. I will be glad to hear from you again.

Sincerely Your Friend,
Elmer S.

Diary Entry Wed. July 10

Did a little painting inside the nurses recreation room. Big evacuation tomorrow.

Diary Entry Thur. July 11

We left the hospital at 7:30. Loaded on a hospital train at Toul. Left Toul at ten o'clock. Arrived at Base hospital #18 at Basiolles.

Was given an examination and a bath. Was made to go to bed.

Diary Entry Fri. July 12

Doctor looked me over and said I was all right. Was given some hospital clothes and am allowed to run around on the hospital grounds. Took a walk with the YMCA man over to Base 116. Run across Ogden while there.

Diary Entry Sat. July 13

A negro was hung over on the other side of the river this morning.

Laid around and read nearly all day. Took in the movies at the "Y" this evening.

Diary Entry Sun. July 14

Laid around and read most of the day. Went to Song Service this evening.

Letter to Mother, July 14, 1918

Y.M.C.A. Paper

On Active Service With the American Expeditionary Force

Dear Mother:

I have just eaten dinner. a rather large one too. Altho it makes me feel lazy I am going to scare up ambition enough to write you a letter. Here's hoping all you folks are all well. I can say for myself I am feeling great. I am well enough to do a good days work if I had it to do. I am sick of these darn hospitals. I'll take the front in preference to one of these places every time. There is at least something up there to keep your mind on here it is dead enough to drive even a lazy man crazy. I am anxious to get back into the game. Perhaps I'll get the guy that tried to get me in the last half of the ninth. Hope I do a better job than he done on me. The piece of shell was left in me, it will never trouble me. It was a small piece 4 by 5 milometers I wanted to keep it in a safe place as a souvenior anyway.

How are all the cows and chickens down on the farm? What is Clarence doing for a living this summer? I haven't had a payday or mail in so long that I have almost forgotten their is such a thing. I'll have a day off to read my mail when I get it.

Well mother this is a very short letter but I don't know of anything more to write about so will make this due for this time. Goodbye.

Your Son,
Elmer

Ok [cannot determine censor's name]

Diary Entry Mon. July 15

Eat and laid around all day.

Newspaper Article, The State Journal, July 15, 1918

OVID BOY RECOVERING FROM SHRAPNEL WOUND

Ovid, July 15.—Private Elmer O. Smith, the Ovid young man, who was severely wounded in action on June 16, is recovering, according to a letter received by his parents, Mr. and Mrs. W.F. Smith, Friday [July 12]. The letter, which was written on June 22, stated he was getting along fine and that he was able to write them about it. He had been at the front only three days when wounded and said he was ashamed at being there such a short time. While working on telephone lines on a bomb-proof on Sunday afternoon, June 16, he with several other men heard a shell explode about 150 yards away and came out to see what was going on, when they heard a second coming. All attempted to enter the dugout again but the second shell exploded about 15 yards from the entrance just as Elmer was entering. A piece of shrapnel struck him in the left side of his back and went through into his chest where it lodged. It just missed his heart. It was not thought necessary to remove the shrapnel yet and probably it will be left in his body. The same shell killed one man and wounded several others.

Elmer was more than pleased with the way Uncle Sam cared for his wounded and stated the American doctors were saving the lives of many wounded boys. He stated it would probably be some time before he would be at the front again.

Private Smith was a member of Battery B, 119th Field artillery and enlisted in Lansing in April, 1917. While in Texas he was transferred to the Headquarter's company.

Diary Entry Tue. July 16

Was transferred from Base 18 to convelescent camp #2 about three miles from the hospital. We work if we feel like. We don't if we don't.

Diary Entry Wed. July 17

Arose at 6:15. Took a 10 minute hike. Breakfasted at 7:30. We were taken out at 9:15 for setting up exercises for 1/2 hr. At 10:30 we were given l hr. drill. Dinner at 12:00. From one to two we were made to lie down and rest. We were given a hike from two until three o clock. At 3:30 we went out on the athletic field and played baseball, soccor, football, or could lay in the shade. Take it from me this is some place.

Diary Entry Thur. July 18

Did light exercises all day. We are getting about four medical examinations a day.

Diary Entry Fri. July 19

I was put in C class this morning so I am fit for duty. Exercised and did light fatigue.

Diary Entry Sat. July 20

Did light exercise and a little drill. Was given a final examination. Passed O.K. Weigh 133 lbs. stripped.

Hurrah for the Allies. They have the Germans on the run up on the Soissons front. Here's hoping they keep them on the run.

I predict the war to be over in three months. [He was off by three weeks!]

Diary Entry Sun. July 21

Laid around this forenoon. Went to a ball game between the Medical Corp and the Convalescents. We were beaten 8–5. If it hadn't been for our negro pitcher and 3rd basemen we would of suffered a beating by a far greater score. Two men got their arm broke during the game. Some tuff bunch we are.

The Huns are still in full retreat at Soissons.

Diary Entry Mon. July 22

Was examined by the doctor this morning and declared fit for service. We left the conv. camp at 11:00 A.M. Went to Neuf Chateau. Took the train their at 2:P.M. Changed to the All American train at Chaumont. Spent a miserable night on the train.

Diary Entry Tue. July 23

Arrived at the re-emplacement camp at St. Aignan at noon. Was given some equip and was classified. St. Aignan, altho small is very beautiful. The large old fortress and chateau built hundreds of years ago on the large hill across the valley is very picturesque.

Diary Entry Wed. July 24

Slept the entire forenoon. Was given gas instruction this afternoon.

Diary Entry Thur. July 25

Was put on a detail at the Q. M. Did not work much in forenoon but had to work like the devil this afternoon.

Diary Entry Fri. July 26

Laid around and read all day long.

Diary Entry Sat. July 27

Read and slept during the day. Saw a few boxing exhibitions at the Y.M.C.A. this evening.

Diary Entry Sun. July 28

Played ball and read most of the day.

Diary Entry Mon. July 29

Was sick all night last night. Feel a little better this morning. Was called out for evacuation. Left St. Aignan at 9:30 A.M. Bound for replacement camp near Bordeaux. Stayed in Tours all afternoon waiting for the evening train to Bordeaux. Dont expect to sleep much.

Official AEF Censoral Postcard to Sister Zelma, July 29, 1918

I am quite well.
And am getting along well and hope to return to duty soon.
Letter follows at first opportunity.
I have received no letter from you lately.

Elmer O. Smith

Diary Entry Tue. July 30

A dam poor night for sleep. Arrived in Bordeaux about noon. Changed cars there. Left for replacement camp Corneau near the ocean. Arrived in camp about dusk.

Diary Entry Wed. July 31

Slept well if I did have hard boards for cushions. This is a new American camp. The country is quite wooded and the dirty black sand reminds me of Grayling, Mich.

Laid around all day. It is very hot hear. Went for a dive in the canal this evening.

Diary Entry Thur. August 1

Drew part of my equipment this forenoon. We were given about an hour of infantry drill with rifles. And about one and a half hrs drill of the seventy fives.

I have caught a deuce of a cold.

Diary Entry Fri. August 2

I was put on a fatigue detail this morning. Spent the rest of the forenoon at the "Y" reading room after the fatigue was done.

Had gas mask drill and standing gun drill this afternoon.

Diary Entry Sat. August 3

Did rifle and squads east and squads west drill this forenoon.

Laid around and read this afternoon. Was notified to be ready to go back to the outfit tomorrow.

Diary Entry Sun. August 4

Packed my equipment and went over to regm'l. hdqs. for inspection. Drew rations for three days. Their is ten in my bunch to leave. Most of them from the 32nd Div.

Skipped a detail this afternoon. But was put on another one after supper to unload horses. At arriving at the train I staid with a baggage detail and was back to my quarters shortly after. Dont expect to leave this camp until Tuesday.

Diary Entry Mon. August 5

Did some "over the top" stuff in a deep ditch for drill this morning. Laid around the rest of the day. Saw a ball game tonight.

Diary Entry Tue. August 6

Laid around and read all day. The 344th Artillery Band gave a concert tonight.

We get up at 5:00 o'clock tomorrow morning. We leave here on the train at 6:30.

Diary Entry Wed. August 7

Was woke up early and was ready to leave Le Courneau at 6:30. Changed cars in La Teste. Arrived in Bordeaux about noon. Stayed their the entire afternoon. Left about 6:30 o clock.

Diary Entry Thur. August 8

Did not rest much last night. Arrived in Tours about 9:00 oclock.

Journeyed thru Orleans and arrived in Nancy Le Sec about midnight. Slept on the cars the duration of the night.

Diary Entry Fri. August 9

We left Nancy Le Sec at 6:30. I am going to Mezy our division hdqs [32nd Division].

Pulled into Chateau Thierry at ten thirty. Had to wait until 3:15 for a train to Mezy. Arrived at Division hdqs. O. K.

Diary Entry Sat. August 10

They decided to keep us hospital men here for a couple of days to police up around the buildings.

Nearly all the buildings in the villages have at least one shell hole thru them while some are leveled to the ground. Graves, shell holes and salvage are to be seen on all sides.

Private Elmer Smith was en route back to his unit, the 119th FA Regiment, after almost eight weeks of recovery and convalescence from his severe wounds. During his absence the 119th and 32nd Division had seen significant combat action in support of the French 6th Army in the Aisne-Marne offensive. The French Commander praised the only American division attached to his Army for their prowess in the battle that became known as the Second Battle of the Marne. But it would not be long before the 119th would again be recommitted to the vicious fighting along the Western Front.

NOTES

1. Headquarters, 119th Field Artillery, American Expeditionary Forces, *Memorandum* (Camp Coetquidan, France: May 31, 1918).

2. American Battle Monuments Commission, *26th Division Summary of Operations in the World War* (Washington, D.C.: U.S. Government Printing Office, 1944), 1.
Russell Gordon Carter, *The 101st Field Artillery: AEF 1917-1919* (Boston MA: Houghton Mifflin Company, 1940), 1.
Colonel Chester B. McCormick, "A Brief History of the 119th Field Artillery," *Honor Roll and Complete War History of Ingham County in the Great World War: 1914-1918* (Lansing MI: The State Journal Company, 1920), 219.

3. *26th Division Summary of Operation*, 5.

4. Carter, *The 101st Field Artillery*, 100-110.

5. Harold H. Borgman, Captain, 119th FA Regiment, *War Record of Battery F, 119th Field Artillery, 32nd Division* (Lansing MI: Library of Michigan), 5.

6. Headquarters Company, 119th FA Regiment, *IMMEDIATE REPORT OF CASUALTY forms for PFC Louis K. Hice and PVT Elmer O. Smith* (Toul Sector, France: June 16, 1918).

7. Headquarters, 119th Field Artillery, American Expeditionary Forces, *Casualty Report* (France: 14 November 1918). A detailed list of soldiers killed in action provides home address and next of kin information. For Louis K. Hice, this was his mother, Mrs. Eva May Hice, who lived at 1109 5th Street, Three Rivers Michigan.

8. MG Henry McCain, Adjutant General of the U.S. Army, *Western Union Telegram informing that PVT Elmer was severely wounded in action on June 16th* (Washington D.C.: War Office, June 23, 1918).

Chapter 8

Back in the Fight at the Front: the Aisne-Marne Offensive

After eight weeks of recovery from his wounds and transport back to his unit, Private Elmer Smith arrived at the 119th FA Headquarters Company on August 11, 1918. For the next three months Private Smith and his unit participated in several significant campaigns and battles. In conjunction with French and British forces, the concerted effort of the entire AEF in attacks against a war weary German Army finally swung the initiative and balance of power toward the Allies. This culminated with the German leadership agreeing to an armistice to end the war on November 11, 1918.

The next three chapters describe Private Smith's participation in the 119th FA's operations over the last three months of the war. The diary entries and letters are supplemented with operational accounts of the unit and the 32nd Division combat elements they supported. The heaviest fighting and hence numerous casualties occurred during this period of almost sustained combat for American forces.

Significant highlights for PVT Smith during this period included:

- Participation in three major campaigns for the 57th FA Brigade and its subordinate FA regiments in support of 32nd and other American or Allied division objectives.
- Several chemical attacks against U.S. forces delivered by German tube artillery.
- Experience with the horrific and raw conditions of the front lines and trenches as the 119th FA moved forward in support of Infantry regiments.

Several 32nd Division maps from the book *The 32nd Division in the World War* are embedded in the description of the campaigns to illustrate the key locations where the Division and its subordinates fought during this period.

Battle Participation

The 119th FA Regiment saw combat in six different major operations in 1918 in France.[1]

- Toul Sector, June 8-23. Attached to 101st FA Regiment, 26th Division. Defensive Sector.
- Center Sector, Haute-Alsace, June 25–July 22. Defensive Sector.
- Aisne-Marne offensive, July 30–August 6.
- Fismes Sector, August 7-22. Also considered part of Aisne-Marne offensive.
- Oise-Aisne offensive, August 23–September 6.
- Meuse-Argonne offensive, September 26–November 3.

Due to the time he spent recovering from the wounds he sustained on June 16, PVT Elmer Smith participated in four of the six major operations. The Defensive Sector mission where Elmer was wounded is described in the previous chapter. The remaining operations are detailed in the next three chapters, corresponding with and as a lead-in to PVT Smith's diary entries.

In the Defensive Sector operations near Toul, the 119th FA primarily conducted counter-battery fire missions in response to German artillery shelling. Starting with the Aisne-Marne Offensive, the 119th became extremely proficient providing fire support to front-line American infantry forces using common Allied artillery tactics including various types of barrages: [2]

- Preliminary artillery barrages to achieve surprise; later termed preparatory or prep fires
- Creeping or rolling barrages behind which the Infantry advanced
- Box barrages to isolate sections of enemy trenches or defensive positions
- Saturation barrages which concentrated the fire of all available arms on a small area to obliterate it

A useful, but not a definitive, source of 119th FA operations was the recollections by Private Leo V. Jacks, a soldier from E Battery. PVT Jacks was a replacement assigned to the 119th in July 1918, serving as a machine gun operator and artillery gun crewman throughout the remainder of the war to include the Aisne-Marne, Oise-Aisne, and Meuse-Argonne campaigns. He wrote part of *Service Record, By an Artilleryman,* during the war and a decade later added additional details on what he experienced in the grueling crucible of combat. His descriptions of events provide compelling accounts of what artillery life on the front lines was like. But it is difficult to decipher exactly where and when most of these battle exploits occurred. Like other sources cited in the book, Jack's commentary is incorporated, as appropriate, to add perspective and intensity to what the unit and its soldiers were encountering.[3]

Counterattack—The Aisne-Marne Offensive

The *History of War* provides a concise overview of the Aisne-Marne Campaign as follows. In the summer of 1918, the Aisne-Marne Offensive was a significant turning point for the Allies in the fighting on the Western Front. Occurring from July 18 to August 6, this campaign was the second phase of the Second Battle of the Marne. The operation's first phase was the German Champagne-Marne Offensive, which commenced on July 15 with attacks east and west of Reims along a 50 mile front. The German attack was the last of its five major spring and summer offensives of 1918 meant to capture Paris and defeat the Allies before the full strength of the AEF could be employed against the German Army.

Twenty-eight German combat divisions consisting of 280,000 soldiers were committed to the offensive. The initial German operations east of Reims made minimal progress, but the German Seventh Army attacks to the west advanced four miles, creating a beachhead on the southern side of the Marne River. At its greatest extent the German salient reached from Soissons in the northwest, to Château Thierry at its southwest corner, and then east along the Marne River. The U.S. 3rd Division was a key part of the Allied force that halted the German advance along the river, earning the nickname "Rock of the Marne" for their brave defense in holding the line.

One positive result of the German successes in the spring of 1918 was the designation of French Marshall Ferdinand Foch as the overall Allied Commander in Chief on the Western Front. Even prior to the German offensive on the Marne, General Foch had been planning a massive counterattack in the area. His plan was to attack with four French armies all around the salient created during the Third Battle of the Aisne from May 27 to June 6, 1918. The main effort was the French Tenth Army commanded by General Charles Mangin who would attack from west to east at the northwest corner of the salient. The Sixth Army led by General Jean Degoutte would provide pressure on the German lines to the south. Further around the front the Fifth Army led by General Henri Berthelot, and the Ninth Army commanded by General M. A. H. de Mitry, would conduct supporting attacks on the salient's southern flank.

The Aisne-Marne Offensive was a multinational operation with over 700,000 Allied soldiers involved. In addition to the French forces, American, British, and Italian divisions participated. The American 1st and 2nd Divisions were with the Tenth Army, while the Sixth and Ninth Armies each contained one U.S. Corps with three American divisions. The U.S. divisions were massive formations with each containing 28,000 soldiers, twice the size of their British, French, or German equivalents. Over 300 French tanks supported the counterattack.

On July 18, the main Allied attack commenced with 14 divisions from the four armies. All along the line the Allies advanced between two and five miles. That night the Germans forces retreated back across the Marne River. The rapid Allied advance threatened German communications within the salient and almost trapped the German forces around Chateau Thierry. Facing this substantial Allied counteroffensive, German General Erich Ludendorff ordered his troops to pull out of the salient and form a new defensive line along the Aisne and Vesle Rivers. The new line began to take form on August 3, the day after Soissons was liberated. On August 6, U.S. forces probed the stabilized front lines and were repelled, ending the offensive.

The Aisne-Marne offensive marked a key turning point in the fighting of 1918. It ended the series of German victories that began with the Somme Offensive in March 1918 and opened the way for the Allied offensives that started on August 8 with the British offensive at Amiens. German leader Ludendorff called it "a great setback" and his gamble to end the war before the full strength of the American army could be deployed had failed.[4]

Summary of 32nd Division Operations in the Aisne-Marne Offensive[5]

Initially in reserve, the 32nd Division was assigned to the French 38th Corps, French Sixth Army on July 27. At 11 a.m., July 30, it relieved the 3rd [U.S.] Division north of Ronch`eres. Later in the day the 64th Infantry Brigade captured Bois des Grimpettes in conjunction with the 28th [U.S.] Division. It also occupied the southwest portion of Bois de Cierges. At 9 a.m., July 31, the 32nd Division relieved the 28th Division.

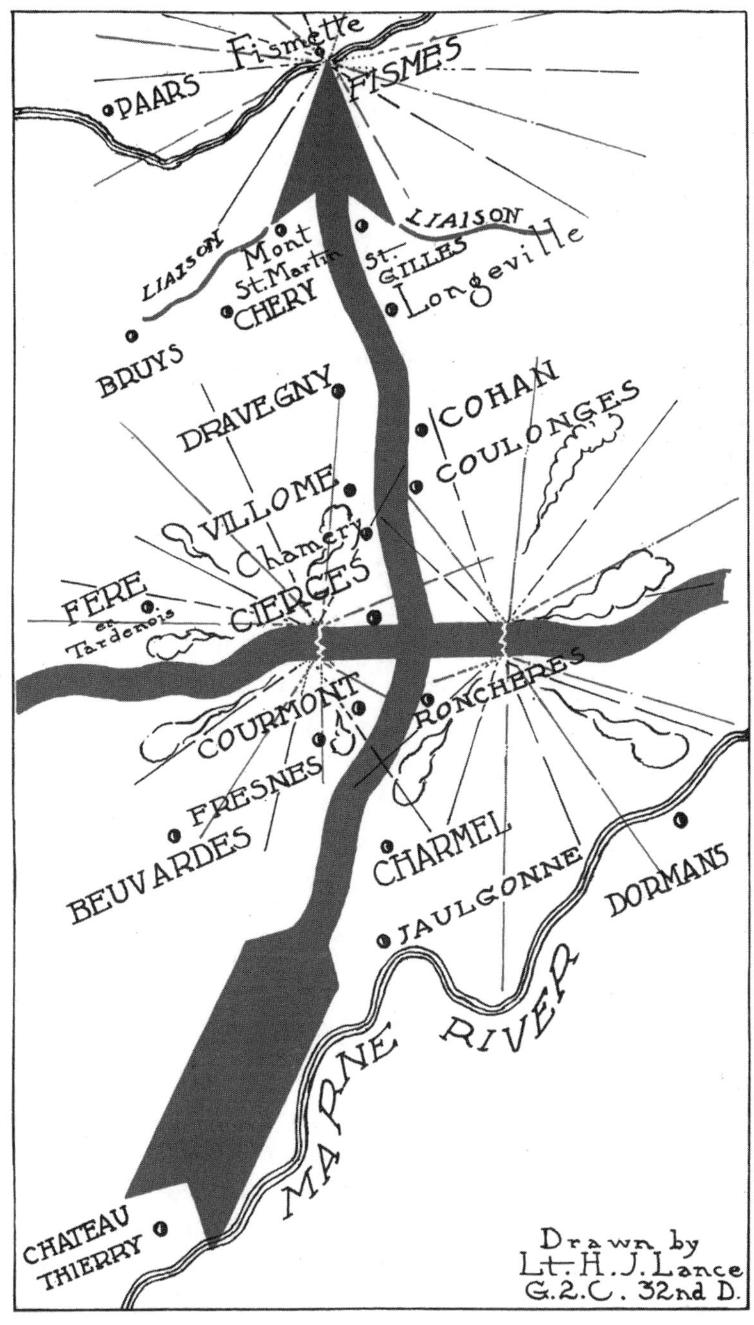

32nd Division Operations in the Aisne-Marne Campaign

The division captured Cierges on July 31 and Bellevue Ferme, Hill 230 and Les Jomblets on August 1.

The German withdrawal to the Vesle River commenced during the night of August 1-2. The attack of the 32nd Division on August 2 made rapid progress, and the division advanced six kilometers to a line north of Dravegny. On August 3 a similar gain carried the division to the north of St. Gilles and Mont St. Martin. The southwest portion of Fismes and Bois de Larribonnet were captured on August 4. Patrols crossed the Vesle River on the 5th and 6th. The occupation of Fismes was complete on that latter day.

The III [U.S.] Corps ordered the 32nd Division relieved by the 28th Division during the night of August 6-7. Command was to pass at daylight, August 7. The relief was accomplished as ordered, and the 32nd Division moved south of an east-west line through Dravegny in Corps reserve. The 57th Field Artillery Brigade (including the 119th FA Regiment) remained in the sector in support of the 28th Division.

Summary of 28th Division Operations from August 7-12[6]

The relief of the 32nd Division was accomplished by the 56th Infantry Brigade, which placed the 2d and 3d Battalions, 112th Infantry [Regiment], in line at Fismes and Bois de Larribonnet respectively. The 57th Field Artillery Brigade, 32nd Division together with the 147th Field Artillery [Regiment][7], 41st Division, and the 3d Battalion, 18th Field Artillery, 3d Division, remained in line, in support of the 28th Division. Command passed at daylight August 7.

The general advance of the III [U.S.] Corps was set for the afternoon of August 7. There were misunderstandings as to H-Hour, however, and the attacks were uncoordinated and unsuccessful. The 28th Division ordered its troops to advance at 7 p.m.

A local operation was conducted at 5 a.m., August 8, after a 1 hour artillery preparation. The 2d Battalion, 112th Infantry, attacked with the mission of cleaning up Fismette. Companies F, G, and H, and a part of Company C crossed the river and established themselves in Fismette and along the dirt road to the east. Fire from the front and flanks forced these companies back into Fismes. After an artillery preparation of 2 ½ hours this battalion attacked again at 1:30 p.m. and secured a foothold in the southern and eastern parts of Fismette.

Several local German attacks were defeated on August 9... The 28th Division ordered the 56th Infantry Brigade to capture the spur northwest of Fismette by attacking at 4:30 a.m., August 10... There was to be a 30 minute artillery preparation prior to the attack, and the advance was to be covered by a rolling barrage.

On August 11 the 28th Division ordered the 111th Infantry to conduct a raid for the purpose of obtaining prisoners and capturing materiel located in the ravines and along the sunken road leading south from Mont de Perte...

Summary of 77th Division Operations from August 13-23[8]

The 77th Division relieved the American 4th Division and elements of the French 62d Division along the Vesle River in the vicinity of Bazoches during the night of August 11-12. On August 13 it relieved elements of the American 28th Division at Chateau de Diable... The 119th Field Artillery, 32nd Division, was attached to the 77th Division on the 13th and remained in support of the division until August 24.

On August 13 the III [U.S.] Corps, believing that the plateau north of the Vesle was held only by a small force, ordered both the 77th and 28th [now to right of the 77th] Divisions to prepare reconnaissances. The force to be employed by each division was to be approximately one company. Artillery preparations and box barrages were ordered.

On the morning of August 22 the Germans attacked the 3rd Battalion, 308th Infantry, in the vicinity of Chateau de Diable. In the course of the fighting the 3d Battalion was forced back to the south bank of the Vesle River.

The 119th FA Regiment in the Aisne-Marne Offensive: From Colonel McCormick's Post-War Summary[9]

The latter part of July, the 119th was rushed into the Second Battle of the Marne, referred to as the Marne-Aisne Offensive. The gallant Michigan men were suddenly confronted with one of the most severe test of their entire career. With new animals and inexperienced drivers, they were forced to march for five days to the vicinity of Chateau Thierry. On account of the shortage of artillery harness the regiment was compelled to drag sixteen American caissons loaded with ammunition this entire distance. To save the animals, everyone except the drivers were compelled to walk and carry full pack, for which they had no previous training.

Entering the lines July 30th in support of the 32nd Division, by rapid advances August 2nd and 3rd the Division forced the enemy from Oureq to the Vesle [Rivers]. This was the first rigorous and reliable test of the ability of the regiment in open warfare. Each organization acquitted itself most creditably in arriving promptly with the first elements of the infantry and assisting in effecting the capture of Fismes.

The 32nd Division was relieved on the 6th and the 119th Field Artillery was left in support of the 28th Division. By the dogged support of the Michigan gunners the infantry was able to capture Chateau de Auble and then, crossing the Vesle, they captured Fismettes. Here the gallant and courageous conduct of the gun crews, which time and again were totally wiped out and the guns destroyed by the enemy shell fire, demonstrated that the rigid discipline and details of their early training had not been without avail. The test came and it was met without faltering. Relieved from duty with the 28th Division on the 12th, you were placed in support of the 77th Division where after 10 days constant strenuous service, under many trying conditions, you were relieved.

From Detroit News Post-War Summary[10]

Just after the reunion [with the 32nd Division after having been attached to the 26th Division], things began to happen around Chateau-Thierry and all the world now knows what those events portended. So the division climbed into those cars which have become the foundation of about half the jokes in France, those boxes labeled, "8 Chevaux—40 Hommes." [8 Horses—40 Men] The destination was the Soisson front and the route was via Paris. Going through that city, the division was given a Paris welcome, American soldiers being comparatively novel then.

Between the cheers of Paris, the flags, the greetings and kisses and Chateau-Thierry, there was only brief interval. The division detrained at Rivecourt and made a night march of 17 miles to Pont St. Maxine, where it bivouacked a day. Then came the order to reinforce the Allies at Chateau-Thierry, 112 miles away.

To Front in Trucks

To the great counterattack, the infantry of the 32d Division went in motor trucks. There were 1,200 of these vehicles and they made a mighty train stretching as far as the eye could see, the freight Michigan and Wisconsin boys, tight-lipped and grim—men who were just ordinary boys back home, but who were to write their names in the History of Human Liberty—heroes.

The artillery traveled overland also, but not in motor trucks. Horseback and afoot, these men went across France day and night until their objective was reached. Shorn of detail and the personal touches and giving only a bare record of achievement, here is what that meant:

To Vaumoise, 45 kilometers (36 miles): to Coulomos, 25 kilometers (18 miles) and so on until Chateau-Thierry was reached, the last march being 28 kilometers (22.4 miles).

Nor was that the end. To reach the battery positions, north of Lacharmel, 30 more kilometers (24 miles) had to be covered. The end of that journey had been reached. The artillery was with the 32d Division up in the front line.

It was just in time for that great drive of 20 kilometers, resulting in the capture of Fismes. After that feat, the 32d, the line being stabilized, was withdrawn for a rest, being relieved by the 28th Division. The artillery, including the 119th, stayed right where it was, because it was needed.

The enemy made a stand and the attempt to force the Vesle failed, but the 28th, with its artillery support, captured Fismette, on the north bank of the Vesle. Colonel McCormick was acting chief of light artillery during the capture of Fismes and Fismette.

Withdrawn August 24

After about a week with the 28th Division, the 119th took a merited rest on the left of the 77th Division and, August 24, was withdrawn…

French 6th Army Commendation for 32nd Division, August 8, 1918[11]

Sixth Army, P.C., August 8, 1918, General Order.

Before the big offensive of July 18, the American troops belonging to the Sixth French Army have distinguished themselves by carrying off in front of the enemy, the wood of the "Marine Brigade" and the village of Vaux and stopping the German offensive on the Marne and at Fossoy.

Since then they have taken the most glorious part in the second battle of the Marne, rivaling the French troops in ardor and bravery. They have during 20 days of ceaseless battle freed numerous French villages and accomplished, through a very difficult country an advance of 40 kilometers that has brought them beyond the Vesle.

Their glorious steps are marked by names that will make illustrious in the future the military history of the United States; Tarcy, the Ourcq, Le Charmet, the Vesle, Sugy, Fismes, Belleau, Chateau of Etrepilly Epieds, Seringes and Nesles.

The young division that was in action for the first time has proven itself worthy of the old tradition of the Regular Army. Its members have had the same lively will to defeat the Boche, the same discipline that causes the orders of the commander to be always executed, whatever may be the difficulties to overcome, and the losses to suffer.

The splendid results obtained are due to the energy and skill of the chief and to the bravery of the men.

I am proud to have commanded such troops.

The General Commanding the Sixth Army, Degoutte.

At the end of each month Elmer Smith's diary had a Memoranda page. He used this page only twice with diary entries. In August he highlighted a key event from the beginning of the month when he was still recovering from his wounds. He received word of and wrote of the key 32nd Division attack with the 119th FA's support in the Aisne-Marne Offensive

Diary Entry, August Memoranda

The 32nd Division drove the Germans from Chateau Thierry on the Marne back to the Vesle river. It was the first drive made by the Americans. The Germans massed their troops on the Marne prepatory to a drive toward Paris. Their counter attacks were repulsed and in turn the Americans counter attacked and drove the German troops back in disorder. The 32nd has received two citations.

Private Elmer Smith was back with the 119th FA from August 11 onward. On his first day back he witnessed the flow of gaunt looking soldiers from his unit who had recently returned from the front. Since Elmer had recently been wounded his duties during this period were relatively moderate. One day he went to the front to bury seven dead horses and ran telephone lines. He also operated the switchboard at the Regimental rear echelon post of command (P.C.) from August 20-23.

Diary Entry Sun. August 11

I kicked on being kept here so they decided to send me up to the regiment. I waited all day for a truck. Finally caught one in the afternoon. Arrived at the hdq's echelon at supper time.

Saw many of the fellows that had just came from the front. They all look pale and thin. This front is a regular hell from what they say.

Diary Entry Mon. August 12

Slept fairly well. Was awakened once by a gas alarm.

Major Kerr [Major Murdock M. Kerr, 119th Medical officer] gave orders I was not to go to the front to stay for a few weeks.

Groomed horses and laid around all day.

Diary Entry Tue. August 13

Outside of a few gas alarms, slept fairly well.

Diary Entry Wed. August 14

Went up to the front and buried seven dead horses that were the victims of some spare parts of an iron foundry from Germany.

Diary Entry Thur. August 15

Did stables and slept all day.

Diary Entry Fri. August 16

Took it easy all day.

Diary Entry Sat. August 17

Groomed the nags and led them to water.

Diary Entry Sun. August 18

Outside of taking care of the horses had it easy all day. Went to services conducted by Chaplain Atkinson.

Diary Entry Mon. August 19

The horses were groomed and cared for. No excitement.

Diary Entry Tue. August 20

Groomed nags this morning. Helped the reg'ml. telephone detail string a line to the P. C. Expect to go to the front and join the detail tomorrow.

Diary Entry Wed. August 21

Helped string a telephone line. We have a switchboard installed here. Lt. Stillwell [1LT William G. Stillwell] left me to operate it. Two men from the P.C. came to assist me and rest up every two days.

Diary Entry Thur. August 22

Laid around and operated the switchboard all day.

Orders came in tonight that the 119th were to move to the rear to rest billits.

F. battery had a number of gas and high explosive casualties this forenoon. Lt. Oates [2LT Morley S. Oates, Battery F] was cut in to [two] by a piece of shell.

The following summary of Battery F's actions describe the horrific effects artillery fire and gas had on the front line elements of the 119th FA that PVT Smith was supporting.

Excerpt from War Record of Battery F

On the night of August 21st Battery "F" was relieved of its mission at "Death Valley" and pulled back to a reserve position, two kilometers south of Chery-Chartreuve, where replacements that had just been received were to be trained in the handling of the guns.

Lt. Oates was in charge of the instruction and the new men arrived at the position on the morning of August 22nd while the veteran crews returned to the echelon for a rest. At about 11:30 a.m. an enemy 105 mm battery opened fire on the woods where "F" Battery was located and also on the woods to the right and left, searching for one of our 155 mm rifles [howitzer] which had been causing them some annoyance.

The men of the Battery who were preparing the new position were suddenly caught in this concentration of mustard gas and high explosive shell which although it lasted a few minutes, was accurately placed and did considerable damage.

Lt. Oates was mortally wounded and died a few moments later at the dressing station. PVT Geo. S. Monroe of South Haven, Michigan, a machine gunner, was instantly killed. Mechanic Walter Gutowsky of Detroit, Michigan, was mortally wounded and died on the way to the dressing station. Ten other men were among those wounded and burned with mustard gas. Lt. Wilson of the Medical Detachment was seriously wounded while administering first aid.

SGTs Doyle, Miller, and Graham with CPL Unroe and PVT Lochbiler deserve special mention for their heroic work in administering first aid and evacuating the wounded, they themselves being badly burned with gas and CPL Unroe and PVT Lochbiler were nearly blinded, but neglected their own injuries to take care of their comrades.

Diary Entry Fri. August 23

We got everything ready to move. Tore down the telephone centrals and was ready to move at ten thirty. Hiked all night. Made Camp about 5:30 in the morning. Was nearly all in. Slept all day. Pulled out on the trucks at seven o clock. Went around Chateau Thierry toward Soissons. Reached a village and stayed all night.

NOTES

1. U.S. War Department, *Battle Participation of Organizations of the American Expeditionary Forces in France, Belgium, and Italy: 1917-1918* (Washington: Government Printing Office, 1920), 39.
   Colonel Chester B. McCormick, "A Brief History of the 119th Field Artillery," *Honor Roll and Complete War History of Ingham County in the Great World War: 1914-1918* (Lansing MI: The State Journal Company, 1920), 219-220.

2. Richard A. Preston, Alex Roland, Sydney F. Wise, *Men In Arms: A History of Warfare and its Interrelationships with Western Society, Fifth Edition* (Fort Worth TX: Harcourt Brace Jovanovich, 1991), 234.
   Byron Farwell, *Over There: The United States in the Great War, 1917-1918* (New York: W.W. Norton and Company, 1999), 45.

3. Leo V. Jacks, *Service Record: By An Artilleryman* (New York: Charles Scribner's Sons, 1928).

4. J. Rickard, "Aisne-Marne Offensive, 18 July-6 August 1918," *History of War* (August 21, 2007) http://www.historyofwar.org/articles/battles_aisne_marne.html, accessed January 5, 2014.
   John F. Votaw, "Aisne-Marne Offensive," *World War I: A Student Encyclopedia* (Santa Barbara CA: ABC-CLIO, 2006), 110-112.
   American Battle Monuments Commission, *American Armies and Battlefields in Europe: A History, Guide, and Reference Book* (Washington, D.C.: U.S. GPO, 1938), 43-104.
   Office of the Chief of Military History, U.S. Army, *The Army Flag and Its Streamers: Aisne-Marne* (Washington, D.C.: U.S. GPO, 1964), http://www.history.army.mil/html/reference/army_flag/wwi.html, accessed March 30, 2015.

5. American Battle Monuments Commission, *32nd Division Summary of Operations in the World War* (Washington, D.C.: U.S. Government Printing Office, 1943), 8.

6. American Battle Monuments Commission, *28th Division Summary of Operations in the World War* (Washington, D.C.: U.S. Government Printing Office, 1944), 24-28.

7. U.S. Army Center of Military History, *Order of Battle of the United States Land Forces in the World War, American Expeditionary Forces: Division, Volume 2* (Washington: U.S. Government Printing Office, 1988 (Reprint originally published 1931-1949), 177. The 147th FA Regiment was assigned to the 41st Division but attached to the 57th FA BDE from June 24, 1918 to April 8, 1919. Hence this 75mm equipped unit

fought alongside the 119th FA for the duration of the war. The 119th was the largest of the three 75 mm FA Regiments.

8. American Battle Monuments Commission, 77th *Division Summary of Operations in the World War* (Washington, D.C.: U.S. Government Printing Office, 1944), 6-10.
9. McCormick, "A Brief History of the 119th Field Artillery," 219-220.
10. L.L. Stevenson, "Pages of Liberty Volume Illustrated by the 119th (Part 2 of series on the 119th FA's war exploits)," *Detroit News*, February 1919.
11. General Jean Degoutte, *General Order* (6th Army Post of Command, August 8, 1918).

The Wilfred and Olive Smith Family

Sitting from left to right Wilfred, Olive, and Elmer. Standing in back from left to right Dee, Zelma, and Clarence. Standing in front, Genevieve. Given that Genevieve was born in December 1913, this portrait was likely taken in late 1916 or early 1917 before Elmer enlisted in the Army and left for war.

Plot map and image showing location of W.F. Smith property near Ovid and Carland, Michigan. The 80 acre farm of Wilfred Smith was an irregular L shaped plot in Section 33, Fairfield Township, Shiawassee County.
Imagery ©2015 TerraMetrics, Map data ©2015 Google

Post card scene of the small unincorporated farming community of Carland, Michigan. The Smith family farm was about two miles from Carland's town center in Shiawassee County. The Smith property was about the same distance to the larger town of Ovid, Clinton County, where the family maintained a post office box for mail.

The W.F. Smith farmhouse adjacent to West Juddville Road near the rural towns of Carland and Ovid, Michigan. This farmhouse was later torn down and another sits in its place today.

The W.F. Smith barn was built in 1910 as painted on its grain silo. Note the two children sitting in the foreground, likely Dee and Genevieve. The barn is still standing today but is dilapidated and appears beyond repair.

The W.F. Smith barn looking south from Juddville Road.

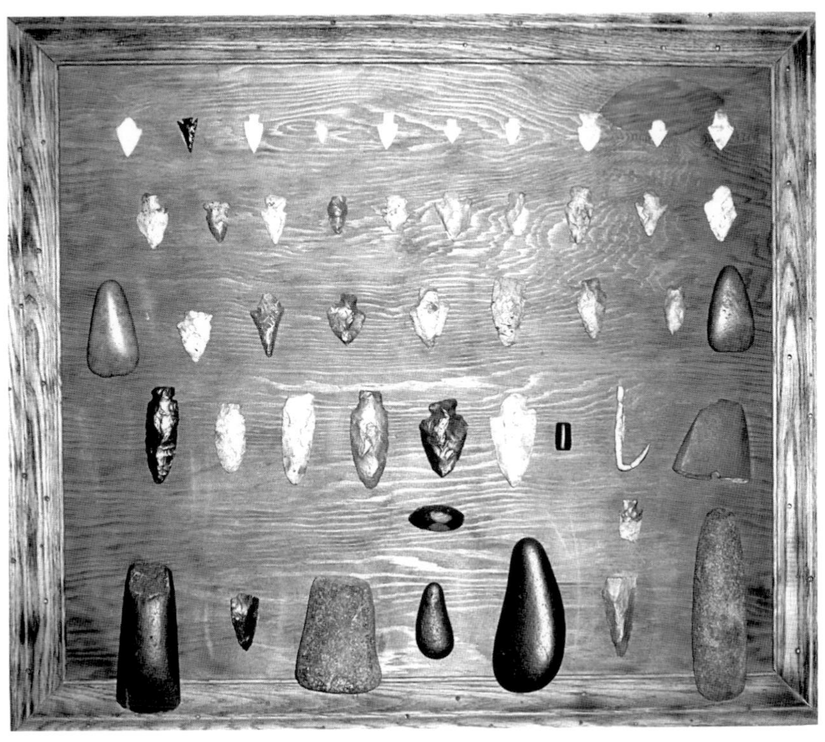

Elmer Smith's boyhood arrowhead collection. Elmer gathered these arrowheads and other Native American artifacts from the creek bed that ran through the eastern side of the Smith property. Artifacts were primarily uncovered and found after major rainstorms or when dredging the waterway for fertile soil.

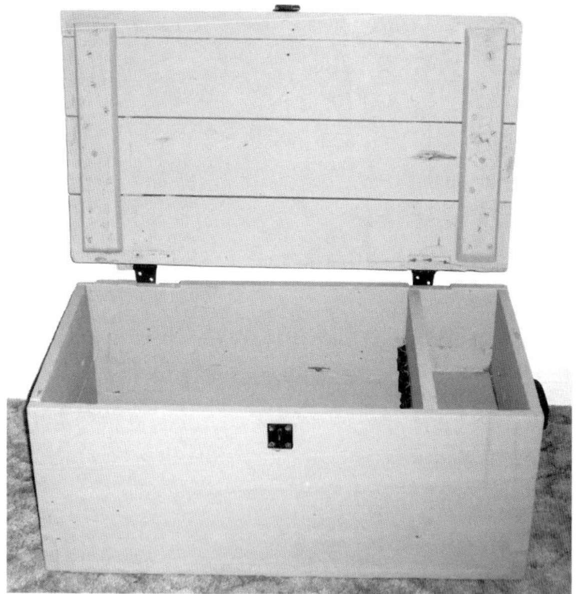

In the summer of 1917, as his unit prepared for mobilization, Elmer asked his father to build a wooden trunk to transport and store his uniforms, equipment, and personal belongings. The trunk accompanied Elmer throughout his Army service, from Lansing and Camp Grayling, Michigan, to Camp MacArthur, Texas, and onward to France. After the war Elmer used the trunk as a tool chest but it remains in good condition today.

Two photographs of Elmer with best friend Frank Nethaway while visiting him at the University of Michigan in Ann Arbor. The Nethaway family owned the farm one mile east of the Smith property near Carland, Michigan. The dirt road to the farm off of W. Juddville Road is still called Nethaway Road. Although three years older, Elmer considered Frank his closest friend. Elmer's older sister Zelma and Frank were the same age and were married in 1922.

A panoramic photograph of Battery B, First Michigan Field Artillery Battalion, assembled at their mobilization site, Camp Grayling in northern Michigan. Elmer is in the middle row, the second soldier kneeling from the right. The First Michigan Artillery and First Michigan Cavalry Squadron were combined to form the 119th Field Artillery Regiment in September 1917.

The First Battalion, Michigan Field Artillery cantonment area at Camp Grayling in September 1917. In the background are the cantonment areas for the 31st and 32nd Infantry Regiments, two Michigan units that also mobilized at the camp.

A panoramic photograph of officers and soldiers of Battery B, 119th FA at Camp MacArthur, likely taken while Private Smith was still a member of the Battery. Elmer was transferred from B Battery to the Regimental Headquarters Company in early January 1918. Due to extensive shadows, Elmer Smith has not been identified in the photo.

A panoramic photograph of the 119th FA Regiment barracks area at Camp MacArthur, Texas. The 119th occupied these billets from October 1917 through early February 1918. The Exchange in the middle of the Regimental Area sold common hygiene and other useful items.

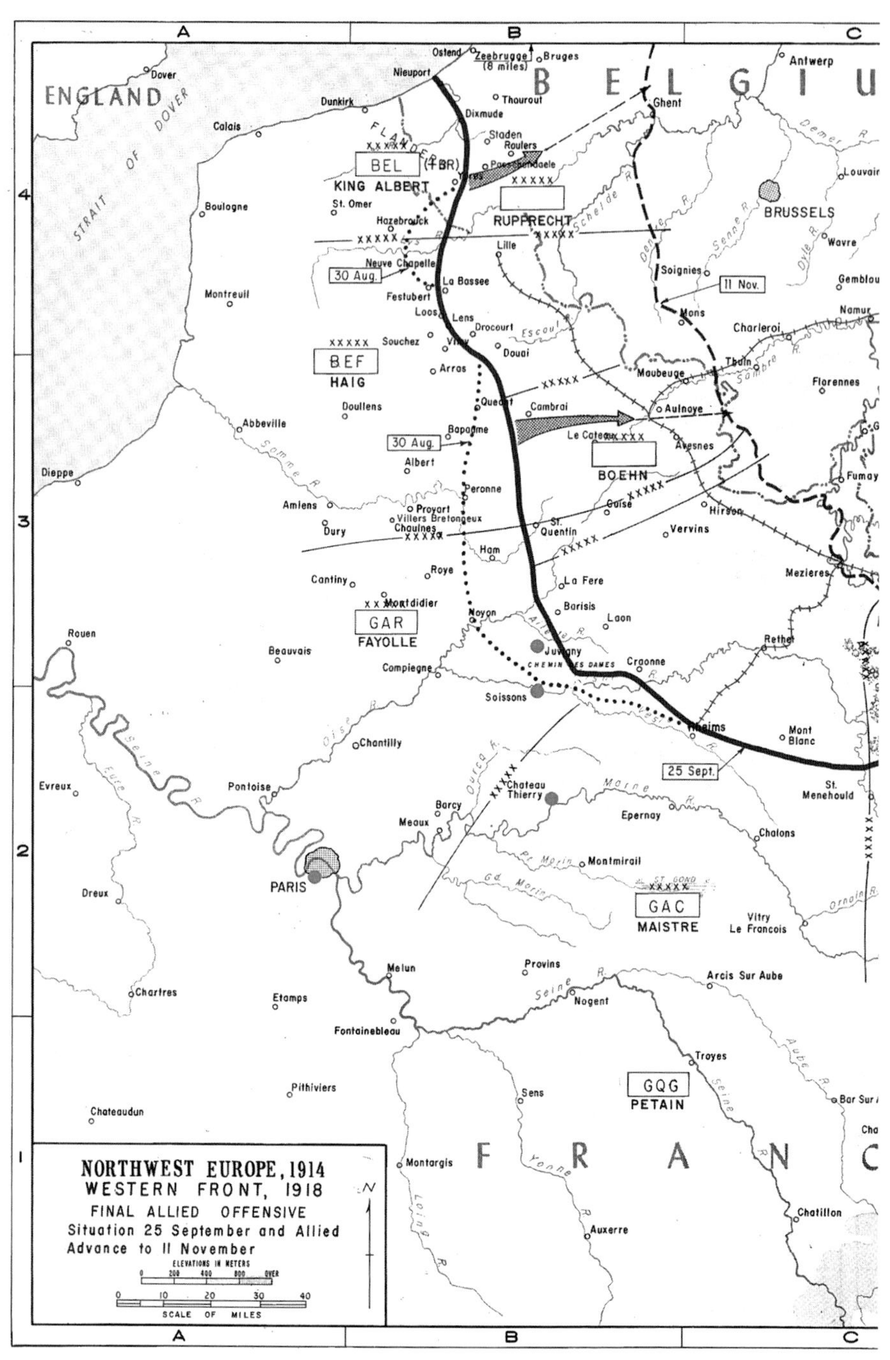

Final Campaign Map of the World War Western Front. Large dots note locations Elmer Smith cited in his diary or letters.

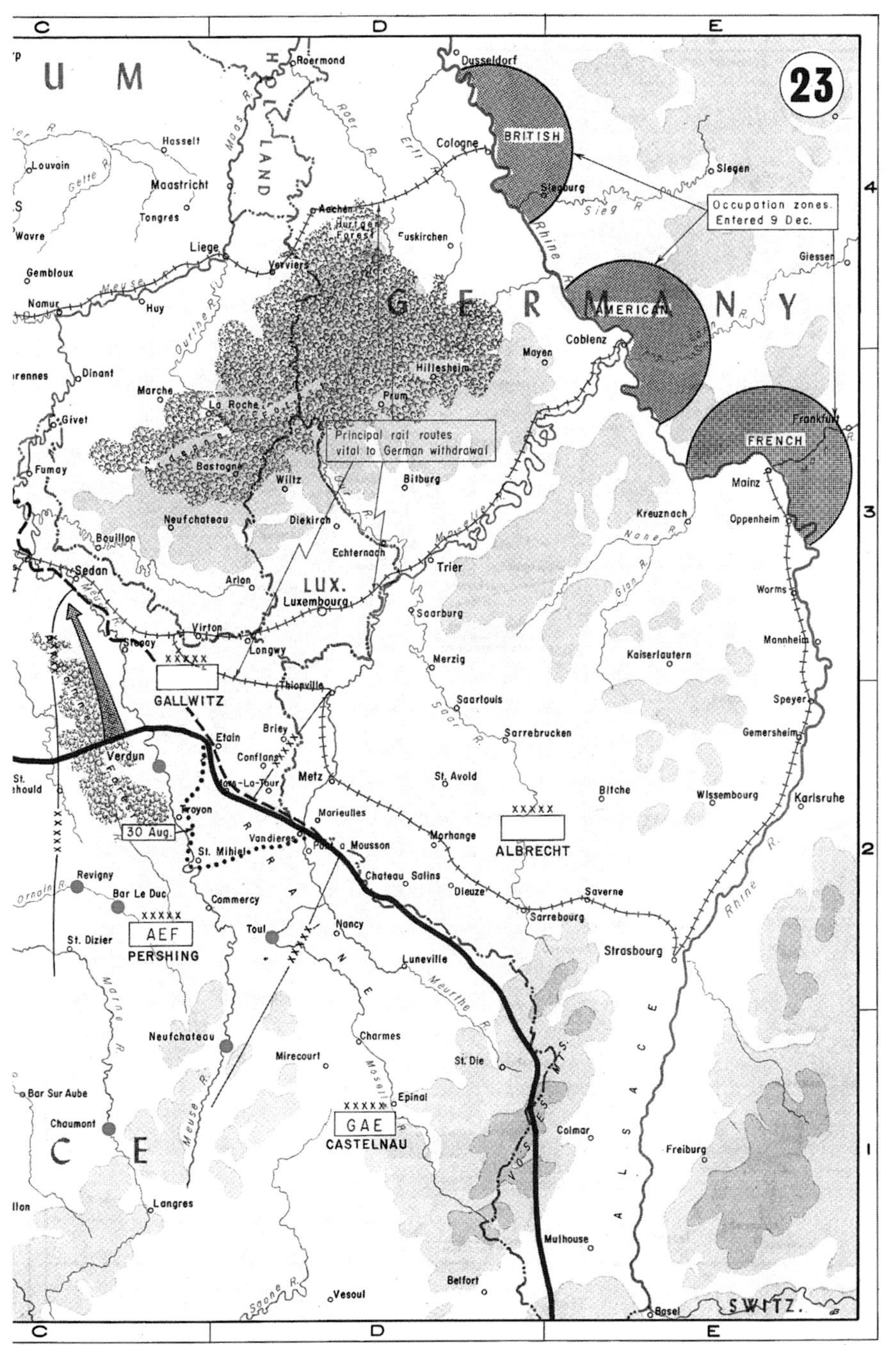

Map courtesy of The Department of History,
United States Military Academy at West Point

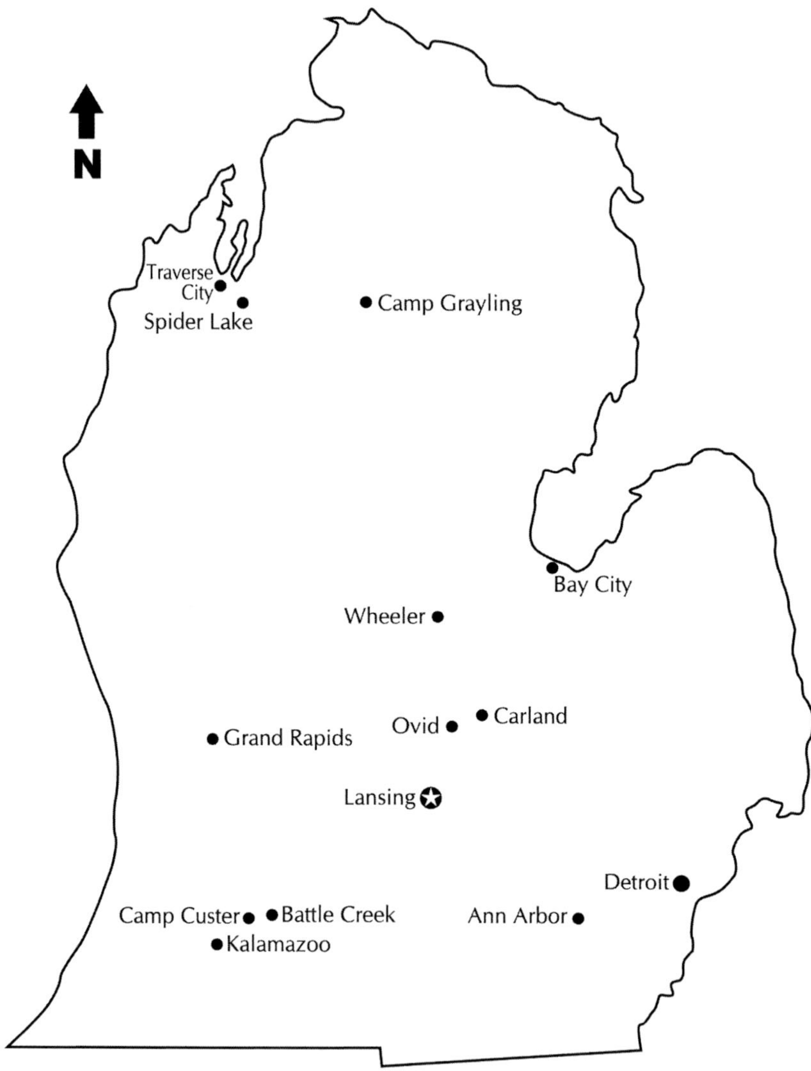

Map of Michigan's Lower Peninsula

A poster-sized roster listing all officers, non-commissioned officers, and soldiers of Battery B who trained for war at Camp MacArthur, Texas.

1—Some Warehouses and Bird's-Eye View.
3—Tent Street.

2—Soldiers' Temporary Homes.
4—Bird's-Eye View Near River.

Selected photos of Camp MacArthur, from *Pictorial Souvenir of Camp MacArthur, Waco, Texas*

Three photographs of Elmer Smith in his field uniform with his gas mask, garrison or overseas cap, and steel "doughboy" helmet. These were likely taken at Camp MacArthur and may have been taken on New Year's Day, 1918, when his first diary entry stated he and two friends were taking photographs.

Private Elmer Smith with an unidentified soldier. It is unknown where this photograph was taken. Elmer does not reference this particular picture in his letters or diary but it may have been one of the photos taken New Year's Day, 1918.

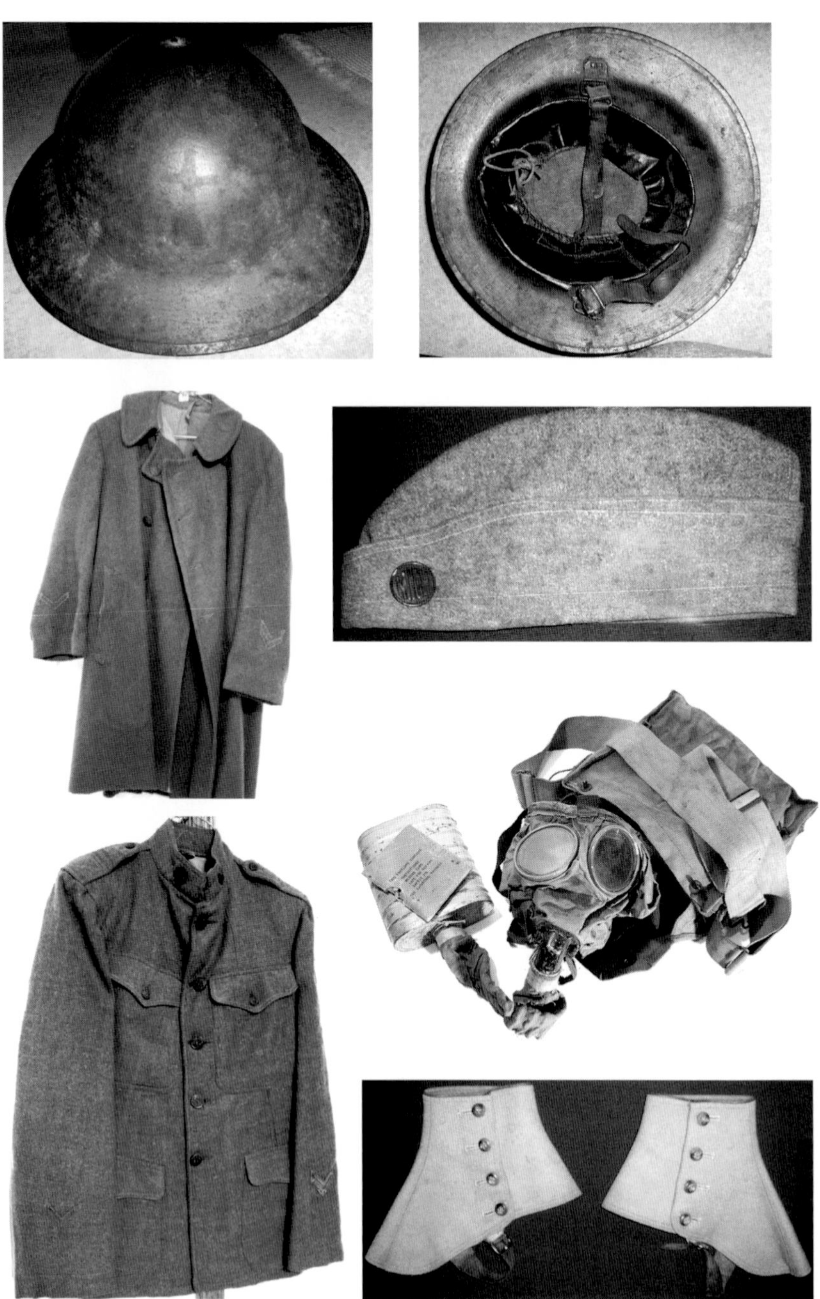

Elmer's uniform items *(clockwise from top left):* helmet, inside of helmet, overseas cap, gas mask, leggings, wool tunic, and wool overcoat.
Gas mask photo courtesy of Bob Umenhofer.

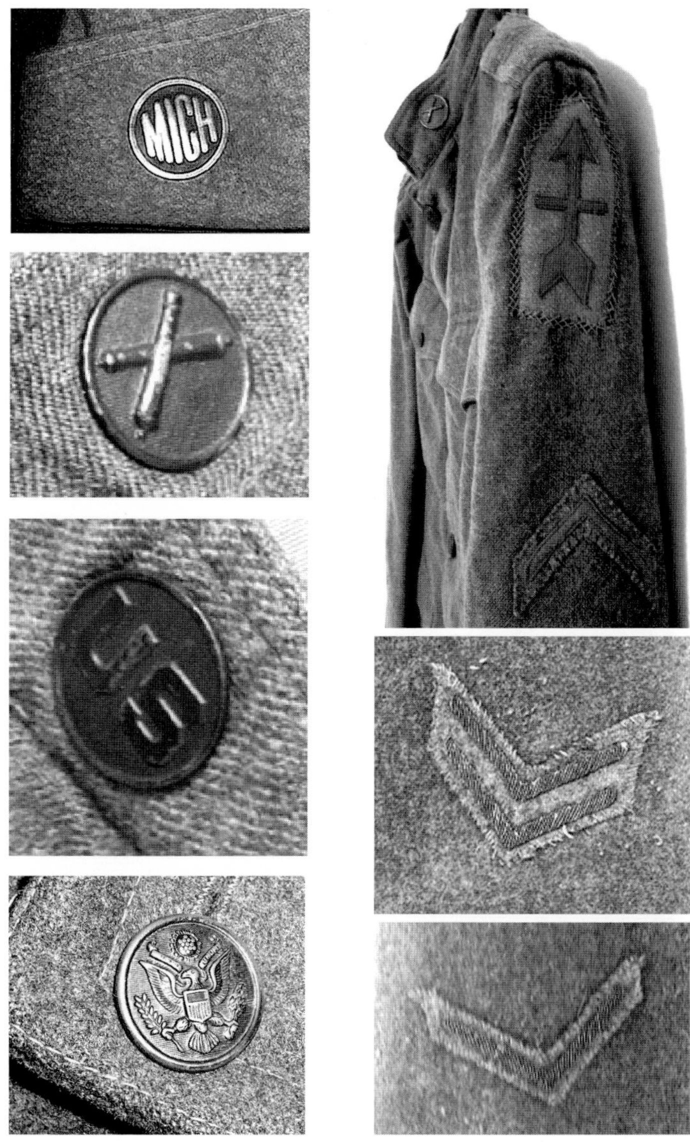

Elmer's uniform accoutrements *(counter-clockwise from top left)*: On the left side of the overseas cap is a circular bronze device with MICH inscribed, depicting his National Guard unit's state of origin; Enlisted man's bronze corps device, left side of collar, Field Artillery Corps, two crossed artillery cannons; Enlisted man's bronze collar service device, right side of collar, US, connoting a Regular Army soldier; Enlisted man's U.S. Army standard uniform button; Overseas Combat Service Chevrons (left cuff); Wound Chevron (right cuff); 32nd Division Shoulder Sleeve Insignia and Private/Private First Class Rank

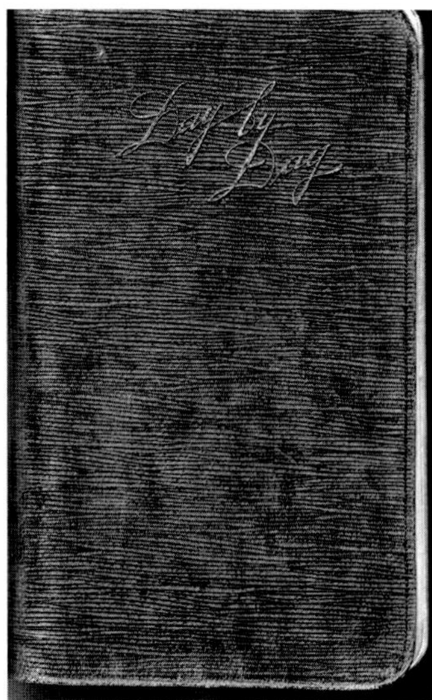

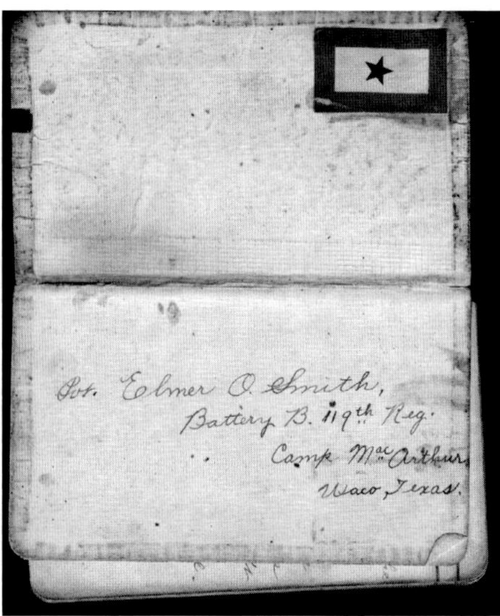

Elmer Smith's 1918 diary cover was entitled "Day by Day." The preformatted diary was printed by the Samuel Ward Manufacturing Company of Boston. On the inside cover of his diary Elmer inscribed his rank, name, unit, and station along with a "Blue Star" sticker which symbolized a soldier deployed overseas in combat.

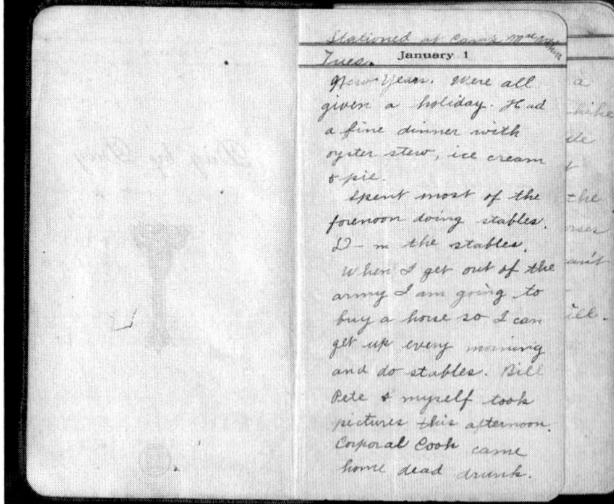

Stationed at Camp McArthur
Tues. January 1

New Year. Were all given a holiday. Had a fine dinner with oyster stew, ice cream & pie.
Spent most of the forenoon doing stables. D—n the stables.
When I get out of the army I am going to buy a horse so I can get up every morning and do stables. Bill Pete & myself took pictures this afternoon. Corporal Cook came home dead drunk.

CALENDAR, 1918

	S	M	T	W	T	F	S
JANUARY	...	...	1	2	3	4	5
	6	7	8	9	10	11	12
	13	14	15	16	17	18	19
	20	21	22	23	24	25	26
	27	28	29	30	31	...	...
	...	...	...	...	...	...	...
FEBRU'Y	...	...	...	...	...	1	2
	3	4	5	6	7	8	9
	10	11	12	13	14	15	16
	17	18	19	20	21	22	23
	24	25	26	27	28	...	...
	...	...	...	...	...	...	...
MARCH	...	...	...	...	...	1	2
	3	4	5	6	7	8	9
	10	11	12	13	14	15	16
	17	18	19	20	21	22	23
	24	25	26	27	28	29	30
	31	...	...	...	...	...	...
APRIL	...	1	2	3	4	5	6
	7	8	9	10	11	12	13
	14	15	16	17	18	19	20
	21	22	23	24	25	26	27
	28	29	30	...	...	...	...
	...	...	...	...	...	...	...
MAY	...	...	...	1	2	3	4
	5	6	7	8	9	10	11
	12	13	14	15	16	17	18
	19	20	21	22	23	24	25
	26	27	28	29	30	31	...
	...	...	...	...	...	...	...
JUNE	...	...	...	...	...	...	1
	2	3	4	5	6	7	8
	9	10	11	12	13	14	15
	16	17	18	19	20	21	22
	23	24	25	26	27	28	29
	30	...	...	...	...	...	...

	S	M	T	W	T	F	S
JULY	...	1	2	3	4	5	6
	7	8	9	10	11	12	13
	14	15	16	17	18	19	20
	21	22	23	24	25	26	27
	28	29	30	31	...	...	...
	...	...	...	...	...	...	...
AUGUST	...	...	...	...	1	2	3
	4	5	6	7	8	9	10
	11	12	13	14	15	16	17
	18	19	20	21	22	23	24
	25	26	27	28	29	30	31
	...	...	...	...	...	...	...
SEPTEMB'R	1	2	3	4	5	6	7
	8	9	10	11	12	13	14
	15	16	17	18	19	20	21
	22	23	24	25	26	27	28
	29	30	...	...	...	...	...
	...	...	...	...	...	...	...
OCTOBER	...	...	1	2	3	4	5
	6	7	8	9	10	11	12
	13	14	15	16	17	18	19
	20	21	22	23	24	25	26
	27	28	29	30	31	...	...
	...	...	...	...	...	...	...
NOVEMB'R	...	...	...	...	...	1	2
	3	4	5	6	7	8	9
	10	11	12	13	14	15	16
	17	18	19	20	21	22	23
	24	25	26	27	28	29	30
	...	...	...	...	...	...	...
DECEMB'R	1	2	3	4	5	6	7
	8	9	10	11	12	13	14
	15	16	17	18	19	20	21
	22	23	24	25	26	27	28
	29	30	31	...	...	...	...
	...	...	...	...	...	...	...

SAMUEL WARD MANUFACTURING CO.
BOSTON

The first diary entry on January 1, 1918, describes how Elmer spent New Year's Day with friends and a fine meal before performing the horse stable duties he disliked so much. His common soldier perspective and sense of humor are evident in this initial entry and throughout the year. *Right:* a small calendar with the year 1917 on one side and 1918 on the other. It likely came with the diary as they were printed by the same company.

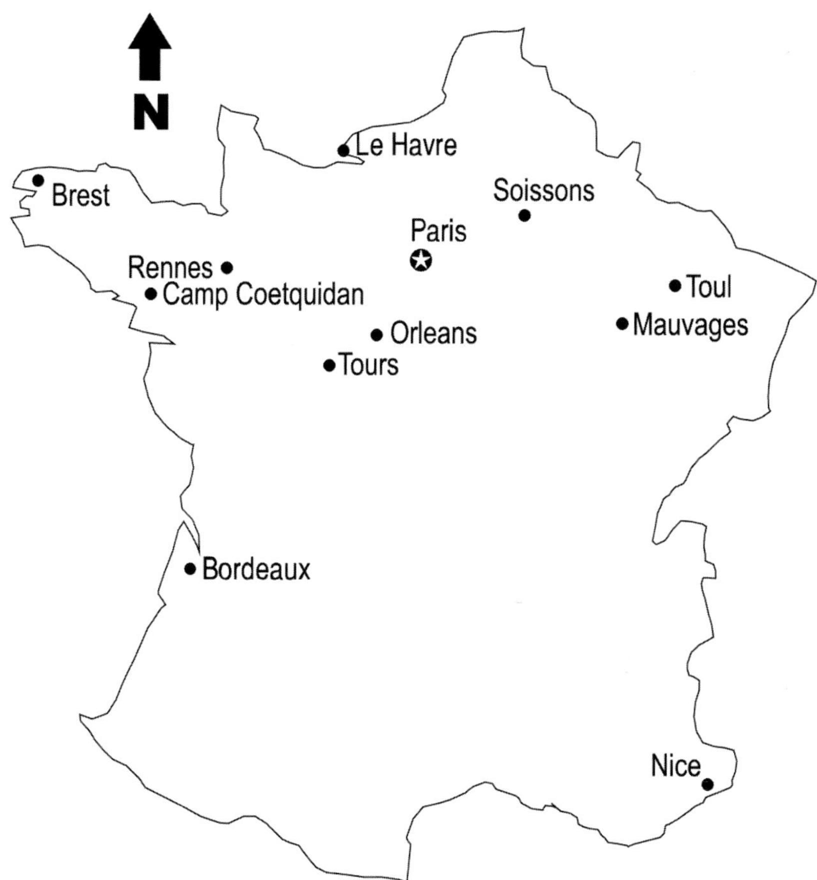

Major locations where Elmer Smith was in France, as cited in his diary and letters.

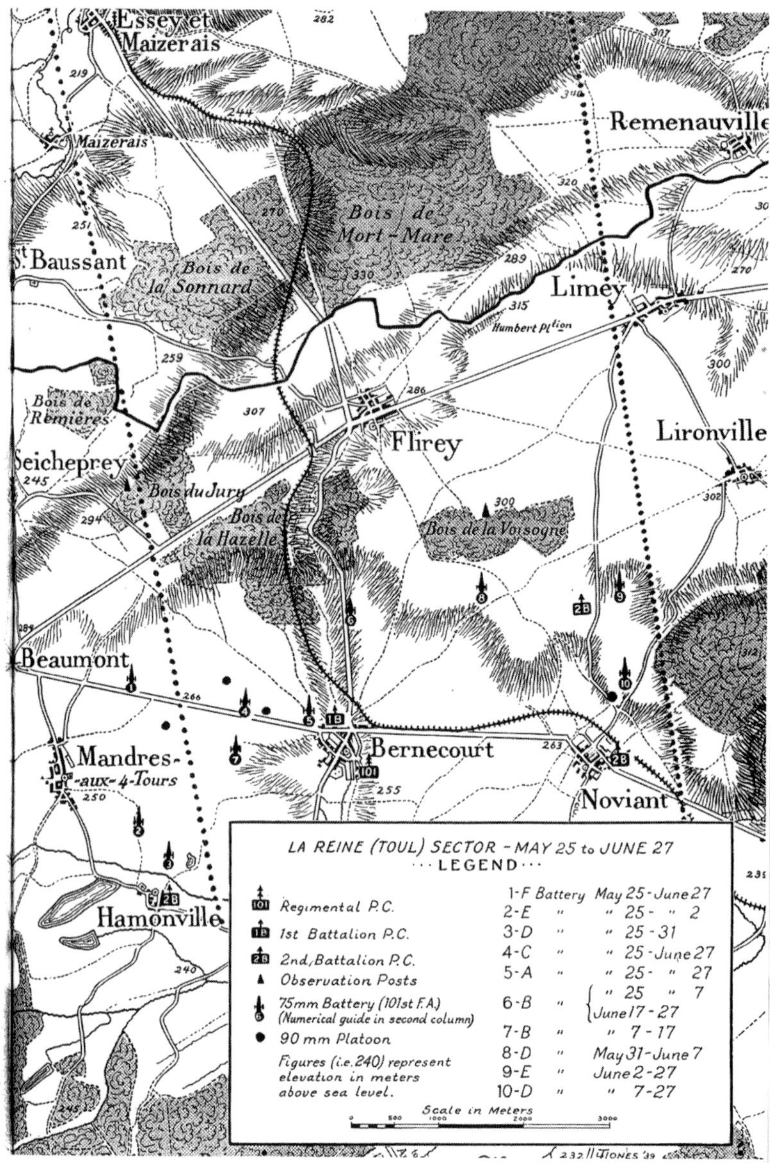

The 101st Artillery map of the Toul area depicts the location of the Regiments' firing batteries and battalion posts of command (P.C.) from May to June 1918. The 119th FA entered the front line in support of the 101st on June 12th and its batteries likely occupied the same positions beside their counterparts. Note the town of Noviant on the right side of the map. It was near this town where German artillery fire wounded Private Elmer Smith and PFC Louis Hice on the afternoon of June 16th. From *The 101st Field Artillery: AEF 1917-1919*.

(WRITE
PLAINLY)

IMMEDIATE REPORT OF CASUALTY
(To be used in place of Form #17, S.D., A.G.O., A.E.F.)

Sent to STATISTICAL SECTION, DIVISION HEADQUARTERS ____ (Hour) 16 June 1918 (Date)
By (Underscore means used) Telegraph, Telephone, Motor Courier, Runner.

1. CASUALTY Seriously wounded
(Killed, Died of Wounds, Died of Disease, Captured, Missing, Seriously Wounded, Slightly Wounded; State which.)

2. NAME Elmer (Christian Name) O. (Initial) Smith (Surname)

3. NUMBER 297020

4. RANK Private

5. ORGANIZATION Hq. (Company) 119th F.A. (Regiment)

6. CAUSE Shell Fire
(Gas, Shell Fire, Shrapnel, Machine Gun Fire, etc. State in full.)

7. PLACE Noviant (At or near what town or village) Toul Sector

8. DATE 16 June 1918

9. HOUR 14:30

10. IN LINE OF DUTY? Yes 11. RESULT OF OWN MISCONDUCT? No

12. IS SOLDIER ENTITLED TO WOUND CHEVRON? Yes

(Fill in in all cases)

13. EMERGENCY ADDRESS ____

14. DATE OF ENLISTMENT ____

15. PLACE OF ENLISTMENT ____

16. WITH WHAT ORGANIZATION DID HE ARRIVE IN FRANCE? ____

This form to be filled in and sent to Div. Hdqtrs. for each casualty. If report is made by telegraph or telephone this form will follow as a confirmation.

____ (Signature)

____ (Rank) ____ (Organization)

The Wound Cards for Private Elmer Smith and PFC Louis Hice *(facing page)*, from the Michigan State Archives. Each shows the preliminary information the 119th FA collected regarding their wounds from artillery shells on June 16th. Elmer's wounds were listed as severe but after seven weeks of healing and convalescence he returned to the 119th for the duration of the war. PFC Hice's wounds were assessed as slight. However, he died the next day and was the first 119th soldier killed in action.

(WRITE
PLAINLY)

IMMEDIATE REPORT OF CASUALTY
(To be used in place of Form #17, S.D., A.G.O., A.E.F.)

Sent to STATISTICAL SECTION, DIVISION HEADQUARTERS ______ 16 June 1918
(Hour) (Date)

By (Underscore means used) Telegraph, Telephone, Motor Courier, Runner.

1. CASUALTY Slighty wounded.
(Killed, Died of Wounds, Died of Disease, Captured, Missing, Seriously Wounded, Slightly Wounded; State which.)

2. NAME Louis K. Hice
(Christian Name) (Initial) (Surname)

3. NUMBER 297018

4. RANK Pvt. 1st Class

5. ORGANIZATION Hq. 119th I.G.
(Company) (Regiment)

6. CAUSE Shell Fire
(Gas, Shell Fire, Shrapnel, Machine Gun Fire, etc. State in full.)

7. PLACE Noviant France
(At or near what town or village)

8. DATE 16 June 1918.

9. HOUR 16:30

10. IN LINE OF DUTY? Yes 11. RESULT OF OWN MISCONDUCT? No.

12. IS SOLDIER ENTITLED TO WOUND CHEVRON? Yes.

(Fill in in all cases)

EMERGENCY ADDRESS ______

No Personal Record

DATE OF ENLISTMENT ______

PLACE OF ENLISTMENT ______

WITH WHAT ORGANIZATION DID HE ARRIVE IN FRANCE? ______

...m to be filled in and sent ... Hdqtrs, for each casualty. ...t is made by telegraph or ... this form will follow as ...ation.

______
(Signature)

______
(Rank) (Organiza...

Form 1204

CLASS OF SERVICE	SYMBOL
Day Message	
Day Letter	Blue
Night Message	Nite
Night Letter	N L

If none of these three symbols appears after the check (number of words) this is a day message. Otherwise its character is indicated by the symbol appearing after the check.

WESTERN UNION TELEGRAM

NEWCOMB CARLTON, PRESIDENT — GEORGE W. E. ATKINS, FIRST VICE-PRESIDENT

CLASS OF SERVICE	SYMBOL
Day Message	
Day Letter	Blue
Night Message	Nite
Night Letter	N L

If none of these three symbols appears after the check (number of words) this is a day message. Otherwise its character is indicated by the symbol appearing after the check.

RECEIVED AT

Wa Washington D.C. 33 Govt.
June 23-1918
Wilfred P Smith
Amel mich
Deeply Regret to inform you that
it is officially Reported that
Private Elmer O Smith Field
artillery was severely wounded
in action June sixteenth
McCain, The Adjutant Genl.

The Western Union Telegram from the War Department Adjutant General's Office, Washington D.C., notifying his parents that Private Elmer Smith was severely wounded in battle on June 16, 1918. The telegram was sent on June 23rd and received on June 24th.

Colonel CHESTER B. McCORMICK
Commanding 119th Regiment, 32nd Division Field Artillery
Captain of Battery A during Mexican trouble; promoted to Major in May, 1917. Made Colonel December 5th, 1917. His regiment became famous for its gallant service around Chateau Thierry. Born in New York state August 29th, 1879. Came to Lansing in 1900.

Colonel Chester B. McCormick was the commander of the 119th FA Regiment throughout the war. For his stellar leadership and superb artillery support to frontline units during combat the Army awarded him the Distinguished Service Medal. From *Honor Roll and Complete War History of Ingham County in the Great World War, 1914 to 1918.*

The 32nd was named the "Red Arrow" Division for its demonstrated ability to pierce the German line and gain ground in every engagement. The soldiers wore the Division shoulder sleeve insignia or unit patch at the top of the left sleeve of their wool tunic and overcoat just below the shoulder. It was also painted on the crown of the helmet stretching to the rear so soldiers could be identified from behind.

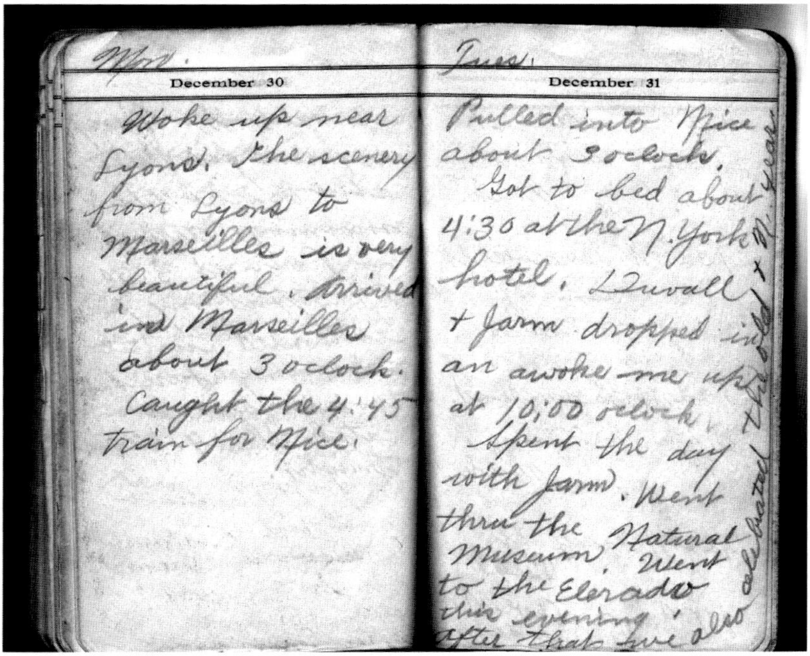
Mon.

December 30

Woke up near Lyons. The scenery from Lyons to Marseilles is very beautiful. Arrived in Marseilles about 3 oclock. Caught the 4:45 train for Nice.

Tues.

December 31

Pulled into Nice about 3 oclock. Got to bed about 4:30 at the N. York hotel. Duvall + Jarm dropped in an awoke me up at 10:00 oclock. Spent the day with Jarm. Went thru the Natural Museum. Went to the Elerado this evening. After that we also celebrated the old + N. Year

The final diary entries

En route to Nice, France, on December 30 and 31, 1918.

ARMEE AMERICAN PERMISSIONAIRE

Date December 28 1918.

No. 36

Name (Nom) Elmer C Smith

Rank (Grade) Pvt 1st Class

Organization Hq. Company, 119th Field Artillery

Under authority of General Orders No. 6, G.H.Q., A.E.F., is authorized to be on Seven days furlough beginning December 28-18 (Date)

He has permission to visit Nice

He does not French. (State whether or not soldier speaks French)

He has all equipment called for under General Orders No. 6, G.H.Q. Amerivan E.F.

He has been in France 10 months and his last Furlough was None (Date)

The address of the A.P.M. at Nice (Destination) is

PHYSICAL EXAMINATION

I have this day examined Elmer D. Smith and find that he is free from Venereal Disease.

Major, M.C., U.S.A.

Chester B. McCormick
Colonel, 119th Field Artillery
Commanding.

Leave Form for Nice, France with stamps for each location Elmer was required to check-in.

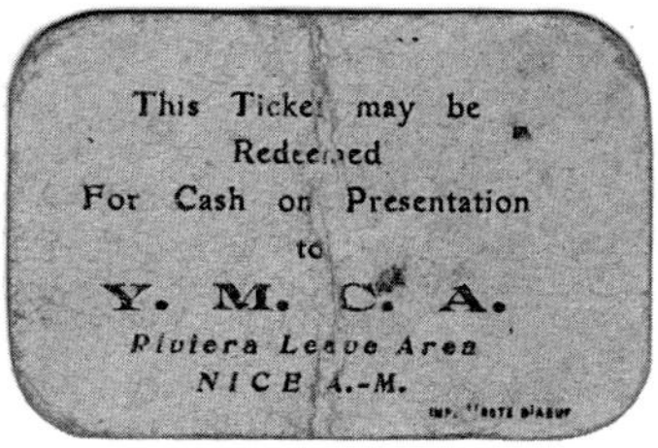

This Ticket may be
Redeemed
For Cash on Presentation
to
Y. M. C. A.
Riviera Leave Area
NICE A.-M.

Leave memorabilia from Nice, France.

SOLDIER'S

INDIVIDUAL PAY RECORD
BOOK

This book will be carried by the soldier in his personal possession

No alterations of any kind will be made in this book. Necessary corrections of erroneous entries will be effected by making a new entry properly authenticated.

It is made the duty of all members of the A. E. F. finding an individual pay record book to mail same to the Chief Quartermaster, A. E. F.

PAID TO INCLUDE	DATE PAID	QUARTERMASTER MAKING PAYMENT
Nov. 30.18	Dec. 1.18	Capt. F. E. Barnum
Dec 31/18	Jan 4/19	Maj. C. E. Mears
Jan 31/19	Feb 9/19	Maj E C Mears
Feb 28/19	Mar 9/19	Maj E C Mears
Mar 31/19	Apr 4/19	Maj E C Mears

1

Soldiers No 297070
NAME Elmer O. Smith
Grade and Organization Pvt. 1 Cl. Hq. Co. 119 F. A.
Occupation Student
Entered service:
From N. G. by draft Aug. 5/17 Yes
Place of rendezvous Lansing Mich (Yes or No)
By draft in National Army, date
Place of reporting
By enlistment in Reg. Army, date
Place of acceptance
Date of opening pay book Oct. 1, 1918
Date of arrival in U. S. from f. s.
Year and date of birth Mar. 5, 1891
Date of application for W. R. Ins. Jan. 1. 18
Amount of War Risk Insurance $ 10000
Serving in 1st enlistment period
Additional pay for Triple TAB, L.V. March 8/19
(Order No. source, date)
Additional pay for
(Order No. source, date)
Due soldier for clothing July 15/17 $

2

GRADE TO WHICH PROMOTED OR REDUCED	TOTAL PAY MONTHLY	CLASS A	CLASS B	ORDINARY CLASS E EXPIRES	LIBERTY LOAN	INSURANCE W.R.	INSURANCE "D"	TOTAL FIXED DEDUCTION	NET PAY MONTHLY
Pvt. 1 Cl.	36.60					6.50		6.50	30.10

MONTHLY ALLOTMENTS

I certify that the entries on opposite page and in first column hereon are correct and that the soldier's signature was written in my presence.

Elmer O. Smith
Soldier's Signature

Schneider
Witnessing Officer's Signature, Rank and Organization

I certify that entries in second column are correct.
Signature.
Rank & Org.

I certify that entries in third column are correct.
Signature.
Rank & Org.

I certify that entries in fourth column are correct.
Signature.
Rank & Org.

Pay Book information pages and pay dates page.

Elmer's former unit, Battery B of the 119th FA Regiment was the first to debark from the U.S.S. Frederick and arrived back on American soil in New York harbor on May 3, 1919. From *Detroit News,* May 4, 1919.

On Tuesday morning, May 13, 1919, a huge victory parade honored the 119th FA Regiment, "Lansing's Own," for its stellar wartime service in France. The parade route through the capital city attracted thousands of citizens who rousingly welcomed back Michigan's proud combat soldiers. Three days later, Elmer Smith was discharged from the U.S. Army and restarted his civilian life. From the Forest Parke Memorial Library of the Capital Area District Library.

ENLISTMENT RECORD.

Name: 267070 Elmer O Smith Grade: Pvt 1st Cl

Enlisted, or Inducted, April 30, 1917, at Lansing Mich

Serving in First enlistment period at date of discharge.

Prior service: * None

Noncommissioned officer: None

Marksmanship, gunner qualification or rating: † None

Horsemanship: None

Battles, engagements, skirmishes, expeditions: Toul Sector 8 June 16 June 1918 Aisne Marne offensive 18 aug - 24 aug 18 Oise Aisne Offensive 27 aug 11 Sept Meuse Argonne Offensive 26 Sept 26

Knowledge of any vocation: Student

Wounds received in service: June 16 at Xivray Shell fragment in Back

Physical condition when discharged: Good

Typhoid prophylaxis completed Aug 11 1917

Paratyphoid prophylaxis completed Oct 30 1917

Married or single: Single

Character: Excellent

Remarks: Travel pay to Lansing Mich No AWOL or AFD under GO 45 WD 1914 B Btry to Hq 119 FA. AEF France May 4 1918. US May 31 1919

Signature of soldier: Elmer O Smith

Corwin Schneider
Capt F.A.

Commanding Hq 119 FA

RECRUITING STATION
GRAND RAPIDS, MICH.
FORWARDED OCT 16 1920
APPROVED BY CAPT. H. M. FALES, U. S. A. RET. ASST. F
FOR VICTORY MEDAL WITH 4 clasps

... Creek, Mich.
MAY 15 1919
Paid in full $109.07
including bonus of $60.00
... F.A. U.S.A.

* Give company and regiment or corps or department, with inclusive dates of service in each enlistment.
† Give date of qualification or rating and number, date, and source of order announcing same.

The 119th FA Headquarters Company Commander, CPT Corwin Schneider signed PFC Smith's Enlistment Record. A stamp in the lower left shows his final pay of $109 which included a $60 bonus and travel pay back to Lansing. It also is stamped in the center right showing that on October 16, 1920, the Grand Rapids, Michigan Army, Recruiting Station Commander approved his request for the World War Victory Medal with four battle clasps.

Honorable Discharge from The United States Army

Received for Record Aug 1 1919
and recorded in Liber No. 2
Record of Discharge of Soldiers.
ARCH W. BURNETT,
County Clerk,
Shiawassee County, Mich.

TO ALL WHOM IT MAY CONCERN:

This is to Certify, That* Elmer O Smith
†297070 Hq Co 119 F A 57 Brig 32 Div.
THE UNITED STATES ARMY, as a TESTIMONIAL OF HONEST AND FAITHFUL SERVICE, is hereby HONORABLY DISCHARGED from the military service of the UNITED STATES by reason of ‡ Cir 106 W D Dec 3 1918

Said Elmer O Smith was born in Ovid, in the State of Michigan

When enlisted he was 20 years of age and by occupation a Student

He had Blue eyes, Lt Brown hair, Fair complexion, and was 5 feet 9 inches in height.

Given under my hand at Camp Custer Mich this 15 day of May, one thousand nine hundred and 19

Certified for
Michigan Bonus June 2, 1921
[signature]
Notary Public.

Chester B McCormick
Col 119 FA
Commanding.

Form No. 525, A. G. O.
Oct. 9-18.

9—3164

*Insert name, Christian name first; e. g., "John Doe."
†Insert Army serial number, grade, company and regiment or arm or corps or department; e. g., "1,620,302"; "Corporal, Company A, 1st Infantry"; "Sergeant, Quartermaster Corps"; "Sergeant, First Class, Medical Department."
‡If discharged prior to expiration of service, give number, date, and source of order or full description of authority therefor.

The 119th FA Regimental Commander, COL Chester McCormick signed PFC Elmer O. Smith's Discharge Certificate. A stamp at the top left shows that on August 1, 1919, Elmer filed this official document with the Shiawassee County Clerk in the Discharge of Soldiers Records. In the lower left corner an entry was added on June 2, 1921, when a Notary certified him to receive a bonus from the State of Michigan for his wartime service.

CAMP PERSONNEL OFFICE
Camp Custer, Michigan.

To Packard Motor Car Co., Detroit, Michigan...

Elmer Smith

has been honorably discharged from the U. S. Army. He is sent to you for employment as

Clerical work

WILMER T. SCOTT,
Major, F. A., U. S. A.
Camp Personnel Adjutant.

C. P. A. 6.

APPLICATION FOR VICTORY MEDAL — DUPLICATE

ENLISTED MEN

Smith, Elmer O. 297070 Pvt Hq Co 119th Field Artillery

(Surname) (Christian name in full) (Army serial number) (Grade and organization—Instr. 1)

TO BE PREPARED ON TYPEWRITER BY APPLICANT

I apply for Victory Medal with appropriate clasps for service in the United States Army in The World War:

Major operations participated in (Instruction 2):

	CAMBRAI		SOMME OFFENSIVE
	SOMME DEFENSIVE	x	OISE-AISNE
	LYS		YPRES-LYS
	AISNE		ST. MIHIEL
	MONTDIDIER-NOYON	x	MEUSE-ARGONNE
	CHAMPAGNE-MARNE		VITTORIO-VENETO
x	AISNE-MARNE		

Defensive sector service (Instruction 3): Toul Sector 6-8 to 6-16, 1918

Service abroad not entitling me to battle clasp, in (Instruction 4)

____FRANCE; ____ITALY; ____SIBERIA; ____RUSSIA; ____ENGLAND

Signature of Applicant (Instr. 6) Elmer O Smith

Address 1324 S Washington ave
Lansing, Michigan

Date 10-16-20

3—7740

TO BE FILLED OUT BY FORWARDING AND APPROVING OFFICER

RECRUITING STATION ... OCT 18 1920

(Station of forwdg. or apprg. officer) (Date)

To The Adjutant General of the Army (____Incls.)

Signature ____

To the Depot Officer, G. S. Depot, Phila., Pa. (Instr. 8)
Approved for Victory Medal.
With battle clasps:*

AISNE-MARNE.
OISE-AISNE 505506
MEUSE-ARGONNE.
DEFENSIVE SECTOR

With clasp for service not entitling to battle clasp:*
NONE

Signature of Approving Officer H W Fales

CAPT. H. W. FALES, U. S. A. RET. ASST. R. O.

(Rank and designation)

(Instructions 7 and 9) *If none, so state.

Top: As part of outprocessing from the Army, the Camp Custer Personnel Adjutant provided a card stating that Elmer Smith was an honorably discharged soldier and could possibly work in the auto industry in Detroit. This card was likely given to all Michigan soldiers but if Elmer wanted to pursue an automobile manufacturing company job he probably would have done so in Lansing at the Oldsmobile or REO Motor Companies.

Bottom: Elmer Smith's formal application for the World War Victory Medal in October, 1920

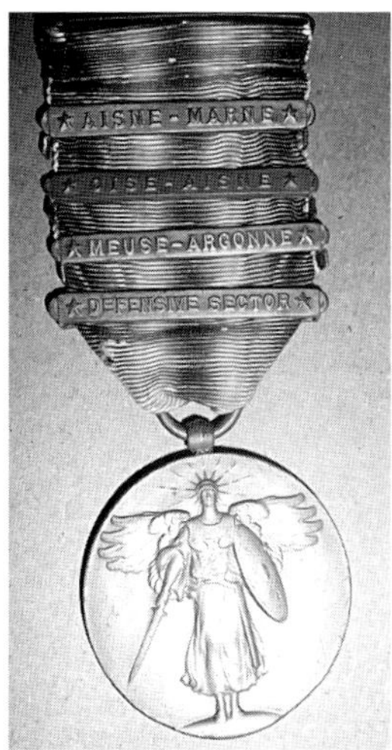

PFC Elmer Smith received three official decorations for his service in the Great War. The first was the World War Victory Medal with four battle clasps for the major battles he fought in. The French government twice awarded his unit and all its soldiers the Croix de Guerre (Cross of War) for distinguished support to French commands during combat. Lastly, he was authorized to wear the Purple Heart Medal for having been wounded in action. The Purple Heart Medal replaced the Wound Chevron after the war but was retroactive to all soldiers wounded during World War I.

After the World War, the U.S. Army began to develop Distinctive Unit Insignia for all of its regiments. In April 1925, it released the insignia for the 119th Field Artillery Regiment. In its upper left corner is the Coat of Arms of Lorraine, France, symbolizing the unit's baptism of fire in the Toul Sector in June 1918. Elmer Smith was one of the first men wounded in action during the Regiment's initial combat operations. The Latin term "Viam Prie Paramus" is the unit's motto translating to, "We Prepare the Way." The 119th's effective artillery preparatory missions amply prepared the way for infantry soldiers throughout its many World War battles.

Elmer shipped several war souvenirs home from France including a German helmet *(above)*, a German 77 mm artillery canister and mortar shell *(left)*, an inert hand grenade, and a cigarette humidor or box made from two brass artillery canisters. The hand grenade was sold in the 1990s. The location of the humidor is unknown. *Shell canister and mortar shell photo courtesy of Bob Umenhofer.*

Elmer and Marge Smith
wedding photo

Elmer and daughter
Margo around 1939

Elmer "Bob" Smith with his Model T Ford

Elmer's parents, Wilfred and Olive Smith, were married for 60 years and raised five children and 10 grandchildren.

Elmer's youngest brother, Dee Smith, served in the U.S. Army Ordnance Corps during World War II but did not deploy overseas.

Elmer Smith and family at their house on Miller Road, Lansing.
From left to right: Steve, Margo, Marge, Sharon, and Elmer.

Elmer Smith built a summer cottage for his family on Spider Lake near Traverse City, Michigan, in 1950. It remains the family's vacation home.

Elmer and Marge in Cheshire, Massachusetts, April 1967, during a visit to see daughter Sharon and her family.

Grandma Marge at home with her and Elmer's first seven grandchildren in the summer of 1969. Grandpa Elmer passed away the previous October, before any of his inquisitive grandkids could ask him to relate stories describing his service in the Great War. But Elmer's storage trunk *(right)* in the basement held his uniforms, and scattered throughout the house were his diary, letters, books and other key documents that convey his story—what he lived through—in surprising detail.

Chapter 9
Fierce Combat in the Oise-Aisne Offensive

WITH LITTLE REST between major operations, the 119th FA methodically moved over 100 miles to support 32nd Division offensive operations to seize the key town of Juvigny as part of the Oise-Aisne Offensive. The 119th played a key role in supporting the 32nd and subsequently the 1st Moroccan Division in this major campaign.[1]

PVT Elmer Smith briefly describes his combat experiences often under intense fire during this operation. These experiences included running communications wire through a field of dead German soldiers, exposure to poisonous gas attacks twice, and having a few more close calls with the destructive effects of German artillery and aircraft bomb attacks. He barely made it back into a cave during an artillery barrage as he ran wire from the Regimental Command Post to the 1st Battalion headquarters, a significant distance while exposed in the open. Although, many 119th soldiers were killed or wounded in the intense fighting, PVT Smith made it through the campaign unscathed—perhaps due to his experience of truly understanding the destructive effects of artillery fire.

Overview of the Oise-Aisne Offensive, August 18–November 11, 1918

The U.S. Army document, *The Army Flag and Its Streamers,* succinctly summarizes the U.S. role in the Oise-Aisne Campaign. In mid-August 1918, the French Army with the multiple U.S. Divisions attached, started a series of drives along their front, which extended about 90 miles (140 km) from Reims westward through Soissons to Ribecourt on the Oise River. These operations continued into late September, when they merged into French Marshall

Foch's final offensives of October–November. About 85,000 American soldiers fought in the Oise-Aisne Campaign including one Corps Headquarters and five divisions.

On August 29, during the initial part of the campaign, the U.S. 32nd Division, as part of General Mangin's French Tenth Army, spearheaded the penetration of the enemy's main line. The next day the Division conducted a "brilliant assault" to capture Juvigny, which secured tactically important high ground for the Allies. The division's 2.5 mile breach of the German lines assisted in causing the enemy to completely abandon the Vesle River line. The 32nd continued to press the attack but by September 2, the division had accumulated over 2600 casualties. The 1st Moroccan Division replaced them and continued the attack to the east.

As part of the French Sixth Army east of Soissons, the III U.S. Corps consisted of the 28th and 77th Divisions. In late August, the III Corps held the western part of the Vesle River sector extending from Braine to Courlandon. In early September, as German forces retired from the Vesle River northward to the Aisne River valley, the III Corps took part in aggressive pursuit operations. Its two divisions carried out successful local attacks, but in fierce fighting failed to break the German line. The two divisions suffered significant casualties—the 28th had over 6700 officers and men wounded or killed and the 77th nearly 4800. The divisions were released to join the American First Army, the 28th starting on September 7 and the 77th on September 14.

No American forces, except the Infantry Regiments of the 93rd Division, under French command, participated in the follow-on Oise-Aisne operations. By November 11, the Oise-Aisne Offensive carried the French armies to the Belgian border.[2]

The 32nd Division in Oise-Aisne Offensive[3]

When the Oise-Aisne Offensive began on August 18, the 32nd Division, less artillery, was in reserve of the American III Corps, French Sixth Army. On August 23, the division was transferred to the French 30th Corps, French Tenth Army. The 57th FA Brigade, which after the relief of the division, served successively with the 28th and 77th Divisions and in III Corps reserve, rejoined the 32nd on August 24. On August 28, the 32nd relieved the French 127th Division west of Juvigny. On the same day it executed a local attack to improve its position.

On August 29, the division took part in the general attack of the French Tenth Army between the Aisne and Oise Rivers. Juvigny was captured on August 30 in a local operation. The general attack was resumed on August 31, the 32nd Division advanced to Bois d'Alsace and the Terny-Sorny to Bethancourt road.

The division was relieved by the French 1st Moroccan Division at 4 a.m., September 2.

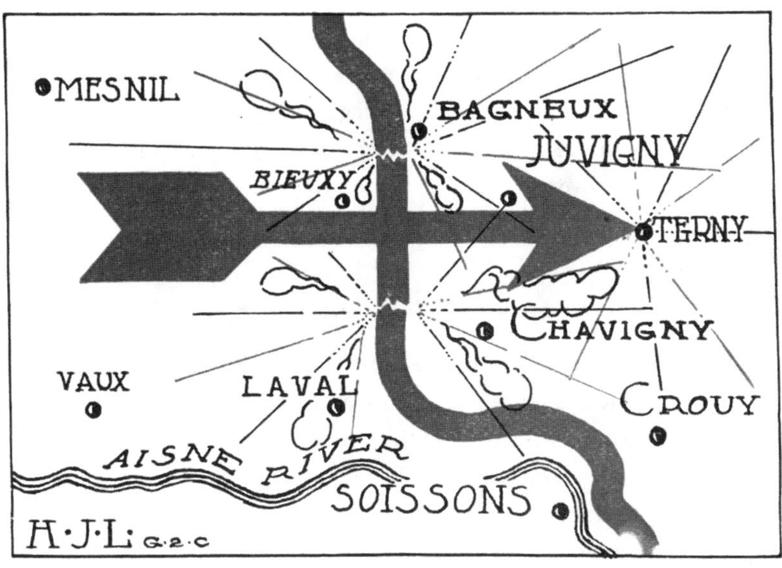

32nd Division Operations in the Oise-Aisne Campaign

The 119th FA in the Oise-Aisne Offensive Excerpt from COL McCormick's Post-War Summary

Again the regiment joined the 32nd Division, which was personally selected by General Mangin [French Tenth Army Commander] to assist the French in a flank attack north of Soissons, which, if successful, would relieve the line along the Vesle and gain the Aisne. Consequently, on the 24th of August, the regiment moved out, and after four days of hard forced marches, covered approximately 140 kilometers. The 28th of August found the 119th again in support of the 32nd Division west of Juvigny, fighting due east and suffering flank fire from the north. Here, after bitter and determined fighting, in which the division withstood several powerful counter-attacks by some of the best enemy divisions, sent to "Hold the lines at all costs," the artillery enabled the infantry to capture Juvigny and reach Torny-Sorny. The brilliant support which the artillery brigade gave to the infantry enabled them to gain the heights of the plateau overlooking the Aisne. The 32nd was relieved on September 1st by the 1st Moroccan Division, where the same determined spirit of the officers and men prevailed, much to the admiration of the French artillery commander of the sector. The selection and occupation of the position in and about Juvigny on the night of September 2nd was a most noteworthy feature in the career of the 119th, as without any daylight reconnaissance, the battalions moved into an unknown country after dark and were in position serving their guns near the village of Juvigny before daylight. On September 6th the regiment was relieved for the Joinville area for rest and re-equipping. However, in the brief stay of five days, little was accomplished in this particular.[4]

From Detroit News Post-War Summary

...General Mangin had selected the 32d Division as being one of the best American shock divisions to put on an attack with the French north of Soisson, for the relief of the line along the Vesle. The artillery was then rushed to the vicinity of Juvigny and was again marched overland, covering 30 kilometers at night.

Near Larcharmel, the artillery made a night march of 45 kilometers and bivouacked in a French forest at Faverolles. This was a great natural cathedral, as carefully kept as a parlor, even after four years of war, with trees fully 60 feet high and all regular and symmetrical. There it was as if there was no war—only peace and a sweetness and cleanness of nature, grateful to the war worn men. But this was only for a night.

TO THE FRONT AGAIN.

The next day, the artillery brigade started forth again. The march was to have been 25 kilometers, but from the front came the cry, "Artillery, more artillery!" It was a plea not to be denied. The 25 kilometers stretched into 50 and for 26 hours officers and men were in the saddle, so great was the congestion of the roads, everything traveling toward the front. And the Supply Train, caught in the congestion, was on the way 36 hours. This was August 27, a date which will live in the minds of Michigan men as long as they breathe. The echelon was established at Vingre.

The animals suffered with the men. Their work had been virtually continuous, supplying ammunition on the east front and going forward in the drive. The horses and mules came into Vingre leaning against one another and some of them supported by men who were supposed to ride them.

And the next day, the artillery took its position with the 32d Division in the vicinity of Juvigny.

...The signal to attack was being waited and August 27 it came and the fight, which lasted until September 1 and resulted in the capture of Juvigny and Tenry-Sorny, began. This attack, which was on the flank, was driven almost straight east. But the division paid the price, particularly on its own left flank.

When the 32d Division was relieved by a Moroccan division, the artillery again remained in the line and, with those wonderful fighters Laffeux was captured. The artillery then was pulled out, taken to Joinville and promised a much needed rest.

But the breathing space was short. At 3 a.m., September 3, the 119th was ordered to be ready to move at daylight. In the wan hours of the dawn the Aisne was crossed at Vic Sur Aisne and, after a march of 40 kilometers (nearly 25 miles), the regiment bivouacked at Mortmont. Early the next day there was a march of 25 kilometers (15 ½ miles), to Villers-Cotterets and there the regiment entrained for Joinville again, thus finishing a march of 402 kilometers (about 250 miles).[5]

Diary Entry Sat. August 24

Moved on to our camp this morning. The regiment pulled in toward night. Stayed all night here.

Diary Entry Sun. August 25

We were woke up at three A.M. Eat at 3:30. Started to hike at 5:00 o clock. Hiked until 1:30 before we eat. Made camp and had supper at six o clock. We were ordered to hike again after supper. On account of sore feet I rode on the trucks. We traveled all night in making ten miles. Found camp in a swamp. We are the only Amex Div. on this front.

Diary Entry Mon. August 26

The French drove the Germans back over this ground about ten days ago.

Diary Entry Tue. August 27

Laid in camp all day.

Diary Entry Wed. August 28

We left camp shortly after noon for the front to take up our position.

Established our hdqs. on the side of a steep hill. We have shacks and bunks to sleep in built by the Germans. Across the road from us are 3 German field [artillery] pieces left by them.

Run a number of telephone lines.

Diary Entry Thur. August 29

Laid around and helped on the lines. They shell the valley below us at all times.

Diary Entry Fri. August 30

Stuck close to the central most of the day. Packed up to move foreward. But because our infantry had to fall back to the railroad we stayed in our position.

Letter to Sister, August 30, 1918

Somewhere In France

Dear Sister:

It has been quite a while since I have written home. I have been so busy and have not had paper when I did have time is the reason why.

I am feeling fine and am as well as ever. I have been back with the regiment for about three weeks now. Needless to say I am at the front. I now sleep in a bunk that was occupied by a Boche a little over a week ago.

I am sending an order in this letter. You need not scrape to fill out the entire order. Use your own judgement in making it up. I do not want you to deny yourself of course. We do not get much chance to buy anything while up here.

I received some of your letters written the middle of July. I have not received those coming to me while I was in the hospital. I guess they on my back trail somewhere.

Well sis I did not finish my letter last night. Will try to tonight. I have been laying a telephone line this afternoon one field we ran it thru was still full of dead Dutchmen [German soldiers, the Netherlands was neutral during World War I. Germany's name for itself is Deutschland]. Well sis I will have to quit. Write often.

Your Brother,
Elmer

Diary Entry Sat. August 31

Took it easy most of the day.

Diary Entry Sun. September 1

We got ready to move foreward tonight. Boche airplanes bombed in our vicinity after dark.

Diary Entry Mon. September 2

We moved up to our new position early this morning. Put our hdqs. in a cave that was occupied by Germans yesterday morning.

Juvigney is the name of the town we are located in. It is all in ruins. Nothing left but a huge pile of stones.

Diary Entry Tue. September 3

Our position we just moved from was blown all to hell by bombs last night. Lucky for us we moved out. Our base moved up near the place after we left it. Two men were killed and several wounded.

We are getting plenty of shelling in our new position. We got a little gas last night.

Diary Entry Wed. September 4

Did some washing and took a bath.

Our P.C. was shelled this afternoon. Had a close call when a shell dropped in front of a cave as I was entering. An ammunition train was blown up and set afire. One Frenchman and four horses were killed during the afternoon. Our telephone lines were blown to the devil and we had to repair them while the shells were still flying. Got a little mustard gas while out on a line tonight.

Diary Entry Thur. September 5

Repaired lines this morning and afternoon. Our batteries moved up tonight. Had a long line to run to the first battalion.

Diary Entry Fri. September 6

Hooray! We were releaved at 4:00 o'clock this morning. We were given orders to get off the front by daylight. Moved back to the old P.C. Started hiking at 2:00 P.M. Stole rides on French trucks most of the afternoon. Camped at Mortamont.

Diary Entry Sat. September 7

We laid around Mortamont until 2:00 o clock. We then moved into a big wood near there and made camp. We expect to entrain shortly.

Diary Entry Sun. September 8

Laid around in the tent this forenoon as it rained. We were told that we would leave here in the morning for Villers Cotteret where we would entrain.

Diary Entry Mon. September 9

I skipped away from the Co. early this morning. Caught a ride on a French truck all the way to Villers Cotteret's.

Stayed around the Y.M.C.A. until the middle of the afternoon. The outfit pulled in about four o'clock. Loaded up and pulled out about nine o clock. Raining hard.

Diary Entry Tue. September 10

Slept fairly well considering the hard floor and rough riding. It rained nearly all day.

Pulled into a station about 6:00 o'clock and unloaded. Hiked to our billets in the village of Danmartin. We are billeted in a Chateau on Danmartin farm.

Diary Entry Wed. September 11

Slept soundly last night as I was nearly all in. Laid around all day long.

Diary Entry Thur. September 12

Awoke feeling fine. Strung up some telephones and had inspections.

Hired a room with Bacheller [Ernest P. Bacheller of Phillips, Maine] from a French lady. The purpose was for the soft feather bed.

Diary Entry Fri. September 13

Fixed up some telephone lines about the village this forenoon.

Did one half hour footdrill this afternoon and laid around the rest of the time.

Diary Entry Sat. September 14

Took care of the switchboard this forenoon. Laid around this afternoon.

Letter to Mother, September 14, 1918

France

Dear Mother:

Will drop you a few lines this afternoon to let you know I am feeling extra fine. I am back in a rest billet now not doing anything except eating and sleeping. I am living principally on bread and milk. This is the first place I have been where I could buy milk. I have been eating about a quart a day. If we stay here very long I fear I will have to rip a couple top bottoms off my pants. Most of the fellows are billeted in a large Chateau but another fellow and myself decided the cold board was not good enough for us, So we got out and hire a room for a few cents a day that has a large feather bed in it one of these that you sink way in out of sight. One of your beds back home would feel like a board beside one of these. You ought to see the bed these french have. Believe me they are real beds. I think if I ever come I will have to bring one home with me. It is very near pay day and I think I will send some money home as I have three months pay coming.

According to your last letter father's health must be improved quite a little or you would not be going back onto the farm next spring. Do you folks intend to go to Florida this winter?

About that order I sent home, I did not stop to think that sugar was so scarce or I would not of put in that order for home made candy. If this letter should reach you in time cancel that part of the order.

Well mother I have written about my limit so will close. I will write again soon if circumstances permit. Don't worry if you don't get my letters regular as sometimes I don't have time to write and when I do have time I don't have writing material. Write and tell me all the news.

Goodbye, Your Son,
Elmer

Former U.S. President Theodore Roosevelt's letter to the 32nd Division, published September 14, 1918

Twenty year old U.S. Army Air Service pilot 2LT Quentin Roosevelt was the youngest son of Teddy Roosevelt. On July 14, 1918, 2LT Roosevelt was killed in action in aerial combat over the Aisne–Marne battlefield. 32nd Division engineer elements located his grave site near Chamery during the Aisne-Marne campaign. Historians surmise that Teddy Roosevelt never recovered from the death of his young son and less than four months after writing the below letter the former President died on January 6, 1919, at age 60.

HEADQUARTERS THIRTY-SECOND DIVISION
AMERICAN EXPEDITIONARY FORCES.

MEMORANDUM:
8 October, 1918.

1. The following letter from Ex-President Theodore Roosevelt has been received by the Division Commander and is published for the information of all concerned:

THE KANSAS CITY STAR

Office of New York Office
THEODORE ROOSEVELT
347 Madison Avenue.
September 13th, 1918.

My Dear General Haan:

I am very much touched indeed by the trouble you have taken in the middle of your absorbing work. I appreciate your letter. I appreciate the sketch of Quentin's grave. It was dreadful to have Quentin killed, but I would not for anything in the world have had him not face death and take his chance.

I most heartily congratulate you, my dear sir, on the great work of your division. By George, your men have hit hard. Will you thank the division for me? We look forward eagerly to seeing you at Sagamore Hill when you return. My dear General, I admire, and I fear I envy, your record.

Faithfully yours,
THEODORE ROOSEVELT

Maj. General W.G. Haan
32nd Division
A.E.F., France.

2. The foregoing letter of thanks was received from Colonel Roosevelt in reply to a letter General Haan sent him with map showing location of his son's grave after the enemy had been defeated on that ground by the 32nd Division. W.G. Haan, Major General, U.S.A., Commanding

119th FA Regiment Orders Listing Soldiers Entitled to Wear the Wound Chevron, September 14, 1918

HEADQUARTERS, 119th FIELD ARTILLERY
AMERICAN EXPEDITIONARY FORCES

FRANCE
14 September 1918.
GENERAL ORDERS: NO. 19

1. In compliance with General Order 110, GHQ, American E.F., the names of officers and men of this command who are entitled to wear the wound chevron covering casualties to this date are published:

[After listing six officers, Private Elmer Smith was the first enlisted man named on the roster as specified below based on the date he was wounded]

Elmer O. Smith, 297070 Pvt. Hq. Co.
June 16/18
Noviant

Diary Entry Sun. September 15

Helped tend switchboard this A.M. Slept nearly all the afternoon.

Diary Entry Mon. September 16

Rested.

Diary Entry Tue. September 17

Packed up our equipment and moved out at 8:30 P.M. Rode the trucks to our first camp at Bienville.

NOTES

1. Colonel Chester B. McCormick, "A Brief History of the 119th Field Artillery," *Honor Roll and Complete War History of Ingham County in the Great World War: 1914-1918* (Lansing MI: The State Journal Company, 1920), 219-220.

2. Office of the Chief of Military History, U.S. Army, *The Army Flag and Its Streamers: Oise-Aisne* (Washington, D.C.: U.S. GPO, 1964), http://www.history.army.mil/html/reference/army_flag/wwi.html, accessed March 30, 2015.
   Colonel James Gordon Steese, *Through War Torn Europe* (Washington D.C.: War Department General Staff, December 19, 1919).
   American Battle Monuments Commission, *American Armies and Battlefields in Europe: A History, Guide, and Reference Book* (Washington, D.C.: U.S. Government Printing Office, 1938), 42, 91-93.
   American Battle Monuments Commission, *32D Division Summary of Operations in the World War* (Washington, D.C.: U.S. Government Printing Office, 1943), 23.
   Byron Farwell, *Over There: The United States in the Great War, 1917-1918* (New York: W.W. Norton and Company, 1999), 152-153.

3. American Battle Monuments Commission, *32D Division Summary of Operations*, 23-31.

4. Colonel Chester B. McCormick, "A Brief History of the 119th Field Artillery," 219-220.

5. L.L. Stevenson, "Pages of Liberty Volume Illustrated by the 119th" (Part 2 of 6 part series on the 119th FA's war exploits), *Detroit News*, February 25, 1919.
   Stevenson, "How War Urge Took 119th, in Rest Billets, to France" (Part 3 of series), *Detroit News*, February 26, 1919.

Chapter 10
The Final Push: the Meuse-Argonne Offensive

On October 27, 1918, according to 119th FA records, Elmer Smith was promoted from Private to Private First Class (PFC) after 18 months in service. Elmer never mentions this in his diary or correspondence. He may not have even known of his promotion until after the fighting was over. His pay records confirm the promotion, showing he earned $36 a month with $6.50 going towards his wartime life insurance policy.[1]

The last campaign PFC Smith fought in was the Meuse-Argonne Offensive. This was the largest U.S. combat operation of World War I. For 38 days, the 119th FA was involved in almost continuous operations supporting Infantry regiments from four different divisions in their mission to attack the German defenses and drive forward to seize key terrain. By early November, the 119th was pulled out of the line to rest and refit after months of moving from one mission to another. Most of their horses had been killed or rendered combat ineffective. This chapter documents the 119th FA's significant contributions in this major campaign.[2]

Overview of the Meuse-Argonne Offensive, September 26–November 11, 1918

The U.S. Army booklet *The Army Flag and Its Streamers* provides a detailed summary of the most significant U.S. campaign of the World War as follows. At the end of August 1918, French Marshall Foch submitted plans to the national commanders for a final offensive along the entire Western Front. The objective was to drive the enemy out of France before winter and end the war by the spring of 1919. The basis for his optimism was the success of Allied attacks all along the front in late July and August. Furthermore, he pointed out, the Allies already had active operations in progress between the Moselle and Meuse, the Oise and Aisne, and on the Somme and Lys Rivers. Foch acknowledged that the Germans could stave off immediate defeat by an orderly evacuation combined with destruction of materiel and communications. Therefore, the overall aim of the fall offensive would be to prevent a methodical step-by-step enemy retirement. As Foch anticipated, the Germans eventually contributed to the success of his strategy. The German High Command could not bring itself to sacrifice the huge stores of supplies collected behind the front lines, and so delayed the withdrawal of its forces.

Foch's broad offensive, planned to begin in the last week of September, called for a gigantic pincer movement with the objective of capturing Aulnoye and Mézières, the two key railroad junctions in the lateral rail system behind the German front. Loss of either of these junctions would seriously hamper the German withdrawal. Despite complaints from the British that they lacked the necessary manpower, a chiefly British army was assigned the task of driving toward Aulnoye. The AEF was designated for the southern arm of the pincers, the thrust on Mézières. Simultaneously the Belgian-French-British army group in Flanders would drive toward Ghent, and the French armies in the Oise-Aisne region would exert pressure all along their front to lend support to the main effort attacks.

The AEF Commander, General John Pershing decided to strike his heaviest blow in a zone about 20 miles (32 km) wide between the Heights of the Meuse River on the east and the western edge of the high, rough and densely wooded Argonne Forest. This difficult terrain, broken by a central north–south ridge dominated the valleys of the Meuse and Aire rivers. Three heavily fortified locations—Montfaucon, Cunel, and Barricourt—as well as other numerous strong points blocked the efforts to penetrate the in-depth German defenses that extended behind the entire front. This fortified system consisted of three main defensive lines tied into the natural defensive features of the terrain and backed up by a fourth line less well-constructed. Pershing hoped to launch an attack with enough momentum to rapidly drive through these lines into the open area beyond, where his troops could then strike at the exposed German flanks and, in a coordinated drive with the French Fourth Army advancing on the left, could cut the Sedan-Mézières railroad.

The task of organizing the U.S. First Army in assembly areas between Verdun and the Argonne Forest in mid-September was complicated by the fact that many of the best American combat divisions were engaged in the St. Mihiel campaign. Some 600,000 AEF soldiers had to be moved into the Argonne sector while 220,000 French moved out. The responsibility for solving this challenging logistical problem fell to COL George C. Marshall, the Assistant Chief of Staff, G-3 (Operations), First Army. In the ten-day period after St. Mihiel, the necessary troop movements were accomplished, but many untried divisions had to be placed in the vanguard of the attacking forces when the offensive commenced on September 26.

On the 20-mile Meuse-Argonne front where the main American attack was to start, Pershing arranged three U.S. Corps side by side. Each Corps had three divisions in line forward and one division in Corps reserve. The respective Corps' initial composition, disposition, and missions were:

- In the center was the V [Fifth] Corps. From right to left were the 79th, 37th, and 91st Divisions with the 32nd in reserve. V Corps was the main effort and would strike the initial decisive blow.
- On the right was the III [Third] Corps. From right to left were the 33rd, 80th, and 4th Divisions with the 3rd in reserve. III Corps would move up the west side of the Meuse.
- On the left was the I [First] Corps. From right to left were the 35th, 28th, and 77th Divisions with the 92nd in reserve. I Corps would advance parallel to the French Fourth Army on its left.

East of the Meuse River, the American front extended another 60 miles (97 km). This sector was held by the French IV Corps, the French II Colonial Corps, and the American IV Corps in the St. Mihiel sector.

To support the First Army offensive, General Pershing assembled 4000 artillery pieces, two-thirds manned by U.S. artillerymen; 190 light French tanks, manned mostly with Americans; and some 820 aircraft, 600 of them flown by Americans.

The Meuse-Argonne Offensive had three main phases. During the initial phase from September 26 to October 3, the First Army advanced through most of the southern Meuse-Argonne region, captured enemy strong points and seized the first two German defense lines. But the attack stalled before the third line due to inadequate tank support, a difficult supply situation, and the inexperience of American troops. These and other factors all contributed to checking the AEF advance.

The second phase occurred from October 4 through the end of the month. After more veteran units replaced the inexperienced divisions, the First Army slowly ground its way through the key third German line known as the Kreimhilde Stellung. The enemy was forced to commit reserves, drawn from other parts of the front, thus aiding the Allied advances elsewhere. In the face of stubborn, entrenched defenders, U.S. gains were limited and casualties were severe. The newly devised enemy tactic of attacking frontline troops with airplanes aided the defenders but First Army air units retaliated with bombing raids, which broke up German preparations for counterattacks. By the end of October the enemy had been cleared from the Argonne and First Army troops were through the German main positions. Two notable incidents of this phase of the campaign were the fight of the "Lost Battalion" of the 77th Division from October 2 to 7, and the feat of CPL (later SGT) Alvin C. York, 82nd Division, who single-handedly killed 15 Germans and captured 132 on October 8.

In mid-October the organization of the U.S. Second Army was completed, at Toul in the St. Mihiel sector. It provided the means for better control of the lengthening American front and resolved the diverse tactical problems this issue presented. Pershing assumed command of the new American Army group and on October 12, named Lieutenant General Hunter Liggett to command the First Army and LTG Robert Bullard to command the Second Army.

The third and final phase of the Meuse-Argonne Offensive occurred from November 1 to 11. Before it started, many of the First Army's exhausted divisions were replaced, roads were built or repaired, supply was improved, and most Allied units serving with the AEF were withdrawn. On November 1, First Army units began the assault against the now strengthened German fourth line of defense. Penetration was rapid and spectacular. The V Corps in the center advanced about six miles (10 km) the first day, compelling the German units west of the Meuse to withdraw hurriedly. On November 4, the III Corps forced a crossing of the Meuse and advanced northeast toward Montmédy. Elements of the V Corps occupied the heights opposite Sedan on November 7, thus finally accomplishing the First Army's chief mission—denial of the Sedan-Mézières railroad to the Germans. Marshal Foch, at this juncture, shifted the First Army's left boundary eastward so that the French Fourth Army might capture Sedan, which had fallen to the Prussians in 1870. American units were closing up along the Meuse and, east of the river, were advancing toward Montmédy, Briey, and Metz, when hostilities ended on November 11.

In his Final Report, General Pershing summarized the outcome of the Meuse-Argonne campaign, the largest battle in American history up to that time, "Between 26 September and 11 November, 22 American and 4 French divisions, on the front extending from southeast of Verdun to the Argonne

Forest, had engaged and decisively beaten 47 different German divisions, representing 25 percent of the enemy's entire divisional strength on the western front."

The First Army suffered total casualties of about 117,000 killed and wounded. It captured 26,000 prisoners, 847 cannon, 3,000 machine guns, and large quantities of material. More than 1.2 million U.S. soldiers had taken part in the 47 day campaign.[3]

Initial 79th and 3d Division Operations, September 26–October 6

Artillery forces were rarely held in reserve. Thus, when the Meuse-Argonne Offensive commenced, the 119th FA was initially attached to the 79th Division operations as part of the V Corps main effort as outlined above. After four days the 3rd Division replaced the 79th on the line. 79th and 3rd Division missions during the first eleven days of the offensive are described from their respective Division Summary of Operations.

79th Division Summary of Operations[4]

The artillery brigade of the 79th Division had not rejoined. Therefore, the 57th Field Artillery Brigade, 32d Division, the 147th Field Artillery Regiment, 41st Division, and French artillery units were attached to it for the attack. This artillery was to join the [First] army and [Fifth] corps artillery in the preparatory fire which was to commence at 2:30 a.m. At 5:30 a.m. the division artillery was to fire a rolling barrage in front of the infantry.

The attack was launched at 5:30 a.m., September 26, covered by a smoke screen and preceded by a barrage… The advance was slow but steady… The advance continued, and about 6 p.m. the [313th Infantry] regiment had completely occupied that portion of the wood within the 79th Division's zone of action.

[On September 27]… about 4 a.m., the 314th Infantry had continued the advance along the Malancourt—Montfaucon road… Before daylight the 314th Infantry had passed over some machine guns. These were dealt with by the 315th Infantry which followed in support.

On the left, the 313th Infantry… renewed the attack about 7 a.m. It was supported by the 316th Infantry and French tanks. After advancing a short distance beyond the north edge of Bois de Cuisy, the troops encountered machine gun fire from the trenches south of Montfaucon. By 9 a.m. these trenches had been passed, the southern slopes of the height of Montfaucon had been reached and an enveloping movement to the right and left of the town begun. By 11 a.m. the enemy had commenced to withdraw from Montfaucon, which was entered by the 313th Infantry about 11:45 a.m.

...the 314th and 315th Infantry Regiments, assisted by the French 343d Tank Company, resumed the advance about 4:30 p.m. Slow progress was made by the infantry, elements of which reached points approximately 1 kilometer south of Nantillois, but these positions were not held.

On the left, after a half hour artillery preparation, the 313th Infantry, elements of the 316th Infantry, three companies of the 311th Machine-Gun Battalion and a few tanks advanced upon Bois de Beuge at 3:30 p.m. The attack was soon stopped by heavy artillery and machine gun fire... Efforts to advance were discontinued by 6 p.m.

[On September 28] after less than an hour's artillery preparation, the infantry advanced upon Nantillois and Bois de Beuge at 7 a.m... On the right, the 315th Infantry advanced without serious opposition until it reached the ridge about 1 km south of Nantillois. Here it came under heavy artillery and machine gun fire. From this point the advance was slow until Nantillois was entered about 10:50 a.m.

On the left, the 316th Infantry at once encountered heavy fire, particularly from Bois de Beuge... In conjunction with the 37th Division to the left, Bois de Beuge was cleared of the enemy about noon... Owing to heavy hostile artillery fire throughout the advance, there was considerable disorganization in the 316th Infantry... The projected attack was not delivered, and the line was consolidated for the night.

At 11 p.m. the V Corps ordered the attack resumed at 7 a.m., September 29. It was to be preceded by a 1 hour artillery preparation. The 79th Division issued orders at 11:30 p.m... One battalion of artillery was assigned to each front-line infantry regiment. One battery of each of these battalions was to be used as infantry guns.

On the right, the 315th Infantry advanced from Hill 274 about 7 a.m. The artillery support during the day was unsatisfactory. Although 15 tanks had been designated to assist in cleaning up the hostile positions... little progress had been made by 9:15 a.m. Three attacks supported by tanks were made in the morning... Elements pushed halfway through Bois des Ogons, but the hostile artillery and machine-gun fire was so intense that this position could not be held.

On the left, the 316th Infantry attacked at 7 a.m.. from the north edge of the wood marked by point 268. Hostile artillery and machine-gun fire was extremely heavy. The 1st Battalion on the left, was stopped after advancing about 400 meters.... the 3d Battalion, together with a platoon of machine-guns, advance into the wood 500 meters to the north. Meanwhile the 2d Battalion in support, had been heavily shelled, and at 10:45 a.m. withdrew into the wood marked by point 268. The 1st Battalion remained pinned to the ground about 400 meters north of the wood... At 12:55 p.m. the 79th Division ordered a defensive position organized along the northern edge of the Bois de Beuge.

3rd Division summary of Operations[5]

The V Corps ordered the relief of the 79th Division, less the attached 57th FA Brigade and 147th FA Regiment, by the 3d Division during the night of September 29-30. The relief commenced about 10:45 a.m. on September 30 and was completed by 6 p.m. the same day.

The zone to be taken over was that of the right division of the V Corps. The 4th Division, III Corps was to the right and the 32[d] Division to the left. The 57th FA Brigade, 32d Division which had been in support of the 79th Division, remained in support of the 3d Division until October 6. The 147th FA, 41st Division, was attached to the 57th FA Brigade during the same period.

From 1 through 3 October, the 3d Division repositioned its forces, conducted reconnaissance patrols, and closed gaps with adjacent units to the left and right.

Field orders of the V Corps... directed an attack... on the heights on both sides of Romagne-sous-Montfaucon... at 5:25 a.m., October 4. The 3d Division was ordered to assist the III Corps, to its right, in the capture of Bois des Ogons, Bois de Cunel, and the heights east of Romagne. A rolling barrage was provided which was to advance at the at rate of 100 meters each four minutes as far as Bois de Cunel, and just south of Cunel. Divisions were ordered to advance independently of one another as far as the combined army first-phase line.

On the right, the 4th Infantry [Regiment] attacked at 5:25 a.m., October 4, following its barrage, and supported by the French 15th Tank Battalion. About 7 a.m. the assault battalion was held up by heavy fire on the northern edge of the wood on Hill 268... About noon, artillery assistance was requested by the 2d Battalion, 4th Infantry, but the artillery fire was put down too close to the troops and did not affect the enemy positions... About 4 p.m. the attack was renewed under cover of a smoke screen. The 2d Battalion, 4th Infantry, was unable to advance. To its left, a detachment of the 2d Battalion, 7th Infantry, succeeded in crossing Ruisseau de Moussin, but on approaching Bois de Cunel, came under fire, and dug in about 200 meters south of the wood... At 5:30 p.m. the tanks withdrew for reorganization, all being out of action.

At 10:50 p.m. the V Corps issued orders directing a resumption of the attack at 6:30 a.m., October 5, with the same zones of action and objectives... The 80th Division was to assist the advance of the 3d Division. At midnight, the 3d Division repeated these instructions to its units in field orders, stating that tanks would not be used in the attack and that the advance would be carried forward by infiltration... The enemy strengthened his position on Hill 253 with additional troops and several pieces of light artillery.

On the right, the 2d Battalion, 4th Infantry attacked just before dawn in a fog, but the fog lifted before the troops could reach the wood on nose 250 and the battalion was stopped by fire from the wood. During the morning, elements of the 4th Infantry succeeded in gaining the wood, but no organized line was established. At 11:05 a.m. another unsuccessful attempt to advance was made after a 15-minute artillery preparation. Again following a 15 minute artillery preparation, the 1st and 2d Battalions, 4th Infantry, attempted at 2 p.m. to gain the wood, but at 4 p.m. no material advance had been made.

At midnight, October 5... the V Corps issued orders... to organize for further attack... Corps and division artillery were given counterbattery missions to prevent hostile artillery fire on front-line infantry. By daylight, October 6, the 3rd Battalion, 4th Infantry, had mopped up all of the wood on nose 250 west of the Nantillois-Cunel road. The front line of the 7th Infantry had been organized by 9 a.m. on the southern slopes of Hill 253, in the positions gained during the night.

In the zone of action of the 4th Infantry, arrangements were made for a barrage on the southern edge of Bois de Cunel and points in the wood from 1 to 4 p.m., after which the 2d and 3d Battalions, 4th Infantry, were to attack Bois de Cunel, clear it and secure the trench which ran through its center. The attack... took place as scheduled, but fire from the Bois de Cunel and the crest of Hill 253 was so intense that no gains could be made.

The 32nd Division in the Meuse-Argonne Offensive

Once committed, the 32d Division again fought fiercely in combat. *In America's Deadliest Battle: Meuse-Argonne, 1918*, Robert H. Ferrell provides a synopsis of the Division exploits and effectiveness.

During the attack of October 4, the other AEF Divisions did what they could. For most of them, this was not much, but one of them did as well as the 1st [Division]. This may have been because, in many ways, the two divisions were alike. The 1st had more training than any other division in the AEF, but the 32nd's commander was an insistent disciplinarian who believed in training and did as much of it as possible. Major General William G. Haan liked to describe his division as a fighting machine, and in a lecture presented after the war, he characterized it as such. The two divisions... came into the line in the Meuse-Argonne at the same time... Their men went up to the front with the same attitude, which was a combination of competence and "getting the job done." Haan and his staff, the men following in full packs, went up through shell-torn fields at night, ready for whatever tasks the commander-in-chief assigned. Just as the 1st had the task of taking back territory lost by the 35th and advancing the line as far as possible, the 32nd, replacing the 91st and 37th, had the task of taking back what the former had lost and securing more if possible.

The 32nd remained in the line longer than the 1st and... ended its stay with the... brilliant attack... the capture of the Cote' Dame Marie eight kilometers north of Montfaucon, at a cost of no casualties. The hill rose three hundred feet above its surroundings and was more than half a mile long and crescent shaped, with rises on each side. The ground in front was rolling fields with patches of scrub oak, offering little cover. The hill was a place from which German officers with field glasses could watch men struggling forward and call in artillery fire. The 32nd took it on October 14.

...On October 17, Haan wrote to Summerall [MG Charles Summerall, former commander of the 1st Division], by then the commander of V Corps, that the 32nd was exhausted and he did not want to hurt the division's morale by keeping it in line. It had been at the front for 20 days and its regiments had been reduced to cadres—the 127th with 216 men in its First Battalion, 160 in the Second, and 139 in the Third. The Third Battalion had 2 officers and 32 men in I Company, 3 officers and 21 men in K Company, 3 officers and 60 men in L Company, and 2 officers and 16 men in M Company. Casualties were 5,833, with 1,179 dead. The Corps commander relieved the division with gratitude.[6]

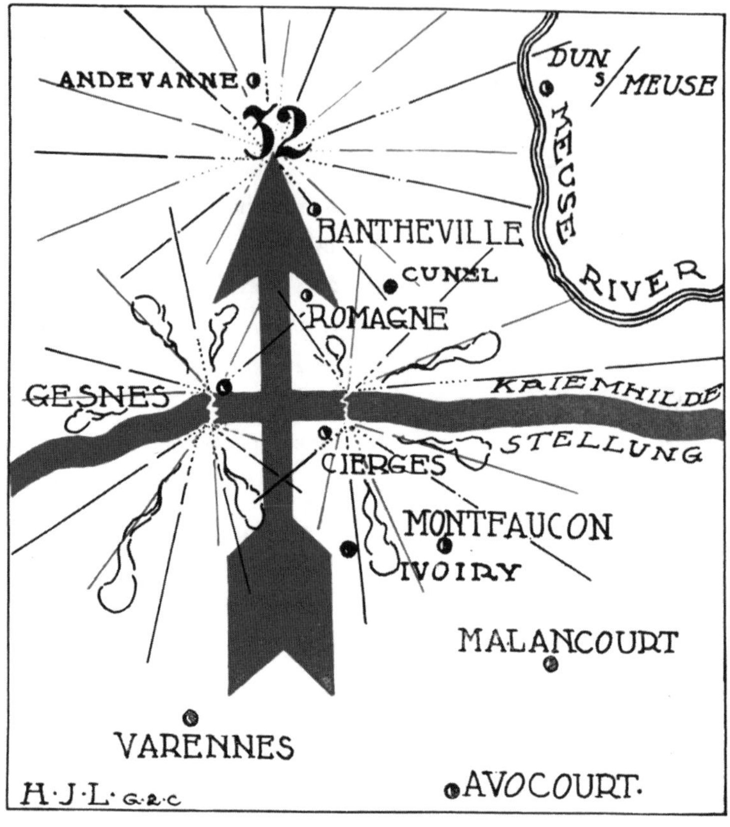

32nd Division Operations in the Meuse-Argonne Campaign

32nd Division Summary of Operations[7]

When the Meuse-Argonne Offensive opened, the 32d Division was in reserve of the V Corps. The 57th Field Artillery Brigade was detached and served with the 79th and 3rd Divisions until October 6.

On September 30, the 32d relieved the 37th Division on the general line, northern edge of the Bois de Beuge—south of Cierges—northern edge of Bois Communal de Cierges. On October 1 the division advanced its center to a line north of Cierges.

During the night of October 3-4, the 32d Division shifted about 2 ½ kilometers to the west, taking over the zone of action of the 91st Division. The 1st Division was to the left of the 32d Division.

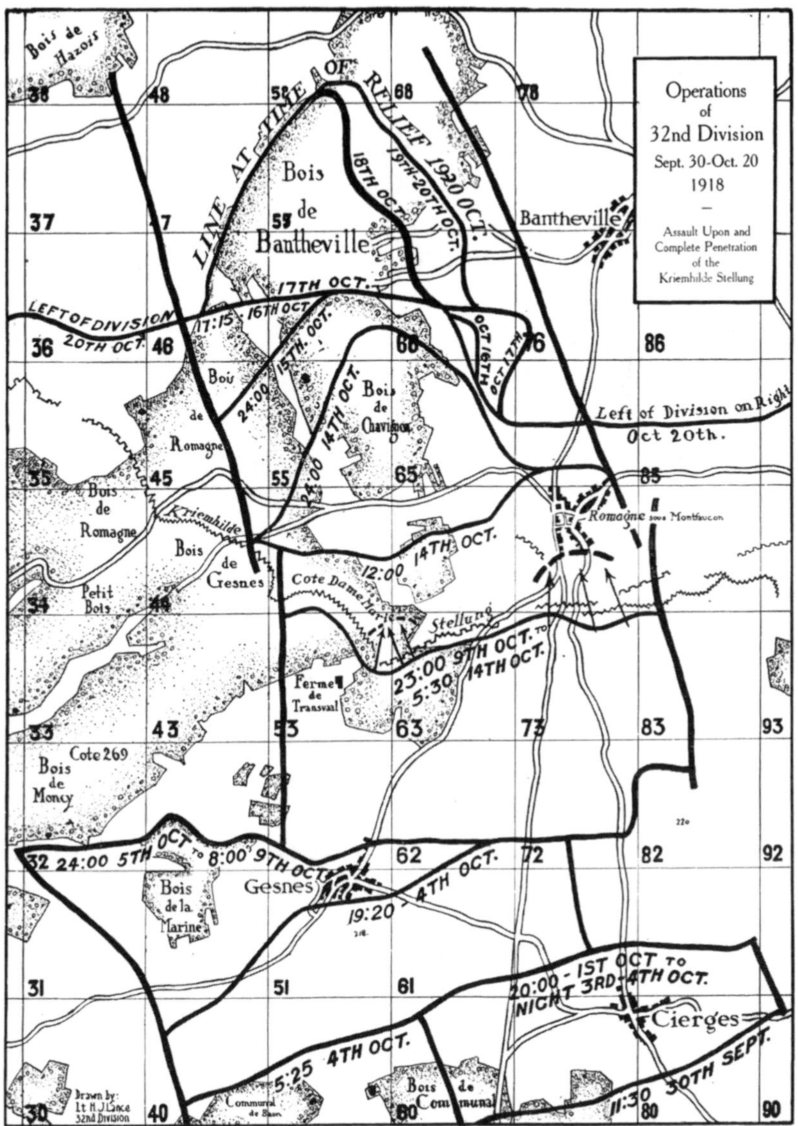

32nd Division Operations Map from the Meuse-Argonne Offensive

The 32d Division attacked on October 4 with the mission of capturing Gesnes and the heights west of Romagne-sous-Montfaucon. By night the division held a line along the Cierges—Gesnes—Exermont road.

On October 5 the attack was renewed with the same objectives and dispositions as on October 4. The line for the night extended east and west through Gesnes. From October 6 to 8 the division readjusted its line, improved its position and made preparations to attack. The 57th FA Brigade and its subordinate FA regiments rejoined the Division during this time.

On October 9 the division attacked and advanced about 2 kilometers. On the 10th a gain of about 1 kilometer was made on the left. The 181st Infantry Brigade, 91st Division, which had been attached to the 1st Division, to the left, was attached to the 32d Division on the latter date. There were no gains on October 11.

During the early morning of October 12 the division extended to the left and took over the zone formerly held by the 181st Infantry Brigade. On this day the 3d Division passed to control of the III Corps, the 32d Division thus becoming the right division of the V Corps. The 42nd Division relieved the 1st Division to the left of the 32d.

No attack was made on October 13. On the 14th the division captured Romagne and gained a line through Chauvignon. The left flank was refused to the southeastern slopes of Hill 288.

The Capture of the Cote Dame Marie on October 14, 1918

As described above, one of the 32d Division's greatest battlefield feats occurred on October 14. The book, *The 32nd Division in the World War,* has a detailed account of the operation which seized the hill mass called the Cote Dame Marie. This key terrain was one of the anchors of the Kreimhilde Stellung, the German Army's third and strongest defensive belt opposing the First U.S. Army in the Meuse-Argonne Offensive.

While the 126th and 128th were thus breaking through the Kreimhilde Stellung, the 127th on the left was flinging itself in vain against the impregnable defenses of the hills which flank La Cote Dame Marie... But, while La Cote Dame Marie was resisting every effort at a frontal conquest, her doom was being sealed by the valiant battalion of the 126th, which had been the first to break through the line in the morning. This battalion drove straight forward, concealed and protected from view of the Cote, and passed the hill on the right. Its objective was north of La Cote Dame Marie, and this objective the battalion reached, there establishing the position which it had extended to the right to meet the 128th.

The support battalion of the 126th, which followed in the wake of the troops who had forged ahead from Hill 258, sent a mopping up party from Company M under command of Captain Strom to make a turning movement to the left and attack the defenders on Dame Marie from the flank. This mopping up party, by an effective use of rifle grenades, put to rout the group which had been holding the German left flank on the hill, and allowed the whole 126th line in the center of the Division sector to move forward to the objective north of Dame Marie.

In the meantime, the 127th had despaired of taking the position frontally or of obtaining a footing from which a further attack might be launched. Accordingly, a maneuver around the German right flank was decided upon and immediately undertaken. It was as successful as Captain Strom's attack… Mopped up on one side and outflanked on the other, there was nothing left for the defenders of the German stronghold to do but give it up. This they did, and when darkness came, and the 127th decided upon an audacious march across the top of Dame Marie, expecting to meet and battle to the death with whatever of the enemy remained, they found the wicked machine gun nests deserted by all but the dead.[8]

The 32nd Division capture of the Cote Dame Marie and penetration of the German's primary defensive line was a significant point in the Meuse-Argonne Offensive. The Division continued the attack the next day as their Summary of Operations describes below.

The attack was resumed on October 15 and an advance made to the northern edge of the Bois de Chauvignon. The left flank was advanced in Bois de Romaigne to the southeast of La Tuilerie Ferme.

No general advance was made on October 16. On the 17th the L-shaped wood east of Bois de Chauvignon and the southern and western portions of the Bois de Bantheville were taken. On the 18th the line was advanced in Bois de Bantheville. This line was held until the 89th Division relieved the Division at 8 a.m., October 20.

After refitting and resupply, the 32d Division was again recommitted to the offensive for the last several days of the war. On November 9, the 32d Division crossed to the east bank of the Meuse and entered the front line as the right Division of the III Corps by taking command of its 128th Infantry Regiment, which, while serving with the 5th Division, had reached Peauvillers, about 10 kilometers east of the Meuse.

The division attacked on November 10 in two columns. The right column advanced three kilometers, but being ahead of the units on its flanks, was forced to return to the line of departure. The left column advanced about three kilometers to about 200 meters west of Thinte Ruisseau where it was abreast of the right column. On November 11 the attack was abandoned because of the Armistice.[9]

The 119th FA Regiment did not support the 32nd Division in the operations during the last three days of the war.

The 89th Division Summary of Operations[10]

The 89th Division, as the right division of the V Corps, relieved the 32nd Division in Bois de Bantheville on October 20. The mopping up of the wood, reorganization of the position and preparations for the general attack of November 1 engaged the division's attention until that date.

Commencing at 5:05 p.m. on the 25th, the enemy placed heavy artillery fire on the northern and eastern edges of Bois de Bantheville and launched an attack against the two left flank battalions of the 357th Infantry, 90th [U.S.] Division. Crossfire from the 89th Division… assisted in breaking up the attack.

By the end of October, the First [U.S.] Army had accomplished the first part of its plan for the Meuse-Argonne Offensive. It had seized the hostile third position in Bois de Foret, on the heights of Cunel and Romagne and on Cote de Chatillon, southeast of Landres et St. Georges. The enemy had been driven from the Argonne Forest, and the left of the First Army was firmly established, in contact with the right of the French Fourth Army, at Grandpre. East of the Meuse, the heights had been cleared as far as the southern portion of Bois de la Grande Montagne. The First Army was now in a position to undertake the second operation, i.e., cut the Carigan-Sedan-Mezieres railroad, and drive the enemy beyond the Meuse.

In addition to the 57th FA Brigade, the 58th FA Brigade, 33d Division, had been placed at the disposal of the 89th Division and remained with it until November 11. The 11th FA, 6th Division, supported the 89th Division from October 26 to November 11. The 57th FA Brigade, 32d Division, including the 147th FA, 41st Division remained with the 89th Division until November 2. The artillery was to fire a 2 hour preparation, to be followed by a rolling barrage. A maching gun barrage was to be fired until the first objective was reached.

The time of the attack was announced at 5:30 A.M., November 1 ... Following the prescribed artillery preparation, the attack was launched as planned ... By evening of November 1 the division had captured Bois de Barricourt ... [On November 2] the 177th Infantry Brigade, which had been ordered to attack at 5:30 A.M., did not do so, as the troops failed to recognize the scattered artillery fire as a barrage. Another barrage at 10 A.M. also proved too weak to be recognized and the troops still did not move forward. The brigade then ordered the regiment to advance, employing only rifle fire and their own accompanying weapons ... the right of the division captured Tailly.

Fire Support for Four Divisions: The 119th FA Regiment in the Meuse-Argonne Offensive

The 119th FA Regiment and its higher headquarters, the 57th FA Brigade, were attached to four different divisions providing 38 straight days of sustained fire support to front-line combat units. The 79th, 3rd, 32nd, and 89th Divisions were each under V Corps command, operating in the designated Corps zone of action. The majority of the Meuse-Argonne Offensive's key objectives were located in the V Corps zone and accordingly, the 119th FA fought in multiple intense battles to seize key terrain from the entrenched German defenses.

Excerpt from COL McCormick's Post-War Summary of Operations[11]

Beginning September 16th, there followed seven nights of exhausting forced marches in mud and rain, entering the Meuse-Argonne offensive. Not only was this a severe test upon the morale of the organization, but the many hard marches began to tell upon the animals that at this time were weak and exhausted. On the night of the 24th, the regiment entered the lines in support of the 79th Division. On the morning of the 26th, after a tremendous artillery preparation, the infantry went over the top on the same ground where a half-million perished on either side in the operations about Verdun in 1916. After many hours' delay in the preparation of roads across "No Man's Land,' the 119th succeeded in reaching positions near Montfaucon, being the first of the division artillery over. After the capture of Montfaucon and Nantillois, both battalions were detailed as supporting artillery under direct command of the infantry colonels. Here the batteries suffered one of the most trying ordeals of their experience in the war. Occupying what were impossible positions in the face of terrible destructive fire of the enemy, without flinching, the men of Michigan again demonstrated as on the Marne, that indomitable dogged spirit of true artillery and stuck to their guns. The 3rd Division relieved the 79th Division on the 4th. Relieved from assignment with the 3rd, the regiment moved into the sector on the left and were again in support of the 32nd Division.

In its third effort in battle, the 32nd Division broke through the famous Kriemhilde line, the last organized line of the enemy's defense on this front. During the nineteen days of almost continuous battle, not a day passed without some progress being made, and during this period a total advance of eight Kilometers was accomplished. This in itself does not seem a great distance, but when it is considered that this progress was made through a well-organized position of great natural strength at a key of that position, it was a task accomplished of which the Division can well feel proud. The work of the batteries was perfect.

The actual penetration of the famous Kriemhilde line was perhaps less difficult than the long approach to the wire defense of that position upon ground where the Division had to first work down a slope and then up another slope for three to four kilometers, where it was constantly under observation and under artillery and machine-gun fire. The excellent maneuvering supported by the artillery, machine guns, Stokes mortars, one-pounder and all the other auxiliary weapons all working together, permitted the accomplishment of the mission and the attaining of the objectives with a minimum loss. Following the breaking through of the Kriemhilde Stellung came the capturing of Gesnes, Cote Dame Marie, Romagne and Bantheville. November 1st found the 119th in support of the 89th Division with the front lines along the north edge of Bois de Bantheville, at which time was launched one of the best organized and most preponderous artillery attacks yet delivered on the western front, covering a front of twenty-five kilometers, in which the guns assisted in smashing the enemy's defense for a depth of eleven kilometers, breaking the backbone of his resistance, cutting his communications into Belgium and climaxing in his submission to the terms of the armistice November 11, 1918.

From Detroit News Post-War Summary[12]

"Our men had hardly scattered to the billets at Joinville before there was a cry for more artillery," said Chaplain Atkinson, adjusting the candles so that the map could be read more readily.

Following this appeal for artillery were seven days and seven nights of marching. Then the 119th went into position in No Man's Land, at Aisnes. For four years war had rolled over this part of France. For five kilometers (3 miles) there was naught but devastation. The terrain looked as though it had been wrought by devils. And in digging the positions grim reminders of the cost of war were exposed.

"I can't describe the appearance of the field at Aisnes," said Colonel McCormick. "The earth was ruined. It was as though a giant had burrowed 20 feet below the surface and then raised himself. As far as you could see it was this way. With it was all kinds of debris, rusty wire, broken guns and other waste. What had been villages were now irregular heaps of mortar, brick and stone. Forests were now only blackened splintered stubs."

HORROR BEYOND WORDS.

It was at this point that the 119th was attached to the 79th Division. Mt. Faucon, which had been the observation post of the German Crown Prince in the battle of Verdun, was the objective. To reach it the vast waste had to be crossed. The infantry got over all right, but it was necessary for the Engineers to build roadways for the artillery. The making of these roads revealed a horror tale that cannot be told.

The 119th waited in the saddle while these roads were being built. For 36 hours they endured this wait, a heavy, soaking, persistent rain falling continually. Meanwhile, the infantry was suffering severely from the enemy's artillery. At last there was an aisle way through the wire and debris and the artillery went over, taking a position about a half mile south of Mt. Faucon.

After Mt. Faucon, Nautillois and Cunel were taken, the 79th was withdrawn and the 3^{d} substituted. The stubborn resistance made by the enemy caused heavy losses and the 119th suffered with the infantry. It was at Nautillois that Major Edward W. Thompson, of South Haven, was killed.

YANK METTLE TESTED.

The 32d Division entered the sector on the left, after the capture of the Cunel Wood and the 119th, with the rest of the artillery brigade, was recalled and placed in support of the Michigan-Wisconsin division. Then ensued a test.

The enemy had fallen back to a prepared position, the Kriemhilde-Strellung line, and there waited the smash, confident that the Yanks were stopped. But they only paused seemingly to put more force into a series of smashing blows. When the enemy recovered from his surprise, he found that the Michigan-Wisconsin infantry and artillery had pushed him out of his concrete and wire, had taken the heights of Coute Dame Marie and had captured Cierges, Gaenes, Romanges and Bautheville.

Then the 32d was relieved by the 89th, the 119th and the other artillery remaining in, however, and preparations were made for the final drive of November 1, when the Americans pushed forward, crossed the Meuse and the enemy was convinced that he had met his master, his defense having been smashed.

1,300 HORSES, 300 LEFT.

The 89th Division went on its way, but the 57th Field Artillery Brigade did not. It couldn't; it was unhorsed. The night of the armistice found the 119th quietly camped in echelon west of Mt. Faucon, preparatory to moving to the rear for rest and re-equipping. Out of more than 1,300 horses, less than 300 remained.

More than 300 had been killed in action. The others had died of exhaustion, due to lack of nutrition, because in bringing up supplies men came first, and from grazing in the gassed areas. Virtually all the animals were gassed, as well as the men. So the regiment was pulled down to Mauvages, 62 miles, by motors, and here it remains.

Counting the 32d as a new division each time it was attached to it, the 119th has been with 19 different divisions, 11 of them combat. It has worn out two sets of guns; it has marched all over Northern France. It has had its share of glory—yes, and its share of dead.

PVT Elmer Smith's Diary Entries

Diary Entry Wed. September 18

Received our pay this morning. Had a big feed at a french home. Moved out again about dark.

Diary Entry Thur. September 19

Stayed with the trucks last night in the village.

Rode nearly all day to our next camp.

The regiment moved out about dark in the rain. I stayed in the barracks all night.

Diary Entry Fri. September 20

Started out and hiked as the trucks could not pull all of us.

Found the camp in a woods. Stayed there until about dark. And then started out on the hike again.

Diary Entry Sat. September 21

Hiked a few kilometers the other side of Vaubecourt. Stayed the rest of the night in barracks. Did not move out of there until about dark. I rode on the truck.

Stayed near the trucks at Dombasle the rest of the night.

Diary Entry Sun. September 22

The telephone truck broke down this morning.

Walked a couple of miles to where the outfit is camped.

Took a bum down to a Y canteen this afternoon after some articles.

The telephone stayed on the broken truck all night to guard the telephone material.

Diary Entry Mon. September 23

Did not sleep much because of so much traffic on the road.

Unloaded part of the telephone material on one of the Quads. The Packard was repaired this afternoon and brought the rest of the telephone equipment.

Found a pretty good bunk in a old shed for tonight.

Diary Entry Tue. September 24

Laid around and played poker all day. We took up our position on the edge of No Mans Land. Laid our telephone lines.

Diary Entry Wed. September 25

Laid around most of the day. Was put on the board operating.

Diary Entry, September Memoranda

This is Verdun. Lets hope this battle will not be as bloody as the first battle of Verdun was. This sector is one of the best fortified sectors on the western front.

Diary Entry Thur. September 26

The drive started at 2:30 this morning by terrific artillery fire. The dough boys went over the top at 5:30. Did not meet much resistance.

We moved out of our position at 4:30 this p.m. to go foreward.

Doughboys are still advancing.

Made camp in No Mans Land.

Excerpt from Service Record, By An Artilleryman

September 26. The avalanche shoved off. To the thundering opening overture of a gigantic cannonade, the Meuse-Argonne battle began… It was a magnificent artillery demonstration, slow and impressive. The deep muffled booming of the howitzers sounded like thunder coming out of a Cyclops' cave. Waves of sound seemed as material as waves of water. We were engulfed in them. They surged, and washed, and echoed from crest to crest in volcanic tones. The great forged-steel bolts passed with a rushing noise like a huge wind… A heavy interdictory fire had been maintained on the communicating roads for a long time but the barrage preceding the infantry attack lasted only two hours, ending shortly after sunrise. There was little retaliatory fire from the enemy at first.

Diary Entry Fri. September 27

We moved foreward this morning. The regiment was tied up in the stream of traffic until the middle of the afternoon. The road across No Mans Land was torn up so travel was difficult.

We established a P.C. in dugouts that looked as tho they had been used by German engineers.

Diary Entry Sat. September 28

Our telephone dugout was full of hand grenades. We moved all of them out this morning.

Diary Entry Sun. September 29

Sit around and operated the board most of the day.

Diary Entry Mon. September 30

We moved up toward our advance position this morning. We ran a telephone line with us on the way up. I was given charge of the reel cart and was to bring it around the knoll into the woods where our line came from. The Germans commenced dropping shells on my back trail. They followed me around and shelled the woods hard we were in.

Diary Entry Tue. October 1

Do not like our new P.C. All we have for a shelter is a small shack not even splinter proof.

The boys ran a line to the Out Post. It got rather warm for them as the Germans observed them.

Diary Entry Wed. October 2

Made flap jacks and fryed them ourselves this morning. Slept part of the afternoon.

The sky was full of Boche planes late this afternoon over seeing what they could see.

We were shelled about 6:00 o clock. The nearest shell landed a few feet away and threw fragments all over the shanty.

Diary Entry Thur. October 3

Moved our P.C. back about a kilometer into a woods.

Diary Entry Fri. October 4

Laid around most of the day. Their were a few shells thrown into our woods.

Diary Entry Sat. October 5

Laid around and fryed pancakes nearly all day. Drew in our lines tonight. Move early in the morning.

Diary Entry Sun. October 6

Moved at about 3:00 o clock this morning.
Ran our lines and set up our telephone central.

Diary Entry Mon. October 7

Operated and ran some wire on the reel cart.

Diary Entry Tue. October 8

Did nothing but operate.

Diary Entry Wed. October 9

The big drive started this morning. Our regiment threw over a heavy barrage.

About 1000 prisoners were brought in from our sector. Infantry advanced about five kilometers.

Expect to move up in the morning.

Excerpt from Service Record, By an Artilleryman

After four days in this miserable place there was a furious fight... and the Germans fell back, many prisoners being taken. Some surrendered by whole companies. They were young and had just been sent to the front. They dropped their rifles and walked out, their hands up, to meet our astonished infantry. I saw about 400 collected by a few doughboys near our gun position and most of them did not seem over 14 or 15 years old, mere boys hardly past grammar school.

When the ragged, cootie-ridden, mud-caked, gas-burned [American] soldiers had straggled in out of the dark that night to assemble in the tiny circle of light around Walter Bone's kitchen for their scanty mess, it was the unanimous verdict that since Wilhelm II [the German Kaiser] had to send children to the front he was in his last ditch.

Diary Entry Thur. October 10

Got our equipment ready to move this morning. Did not move foreward until six o clock. Our batteries moved close enough to the front to be under enemy machine gun fire. Our P.C. is in a dirt pit. A battery of 75's are above us and a battery of 90's about 100 yds. in rear of us.

Diary Entry Fri. October 11

Operated the switchboard this forenoon. Our batteries are under heavy shell fire. C battery had a direct hit on the wheel of one of their piece's. One man was killed and three wounded.

Diary Entry Sat. October 12

Took a trip over to the First battalion station this morning. Their are ten Americans to one dead Boche lying on the ground. Some Americans are blown to pieces. All I could see left of one was his legs.

Diary Entry Sun. October 13

Wrote letters home this forenoon. Laid around most of the afternoon.

The communique of last night stated the Germans agreed to all the rules laid down by Pres. Wilson and also to evacuate.

Diary Entry Mon. October 14

Laid around and gaffed about peace most all day.

Letter from Mr. Chas. Ebersol to Mr. W.F. Smith, October 14, 1918 (see earlier returned letter to Elmer Smith of July 3, 1918 that accompanied this)

Lansing Business University

THE CAPITAL BUSINESS SCHOOL OPEN ALL YEAR

Chas E. Ebersol, B.A., B.D., President

Lansing, Michigan

October 14, 1918.

Mr. W.F. Smith,
Carland, Mich.

Dear Mr. Smith:

The enclosed letter for your son was sent to him at his new address when I dated it, but for some reason it must have been wrongly reported in the paper so that the letter has wandered around France and finally came back to me.

Will you kindly put the correct address on it this time and we will send it again hoping that it will reach him.

Cordially yours,
Chas E. Ebersol
CEE/ZHM

Diary Entry Tue. October 15

We agreed that the peace talk is all bosh. So we threw over a barrage and went after the Huns.

Diary Entry Wed. October 16

It is raining to beat the devil. Mud. Worse than Flanders or Texas. The Boche dropped a few Whiz Bangs near us tonight.

Memorandum from 32nd Division Commander on combat tactics to hold ground gained

P.C. 32d Division
October 16, 1918.

MEMORANDUM FOR BRIGADE COMMANDERS

1. In a talk with General Pershing yesterday he told me in most emphatic terms that every meter of ground gained must be held at all cost; therefore, when our line is stabilized at any time or if we stop advancing, the line must be organized on the front elements. The front elements must not be drawn back to organize on a line further back, and the front elements must be held by those troops in those lines who must have positive orders not to fall back under any circumstances in case of attack; they must fight it out on the spot. This does not prevent the organization in depth of other positions toward the rear. These positions to be covered with machine guns, Chauchat rifles and combat groups, generally.

2. In the present instance the main line of resistance, indicated in Corps field order of yesterday, will be organized with a view to its occupation by the Divisional Machine Gun Battalion. No infantry troops will be assigned to this line. The Engineer Regiment will be designated as a Provisional Reserve, and this Regiment, together with the Machine Gun Battalion, is amble to hold this line against any attack that may be expected from the enemy, in case of a reverse to our troops in advance of this line, a matter that does not give me much concern at the present time. In organizing the ground in depth care must be taken that the withdrawal of any troops in moving them further to the rear may not be construed into a withdrawal. This may have a bad effect to the troops that may be left on the outpost line.

3. The outpost line must be held by those troops which are going to be used in case an advance is ordered and the front line everywhere must be well defined, so that in case an advance is ordered this advance can be supported by artillery.

G. Haan
Major General, U.S.A. Commanding.

Diary Entry Thur. October 17

Wallowed around in the mud most of the day. We were shelled for a few minutes tonight. They landed to close for comfort.

Diary Entry Fri. October 18

Rained to beat the devil.

Diary Entry Sat. October 19

Rained some more. Wrote letters and layed around.

Diary Entry Sun. October 20

All of our telephone lines were shot out last night. The fellows were out on lines most of the night.

Excerpt from Service Record, By An Artilleryman

The same night one of our telephone men gave an unusual exhibition of courage. German shell-fire broke the wires and he had to repair them. Day work was less thought of, even when heavy firing was in progress, but night work was unusually hazardous. Ordinarily three or four men in the telephone squad were available for duty, and it was seldom that one man was asked to make two trips on the same night. But on this evening every other man in the squad was wounded or sick. When the operator announced that he could not make connections some one had to go out find the injury, and repair it.

Robert Moore was the surviving lineman. He went out promptly, settled the trouble, and got back, after one or two narrow escapes. In less than an hour another break was reported. Moore went again rather thoughtfully. After midnight a third break was announced. Moore rose with an evident effort. German guns were busy, shrapnel was spattering about, and planes were dropping bombs on the paths. It was clear that he did not value very highly his chance of getting back. But he did come in and without injury.

At three o'clock a fourth break was reported and Moore was roused again. There was a curious expression on his face, but in a moment he got into motion and went gamely on his fourth trip. Fortune favored his courage, for he once more passed through the scattering rain of

German fire unhurt. Returning, he was so weak from exhaustion and strain he could barely stand.

Diary Entry Mon. October 21

We packed up telephone equipment and moved our P.C. up about three kilometers. Our new P.C. is in a horse shoe shape of a large hill that over looks the whole country. We are using Boche barracks and bungalows.

Diary Entry Tue. October 22

Ran a few telephone lines this morning.

Diary Entry Wed. October 23

Orders came in for a three day rest of all the light artillery. Except the telephone detail. We have to stay and keep up communication.

Diary Entry Thur. October 24

Laid around and wrote a few letters. Nothing much to do as their is not many calls coming over the lines.

The Ichelon was bombed by the Boche last night. Fifteen casuals reported.

Diary Entry Fri. October 25

Went to the Y.M.C.A. this afternoon to have an order filled out.

They were shelling the town and before our turn came in line, the M.P.'s [Military Police] placed everybody under arrest. I put my blue band on my arm and said to hell with the M.P.'s and marched out of town.

Diary Entry Sat. October 26

Shaved, went out and repaired a line and made another trip to the "Y".

We were not placed under arrest this time but we could not get our order filled.

The Germans are dropping a few Whiz Bangs around us.

Letter to Sister, October 26, 1918

France

Dear Sister:

Will drop you a few lines tonight. I received your letter of Sept 22 a few days ago. I can't understand why you people are not receiving my letters. Their was quite a space of time I did not write many letters. But not such a long space of time you mentioned.

It is strange I did not even know you had had a operation until mother asked me if I knew about it in one of her recent letters. I am planning on paying you what I owe you if my service record ever gets back so I can draw all my back pay.

I presume those two large orders I sent home will nearly bankrupt the firm of Smith & Co. I dare say you will not be able to send everything I ordered. I sent my three pound X-mas order to Frank. I was so late in sending it I don't know as he will get it in time to fill it. As it has to be on the way back by Nov. 20.

You ask me something about the Y.M.C.A. once. They are not very satisfactory to most of the boys on the front. I haven't heard a man speak a good word for them since I have been to the front. The Red Cross, Salvation Army and K. of C. suits the men far more. I know that's where my donation would go.

Gee I would like to see one of mother's good old fashioned dinners of apple pie, fried chicken, hot biscuits and gravy. We are getting good grub but there is nothing that comes up to mother's cooking.

Well Zelma this is a very short letter but is better than nothing. Will write again soon.

Your Brother,
Elmer

W G Stillwell [Censor Review] 119 FA

Diary Entry Sun. October 27

Lolled around most of the day.

Drew new clothes and pay.

Diary Entry Mon. October 28

The Boche snapped quite a few caps in our valley last night. Their sure was some assortment of Whiz Bangs, Seventy sevens, and one hundred fifties.

Nobody hurt in our Co.

Dug a cute little dug out into the hill side. When George commences snapping caps at us tonight, into the dug out head first.

Diary Entry Tue. October 29

Laid around most of the day. Took my regular shift on the board.

Diary Entry Tue. October 30

S.O.S.

Diary Entry Thur. October 31

Was very busy on the switch board today and tonight. They are preparing a big barrage for tomorrow morning.

Diary Entry Fri. November 1

The barrage started at 3:30 A.M. sharp. It lasted for three hours and was certainly one of the hardest barrages I ever saw. Our dough boys advanced with out much resistance except for a few machine guns. Their was a number of machine guns and artillery pieces captured. The infantry advanced about fifteen kilometers today. Well will I remember this Halloween celebration.

Diary Entry Sat. November 2

We did not advance with the rest of the artillery as our brigade is to go back for the first real rest since we went on the front June 14.

We pulled out about dark for the combat echelon.

We had not gotten very far past an ammunition train when the whole thing went up in a flare.

The ammunition was composed of three inch shells. They sounded about like a million fire crackers. It illuminated the country for miles.

Excerpt from Service Record, By An Artilleryman

One effort was made to get our regiment to go forward in the pursuit. It could not be done. Out of 1,700 men with which the regiment had started there were less than 1,000 now and nearly 700 of them were replacements. We had marched over 600 miles during the actions of summer and fall, and a total assignment of 1,459 horses had dwindled to a little over 300, and they were so sick and weak and starved they seemed about to die. Our own battery was almost horseless. Everyone was in rags, uniforms torn by barbed wire and brambles, the men gaunt and famished, and many sick from prolonged exertion, gas, lice, wet, and cold. The regiment tottered and stood still.

Diary Entry Sun. November 3

Slept under a tarpaulin last night. Moved over into a little house that the Frenchmen had just moved out of.

Stayed there all this day.

Diary Entry Mon. November 4

Laid around all day.

Diary Entry Tue. November 5

Bought 90 bars of chocolate for our detail this morning.

Rolled our rolls and pulled out for the rear echelon about 12:00 o clock. Arrived their and made our home in a deep dug out.

Diary Entry Wed. November 6

Stood around and listened to the band rehearsel this forenoon. Unpacked and repacked our telephone wagon this afternoon.

Diary Entry Thur. November 7

We moved back toward the rear this afternoon. Pulled into an old orchard to make camp about 8:30. It is raining.

Diary Entry Fri. November 8

Left the orchard about ten o clock. Hiked to the woods where we made camp when first coming on this front. The telephone detail was assigned a building by themselves.

Diary Entry Sat. November 9

Laid around and cleaned up.

Diary Entry Sun. November 10

Set up the switch board and put in some lines. Worked most of the day.

NOTES

1. General Orders Number 126, *Soldier's Individual Pay Record Book for PFC Elmer O.Smith* (France: General Headquarters (GHQ), American Expeditionary Forces, August 1, 1918).

2. Colonel Chester B. McCormick, "A Brief History of the 119th Field Artillery," *Honor Roll and Complete War History of Ingham County in the Great World War: 1914-1918* (Lansing MI: The State Journal Company, 1920), 220.

3. Office of the Chief of Military History, U.S. Army, *The Army Flag and Its Streamers: Meuse-Argonne* (Washington, D.C.: U.S. GPO, 1964), http://www.history.army.mil/html/reference/army_flag/wwi.html, accessed March 30, 2015.
   American Battle Monuments Commission, *American Armies and Battlefields in Europe: A History, Guide, and Reference Book* (Washington, D.C.: U.S. Government Printing Office, 1938), 167-328.
   Robert H. Ferrell, *America's Deadliest Battle: Meuse-Argonne, 1918* (Lawrence, KS: University Press of Kansas, 2007), 41-55, 94-95, 130-135.
   Byron Farwell, *Over There: The United States in the Great War, 1917-1918* (New York: W.W. Norton and Company, 1999), 229-244.

4. American Battle Monuments Commission, 79th *Division Summary of Operations in the World War* (Washington, D.C.: U.S. Government Printing Office, 1943), 12-22.

5. American Battle Monuments Commission, *3^{D} Division Summary of Operations in the World War* (Washington, D.C.: U.S. Government Printing Office, 1943), 57-66.

6. Robert H. Ferrell, *America's Deadliest Battle: Meuse Argonne, 1918* (Lawrence, KS: University Press of Kansas, 2007), 100-102.

7. American Battle Monuments Commission, *32^{D} Division Summary of Operations in the World War* (Washington, D.C.: U.S. Government Printing Office, 1943), 33-57.

8. Joint War History Commissions of Michigan and Wisconsin, *The 32ND Division in the World War 1917–1919* (Milwaukee, WI: Wisconsin Printing Company, 1920), 107.

9. American Battle Monuments Commission, *32^{D} Division Summary of Operations in the World War* (Washington, D.C.: U.S. Government Printing Office, 1943), 57-69.

10. American Battle Monuments Commission, 89th *Division Summary of Operations in the World War* (Washington, D.C.: U.S. Government Printing Office, 1943), 57-69.

11. Colonel Chester B. McCormick, "A Brief History of the 119th Field Artillery," 220.

12. L.L. Stevenson, "Somber and Gay Mingle in 119th's War Picture," (Part 4 of 6 part series on the 119th FA's war exploits) *The Detroit News,* February 27, 1919.

Chapter 11
The Armistice and Duty Afterwards

In the first week of November, 1918, the 57th FA Brigade and subordinate FA regiments were pulled off the front line. They were expecting to recuperate for a short period before being committed once again into combat against the German Army. But German forces reeling from relentless Allied offensive operations began to show significant weariness after more than four years of sustained fighting. The recent offensive gains of General Pershing's AEF in conjunction with the French and British Armies on their flanks, demonstrated that the Allies had indeed changed the tide of the war. The German leadership saw that the significant influx of manpower and fighting spirit the U.S. added to the Allies would eventually push the front east into Germany proper. With a weakened Army stretched toward the breaking point, the German leader, Kaiser Wilhelm relented and abdicated. At 11:00 a.m. on November 11, 1918, the Armistice was official. A month of negotiations was agreed to, and "The Great War" was over. Word was quickly disseminated that morning to all American soldiers who soon realized the grueling, though short-lived conflict was over. The Americans truly felt their military might had provided the death knell for the German war machine.[1] But most of all they longed to return to their country and restart the lives they left behind. PFC Elmer Smith was no exception. Wounded in his initial time at the front and living through three subsequent campaigns, made him realize he had clearly performed his duty and contributed to the winning Allied war effort.

AEF casualty figures in five months of severe fighting were significant. Total estimated American casualties were 365,489, of which approximately 53,000 were killed in action, 54,574 died of disease or other natural causes, and approximately 260,000 were wounded or disabled. The casualty figures include the 350 American women who died in service to the nation during the conflict. The 32nd Division suffered many casualties as well, including 3,028 who died in battle or of wounds, and another 10,233 wounded in action. The 32nd's battle related deaths were higher than any National Guard Division and fourth highest overall for all divisions.[2]

After the armistice, the U.S. Army immediately designated certain Infantry brigades, to include those of the 32nd Division, to perform Occupation duty in Germany under the command of the newly formed 3rd U.S. Army commanded by MG Joseph Dickman.[3] But this did not include the 119th FA Regiment. The 119th FA's few horses, equipment, and their worn artillery pieces, were turned over to the French. Hiking and inspections continued to fill daily schedules.

Colonel McCormick, like other commanders, had to maintain good order and discipline within his unit as they bided their time awaiting transportation back to the U.S. He had to keep his soldiers out of trouble and bring them home safely now that they had survived the rigors of war. On December 27, he issued two orders. The first—ruled off limits any café serving alcohol during drill hours or after 8:30 p.m. The second—ordered unit sentinels on daily guard duty to arrest all enlisted men improperly dressed outside of their billets. Elmer made no specific mention of these policies. He departed the next day on his furlough and it is likely this was not an issue when he returned two weeks later.[4]

Elmer Smith had one small brush with trouble. On Sunday, November 24, he and two soldiers were returning from a day pass to Mussey, the town in which the 119th was garrisoned. When the train failed to stop at the town, they proceeded to jump off as it was moving about 35 miles per hour. Elmer suffered a black eye, a sprained wrist, and a wrenched shoulder. Luckily, no one was seriously hurt and after a week's recuperation he was fine again.

Per its pre-printed dated pages, Elmer Smith only kept his wartime diary for 1918. Hence, this chapter focuses on the last two months of that year until Elmer went on his furlough to Nice, France.

Diary Entry Mon. November 11

As we operators do not stand any formations we have it very soft. Sitting around and smoking is all we do.

Hooray! The armistice to Germany was signed at 6:00 o'clock this morning.

Hostilities ceased at 11:00 o clock.

Peace in fourteen days. Yip.

Blackjack Pershing was right when he said "Hell, Heaven or Hoboken" by Xmas.

Diary Entry Tue. November 12

Layed around this forenoon. Helped to run a brigade line this afternoon.

Heard the terms of the armistice. It sure was a humdinger. Our slogan is now, "When do we go home".

Letter to Mother, November 12, 1918

YMCA letterhead

Dear Mother:

Well dear little mother I am coming back to you sometime in the future. Gee I can tell you we were no sore bunch when we heard the Armistice was signed. It sure was a stiff one and peace can not help but come. I wasn't on the front when the last shot was fired as we had just pulled back for a rest a few days before that. Four fronts I have been on and each front was worse than the last. Verdon [sic] was the last one. Well mother I can't think of anything else to write about. The only think I am looking forward to is of getting rid of the cooties and getting some real old civilian clothes on once more. Goodbye.

Your Son,
Elmer

Diary Entry Wed. November 13

Took a good hot bath this afternoon. It is the first real bath I have had in four months.

We are getting things ready to move. Lets hope its toward the coast.

Rumors fly around like leaves. Such as, 4th and 32nd Division home by Xmas. We are to be paid off in American money. Crown Prince has been assinated. Some manure pile dope.

Diary Entry Thur. November 14

Went to Villers sur-Cousances and was decotized.

November 14, 1918 Memorandum of 119th FA Regiment Killed and Wounded in Action

Headquarters, 119th Field Artillery
AMERICAN EXPEDITIONARY FORCES
FRANCE
14 November 1918.

FROM: Personnel Adjutant
TO: Statistical Officer, 57th F.A. Brigade
SUBJECT: Casualty Report

1. In compliance with letter from Headquarters Army Artillery, 1st Army, dated 13 November 1918, the following report of casualties is submitted:

KILLED IN ACTION

30 Soldiers' Names, Ranks, Service #s, Unit, Date KIA, How Killed (Shell Fire, Aerial Fire)

ACCIDENTLY KILLED

3 Soldiers' Names, (Overturned Caisson, Drowned)

WOUNDED IN ACTION

Incomplete List, 54 Soldiers through August 9, 1918 including Private Elmer O. Smith.

Diary Entry Fri. November 15

Expect orders to move tomorrow.

Diary Entry Sat. November 16

Left camp early this morning. Hiked all day with out any thing to eat. The whole regiment are nearly ready for the hospital from the effects.

Camped in a large woods.

Diary Entry Sun. November 17

We had reveille and breakfast before daylight. Started hiking soon after breakfast. Reached Brabant Le Roi where we are to be billeted about ten o clock.

After getting settled in a barracks we were kicked out by some French aviators. Durn the French. If I ever join the army again it will be to fight Frenchmen.

Diary Entry Mon. November 18

Located our telephone central and strung lines.

Diary Entry Tue. November 19

Strung a few more lines and straightened up the Central.

Diary Entry Wed. November 20

Went to Revigney this morning. Laid around this afternoon.

Diary Entry Thur. November 21

Laid around. I am not on duty with the company.

Diary Entry Fri. November 22

Moved to Mussey. Took up all of our lines.

Diary Entry Sat. November 23

Strung lines and located the central today.

Diary Entry Sun. November 24

This is Fathers Day.

Seven of us got a pass to Bar le Duc this A.M. Had a fine time there. Three of us hopped a troop train for Mussey. The train failed to slow down by Mussey so we were fools enough to jump off all tho the train was going about 35 per. Result: One black eye, a wrenched arm and a sprained wrist. Crippen [Ray L. Crippen of Lansing] suffered about the same. Wheeler [Joseph Wheeler of South Haven, Michigan] was not hurt.

Diary Entry Mon. November 25

Did not sleep much last night as my arm ached continually. Went to the infirmary and had it put into a sling.

Diary Entry Tue. November 26

My arm ached all day and was not able to sleep any last night.

Diary Entry Wed. November 27

Slept better last night. The arm is not aching much today. Was able to take it out of the sling.

Diary Entry Thur. November 28

Had a fine Thanksgiving dinner of Roast beef, mashed potatoes, brown gravey, salad, pie, cake, and grapes.

Eat to much as usual.

The band furnished music during the meal.

Diary Entry Fri. November 29

Laid around all day long.

Letter to Sister, November 29, 1918

Dear Sister:

I will drop you a few lines tonight before going to bed. I am feeling fine and ought to be getting fat as all I do is lie around & eat. I do not hike & drill with the rest of the Co. The Colonel has to have his telephone at every place we go so all I do is sit around and & operate the switch board. I don't know when we will get home. I hope by next spring at least. Do you ever hear much of the 32nd Div. We are not with them now all tho I hope we are before we go home. They are in

Germany now. We have been made Army Artillery. We have not much equipment. Our horses have been killed or have died and a number of our pieces have been taken in as worn out. I came back to the outfit at Chateau Tierry front. From there we went to Soissons and took part in the battle of Juvigney. I had some very narrow escapes there of course. From there we came down to Verdun & Argonne. This was the worst front the regiment was on. Many time I have been out there and never thot I had a very big chance of seeing the dugout again. But luck was with me and so here I am with my little done that helps to make history.

I had a little accident a week ago. A number of us went to the Bar Le Duc which is a few kilometers from the village we are billeted in. We spent the day there and had a fine time. Of course spending all of our money. We started for home late. As we neared the railroad yards a troop train was pulling thru our way. Three of us managed to get on. As the train neared our village it failed to slow up. Well while it was going about thirty five miles per hour, we unboarded. A black eye, wrenched arm and bruises is all I got out of it. One of the fellows was not hurt at all and the other was hurt worse than I. We were all a bunch of dam fools anyway.

Well will close for this time. Goodbye.

Your Brother,
Elmer

Diary Entry Sat. November 30

The Colonel is clamping down on everybody. Gee I guess he thinks we are going to have another war.

Diary Entry Sun. December 1

Laid around all day.

Diary Entry Mon. December 2

Everybody except we operators are drilling to beat the devil.

Diary Entry Tue. December 3

A General from the first army reviewed the regiment and also made an inspection.

The 119th was checked as first. The 121st 2nd, 120th 3rd, 147th 4th by the inspection.

Diary Entry Wed. December 4

We had a show down inspection this afternoon. Was checked up on every thing.

The motor school bunch came back tonight as the order was countermanded.

Diary Entry Thur. December 5

Did nothing much but get my hair cut.

Diary Entry Fri. December 6

S.O.S.

Letter to Mother, December 6, 1918

YMCA letterhead On Active Service with the American Expeditionary Force

Dear Mother:

I received your letter of Nov. 3rd a couple of days ago, I am glad to hear that you people are all well. You were lucky in escaping the "Flu" you certainly must of had it hard over there. I have heard of but a few cases of it among the soldiers over here. I haven't received my boxes yet, but I am looking for them in every mail. The X-mas boxes are just coming in. I sent the label to Frank.

I hope Jap buys the farm. You people would be benefitted quite a little. You need a smaller place. I have commenced to figure how much it is going to cost me for clothes when I get back. I just about figure prices must be up, what I have left out of my $100 Liberty bond will buy a good cigar. I just finished paying for my bond just a couple months ago.

I haven't heard anymore about coming back. But I look to coming back the last of Jan. or the first of Feb. We are attached to the 88th Division now. They are under orders to go back sometime this month. But I hardly think we will go back with them all tho such a thing could be possible,

The first thing I am going to do when I get back is look for a good job. Just think I will be 22 my next birthday. Old enough to get married, But I feel like a young kid. Well mother will quit for this time.

Goodbye,
Your Son,
Elmer

Diary Entry Sat. December 7

We had an inspection this morning. The Co. laid around this afternoon.

Diary Entry Sun. December 8

I received a pass for Bar le Duc today. Had a fine time.

Diary Entry Mon. December 9

Laid around and recuperated from yesterday.

Diary Entry Tue. December 10

Nothing to do but sit around and operate the board and read.

Diary Entry Wed. December 11

Eat, slept and sit around.

Diary Entry Thur. December 12

Went out and drilled with the Co. today.

Diary Entry Fri. December 13

Pete [Edward Everett Williams of North Adams, Michigan] and Bach. [Ernest P. Bacheller of Phillips, Maine] came back from their furloughs at Nice. They had such a nice time I was induced to put my name in for one.

Diary Entry Sat. December 14

We had a inspection by Capt. Schenider [CPT Corwin J. Schneider, Headquarters Company Commander]. Laid around this afternoon.

Letter to Mother, December 14, 1918

Mussey

Dear Mother:

I received the box a few days ago. It arrived in fine condition and certainly was appreciated by me. Gee it tasted the best of anything I have had for a deuce of awhile.

I suppose we will be traveling toward a embarkment center soon. I believe we will be on high seas by the middle of Jan. or the first of Feb. I am figuring on getting a furlough to Nice in a couple of weeks if I can scare up the money. A number of the fellows have been there and have had fine times.

Zelmas letter of Nov. 24th just arrived. You can tell Clarence that he need not mind about the insect powder. I have gotten beyond the stage of its use. But I have seen the time when some would have been welcomed. I have some trouble with my arm. We received a shot of diptheria serum last mon. By good rights I shouldn't have been shot at all as I had two of them last spring. The result is that my arm is swelling up to about again it's normal size. And it keeps a swelling more. I went to the infirmary with it this morning. They painted it up with iodine. It relived the itching part of it. Their was great large blotches broke out on it and it itched like the devil.

Well I must close for this time. If we remain Army Artillery. You can look, for me home for my birthday [March 5].

Your Son,
Elmer

Diary Entry Sun. December 15

Services was conducted by Chaplain Atkinson in our barracks this morning.

Jarm [William Jarm] and I walked to Fains this afternoon. We watched the French dance and got pretty well tanked up on beer and rum.

Diary Entry Mon. December 16

Slept rather late this morning caused by effects.

It is rumored the 32nd Div. dough boys have been relieved and the whole division including us are to be sent home soon.

Diary Entry Tue. December 17

It is rumored we will move soon. Lets hope so if its toward home.

Diary Entry Wed. December 18

Cleaned up. Read the rest of the time while not on duty.

Diary Entry Thur. December 19

Laid around most of the day. Tuff job I have. Watching the Co. drill.

Diary Entry Fri. December 20

Worked like the deuce this afternoon taking up our telephone wires.

Jarm and I dined out tonight on steak french fried and beer.

Reveille is 2:30 tomorrow morning. Expect to load at Revigney.

Diary Entry Sat. December 21

Was awakened at 2:30. A deuce of a time to get up. Made our rolls and started to hike to Revigney at 3:30.

Reached Revigney at 6:00 oclock. Had breakfast and then started loading the train. Had every thing loaded by nine o clock. Did not pull out until 3 P.M.

Arrived in a little jerk water town [Mauvages] about 6 o'clock. Unloaded and had supper. Trucks took us to our billets about 20 kilometers.

Diary Entry Sun. December 22

Slept until 10:30 this morning. Had corn meal for breakfast. Straightened up the billet this afternoon. Its a peach too. You can lie and watch the stars go by over head and then roll over and watch the cows go thru underneath. And its only about 25 above zero. The name of this town is Mauvages.

Diary Entry Mon. December 23

We have to put up a telephone central so commenced work this morning. The central is situated in a cow stable. We ran nearly all of our lines today. Jarm [Bill Jarm of Niles, Michigan] and Duval [H. Blair DuVall of McBain, Michigan] went on their furlough to Nice tonight.

Diary Entry Tue. December 24

Moved my bed in the central. Now have a nice warm place to sleep. This does not seem much like a Xmas eve to me.

Diary Entry Wed. December 25

Did not get up very early this morning. Had a very good dinner. Candy was issued with rations today. The Y.M.C.A. gave away small packages with chocolate and cigarettes in them. How in hell could they afford to do it. It is the first I ever saw them give any thing away. Went to a show put on by the band tonight.

Diary Entry Thur. December 26

It is getting quite cold. Did not do much today but read.

Diary Entry Fri. December 27

I was notified I could have my furlough now.
Chose Nice. Expect to leave in the morning.

NOTES

1. Byron Farwell, *Over There: The United States in the Great War, 1917-1918* (New York: W.W. Norton and Company, 1999), 253-266.

2. U.S. War Department, *The War With Germany: A Statistical Summary* (Washington, D.C.: U.S. GPO, May 1919), 117.

3. Byron Farwell, *Over There: The United States in the Great War, 1917-1918* (New York: W.W. Norton and Company, 1999), 253-266.
   American Battle Monuments Commission, *32^{D} Division Summary of Operations in the World War* (Washington, D.C.: U.S. Government Printing Office, 1943), 68.

4. Headquarters, 119th Field Artillery, American Expeditionary Forces, *Memorandum* (Mauvages, France: December 27, 1918).
   Headquarters, 119th Field Artillery, American Expeditionary Forces, *Memorandum for Guard* (Mauvages, France: December 27, 1918).

Chapter 12
Summary of Combat Service

During the months following the conflict, American soldiers and leaders began to write and speak about their combat experiences. Unit After-Action-Reports were written. With censorship controls lifted, many newspaper and other accounts of combat operations surfaced as the American press finally gathered enough information to provide suitable accounts of the fighting of local units in the overall effort.

This chapter incorporates several commendation letters that commanders and political leaders wrote about the combat exploits of the 32nd Division and the 119th FA Regiment. Proud unit leaders wrote summaries of the intense combat operations in which their units participated. Also included are several post-war newspaper articles written about the 119th FA Regiment. Only through these summaries did the significant accomplishments of the 32nd Division and its subordinates, including the 119th FA Regiment, come to light for history to document.

PFC Elmer Smith was a member of one of the best artillery regiments in the U.S. Army. The 119th was very proficient at rapidly firing artillery with most crews able to fire up to 25 rounds a minute. Captured German soldiers even remarked about wanting to see the "machine gun" artillery thinking the 119th had unique equipment that allowed them to fire so quickly.[1]

At the start of his soldier address book, Elmer documented the time he was at the front involved in combat operations, totaling 63 days. He wrote:

> *Toul, June 14th–16th*
> *Chateau Thierry, Aug. 14th–Aug 23rd*
> *Soissons, Aug. 28th–Sept. 6*
> *Argonne, Sept. 24–Nov. 2.*

For his actions in combat in France, PFC Smith was awarded three medals—the Purple Heart, the World War I Victory Medal, and the French Croix de Guerre (Cross of War).

The U.S. Army did not establish the Purple Heart Medal until 1932. It was created to formally and retroactively recognize the many soldiers wounded in the World War. During the war, wounded soldiers received a Wound Chevron worn on the bottom of the right sleeve of their jerkin or wool tunic. A Wound Certificate might also be awarded. At the top it stated, "Columbia Gives to Her Son the Accolade of the New Chivalry of Humanity." At the bottom the soldier's name, rank, and unit were inscribed, followed by, "Served with Honor in the World War and Was Wounded in Action," with U.S. President Woodrow Wilson's signature. Elmer Smith did not have this certificate in his records and likely did not receive one as he preserved most of his other military documents.[2]

The U.S. Army established the World War I Victory Medal in 1919. All soldiers who served during the war received the Victory Medal, with those seeing combat overseas awarded additional Battle and Service Clasps. All 32nd Division and 119th FA Regiment soldiers received four Battle Clasps for the following campaigns: Defensive Sector, Aisne-Marne, Oise-Aisne, and Meuse-Argonne. Soldiers deployed to Europe who did not directly participate in any campaign were awarded a Service Clasp for the country to which they were deployed.[3]

The French Government established the Croix de Guerre in 1915 to recognize Allied units and soldiers mentioned in official dispatches for gallantry in action. The 119th FA Regiment was attached several times to French Corps or Armies and their brave fighting was often highlighted after the end of specific battles. The 119th received the recognition twice and thus the unit is listed as being awarded the Croix de Guerre with 1 Silver Star.[4]

For superbly leading the 119th FA Regiment throughout the war, the U.S. Army awarded Colonel Chester B. McCormick the Distinguished Service Medal. His medal citation reads: [5]

> *The President of the United States of America, authorized by Act of Congress, July 9, 1918, takes pleasure in presenting the Army Distinguished Service Medal to Colonel (Field Artillery) Chester B. McCormick, United States Army, for exceptionally meritorious and distinguished services to the Government of the United States, in a duty of great responsibility during the World*

War, while Commanding the 119th Field Artillery and at times the 57th Artillery Brigade during the Meuse-Argonne offensive. During these operations Colonel McCormick displayed marked judgment and devotion to duty, and by the skillful handling of his command contributed materially to the success of the 57th Artillery Brigade in supporting the 32d and at other times five other divisions.

Newspaper Article, Detroit Free Press, January 1919

State Thanks Valient 32nd

Legislative Resolutions Commend National Guardsmen and Naval Militia

7,000 "Les Terribles" Met 1,200 Casualties

Colonel Bersey Tells Lawmakers Division Was Cited for Bravery Five Times

By H.N. Duff—Staff Correspondent of the Detroit Free Press

Lansing, Michigan, January 2nd—Michigan's National Guard veterans of the Mexican border campaign and more recently the kingpin organization of Pershing's shock troops, Thursday night had cabled to them the thanks and congratulations of the state as represented by her two legislative bodies.

Accompanied by cheers, a resolution embodying the state's recognition of the wonderful fighting ability of "The Terrible One's," as the French dubbed them, went through the joint session of the senate and house this afternoon.

There was no discussion, simply an apparent hate on the part of everybody to perform a duty all recognized.

Adjutant General John S. Bersey, sole staff officer of the guard left in Michigan, put before the assembled legislators some cold facts regarding the record of the Wolverine "bearcats" overseas. His statement being punctured time and again with applause.

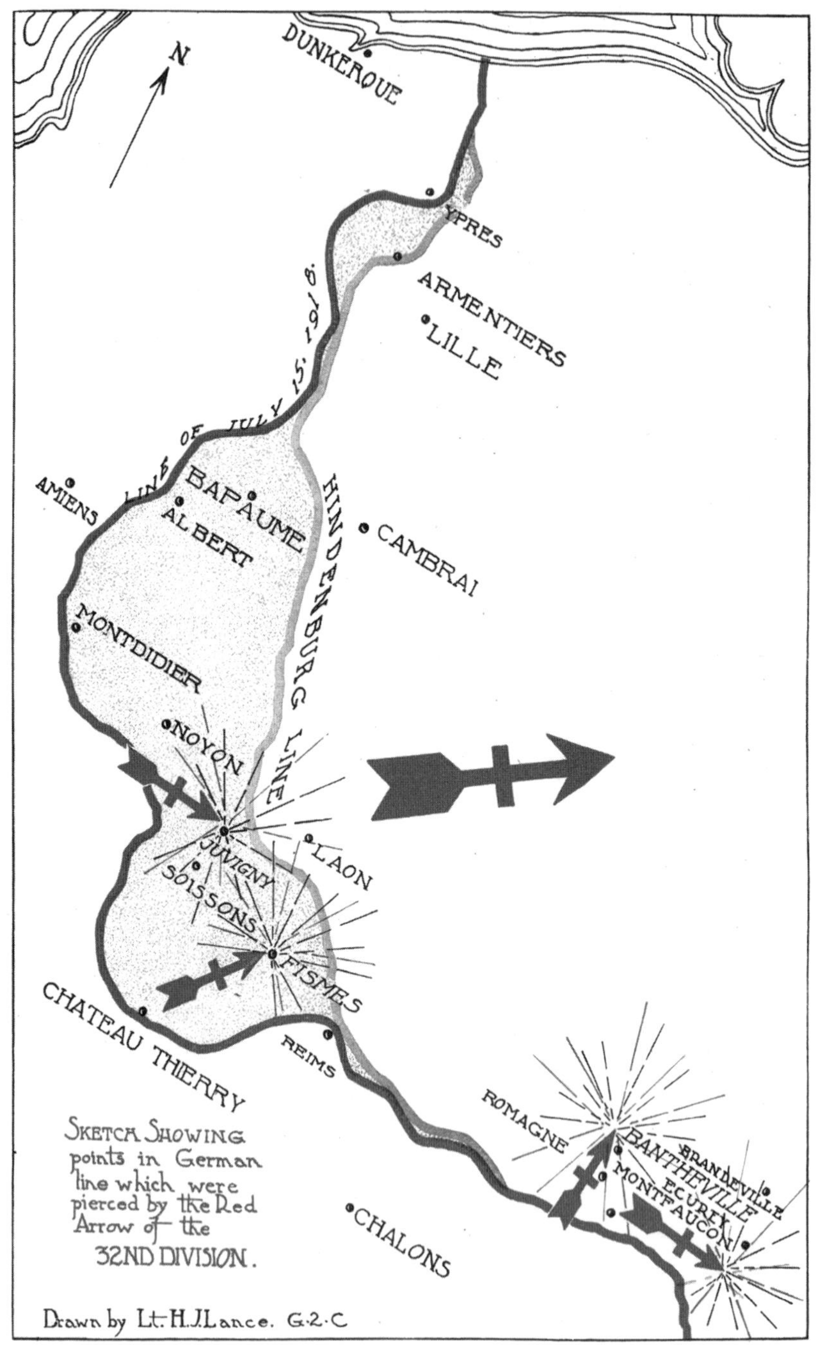

Summary of 32nd Division Campaigns

GOV. SLEEPER PRAISES MEN.

All in all the formal tender of the thanks of the commonwealth formed the feature of the combined session of the two legislative houses called mainly to listen to the inaugural address of Governor Sleeper.

The governor referred repeatedly to the wonderful work of the Michigan National Guard on the other side of the water and introduction of the joint resolution by Senator Forrester, a few moments later made a fitting climax. Frank A. Smith, representative from the Missaukee District, moved the adoption of the resolution.

"Whereas the members of the Michigan National Guard, incorporated in the Thirty-second and Forty-second divisions of the United States Army, have by their deeds of valor brought honor and glory to their native state.

Therefore, be it resolved that the legislature of the state of Michigan, in the joint session assembled, hereby extends to these brave soldiers its hearty congratulations on their splendid achievements, and assure them of its earnest desire to serve them in every possible way.

And, be it further resolved that a copy of this resolution be cabled forthwith to the commanding general of the Thirty-second division named above."

NAVAL MILITIA ALSO THANKED.

Following this came a resolution extending thanks to the former Michigan Naval Militia, scattered as they are to a four winds and due to that fact no cabling will be done them. The naval resolution read:

"Whereas the members of the Michigan Naval Militia have singally distinguished themselves in the great war now happily ended:

Therefore, Be it Resolved, that the legislature of the state of Michigan in joint session assembled, hereby gives expression to its high appreciation of the service thus rendered to the cause of freedom and to its pride and satisfaction in the fact that this great commonwealth has been so worthily represented on the high seas and wherever duty has called these valiant sailor lads."

7,000 OVERSEAS; 1,200 CASUALTIES.

Colonel Bersey's statement of facts regarding the National Guard astounded many. Figures presented showed that up to December 9 approximately 1,200 Michigan National Guardsmen had been on the casualty list. This was from a total enlistment overseas of 7,000.

"Because of the high rating of the Michigan and Wisconsin units in the Thirty-second division, that division was sent overseas first among National Guard divisions, except the Rainbow, which was made up of representatives of all states, including Michigan, and which had the Detroit ambulance company in it. Once landed the Thirty-second was given some preliminary training and then were plunged right into the fighting. The history of the engagements at the Oureq, at Soissons, at St. Mihiel, at Chateau Thierry and even at Metz, cannot be written without praise for the Michigan soldiers.

WOLVERINES CITED FIVE TIMES.

Five times, I understand, they were cited for bravery and heroic conduct in the French orders. The French, who had seen all of the Allied troops, called them the "Terrible Ones," thus giving them practically first place in their estimation. The Germans, captured also wanted to see the wonderful machine gun artillery of the Michigan men, so astounded were they at the rapidity with which Colonel McCormick and his men could make the French firing pieces work."

Colonel Bersey's unofficial compilation up to the official report of December 9 showed this for Michigan National Guardsmen: Killed in action, 226; wounded severely, 508; wounded slightly, 130; wounded, degree undetermined, 105; died of wounds, 87; died of disease, 2; missing, 110; died of accident, 1; total 1169.

Newspaper Articles, Six Part Series, The Detroit News, February, March 1919

119th Waits on Tiptoes, Home or Germany Order

Even Some of Wagons Loaded at Grayling, in 1914, Left; Artillery Regiment's Michigan-Given Standard Still Flies.

(No. 1 of 6) Monday, February 24, 1919

This is the first of a series of six articles dealing with the One Hundred and Nineteenth Field Artillery, largely Detroit and other Michigan men, from the old First Michigan Field Artillery (National Guard), now in the Fifty-seventh Brigade as part of the Eighty-eighth Division. Formerly the regiment was in the Thirty-second Division.)

By L.L. Stevenson (Special Correspondent, *The Detroit News*)

Mauvages, France (By Mail.)—They are painting the camouflage off the guns. The escort wagons, the same wagons that took food across No Man's Land, are being made spick and span. New animals are being issued. A minstrel show, with Lieut. Peckham as director and Chaplain Atkinson in general charge, is being rehearsed. The Y.M.C.A. hut is being doubled in size to accommodate the men.

The 119th is resting. It is time. They have reached the time of which Kipling wrote when he mentioned the last picture. The 119th was in the line from June 11 to November 2. The men therein have been gassed, bombed, shot at. They know the song of shrapnel. They can imitate vividly the sound of the avions of the enemy. They have seen sights that add years in the passing of seconds. Their eyes have beheld the great mystery.

SOME OF THEIR WORK.

Across France they have marched. They have climbed from the caissons and wagons and lugged their packs in the great loop from west to east, on up north and back again almost to the starting point, that the exhausted animals might rest a bit. In the darkness of the night they have supported the bodies of these animals with their own, that they might not fall, for should their horses fall, they would not be able to rise.

Twenty-four hours in the saddle, 36 hours in the saddle; the 119th knows what this means. The 119th knows also the haste of getting to the front, of lining up in position while the enemy was doing his best to blow the members into eternity. Yes, and more—much more, the telling of which must be left to the men who experienced it, for they are the only ones by whom it can ever be told, if it is possible for them to give the picture. It is too recent now for detail.

Perhaps, if this regiment swings up the streets of Detroit, perhaps if it parades in the capital of Michigan, the warmth of the welcome may melt this reserve, may relieve the feeling of unreality and bring words where there is now only silence. And the men of the 119th are dreaming of this time.

PICTURES OF HOME.

Here in this little town of Mauvages, with its two streets, its mud, its fraternizing animals and fowls, its pleasant population who regard the Americans with entire friendliness and its souvenirs—wrecked buildings, mostly—of night visits with Jerry—they reconstruct pictures of Detroit and Lansing. Yes, and more.

The 119th no longer is an all-Michigan organization. Changes have been wrought in the personnel of the officers and men, just as changes have been wrought in the material. The 57th Field Artillery Brigade, of which the 119th Field Artillery is a part, never gave up a yard of ground. The price was lives. Now, in the 119th there are officers and men from 40 different states. Yet the old skeleton is there; the standard of the regiment was presented by the state of Michigan and the feelings towards their home state of those who are left have not changed in the slightest.

Those guns, which I mentioned at first, are like the regiment. They are not the ones which the regiment used in training. They have never seen the state of Michigan. They are the second set. The others were worn out in action.

LOADED AT GRAYLING, IN 1917.

So it is with the wagons. Some of them were loaded on flat cars up at Grayling, September 24, 1917. But these are few. Down underneath the olive drab paint of others is a coating of gray. They were taken from the enemy and used against him. Wood from German ammunition cases keeps the regiment warm now.

But this is in the past. Thoughts at present turn to the future. The 57th Field Artillery Brigade—and by the way, the assistant adjutant is Lieutenant Stanaford, Detroit—is a part of the 88th Division now. Officers and men are wondering if they will be reassigned to the 32nd Division and sent on to Germany or sent home with the 88th. Home or Germany, that is the question.

It enters into the daily life here in Mauvages. Life here is not strenuous—it is merely busy. There is much to be done—things that could not be attended to back in the States. Nobody loafs, but the old, fierce strain of the days from June 11 to November 2, is ended. Consequently, there is more time for routine.

BAND PLAYING AGAIN.

Take the band, for example, the band of which Edward W. Thomas, Detroit, is the leader and Kenneth (Chick) Miller, also of Detroit, is drum major. For four months, the musicians of this organization, many of whom used to play in Detroit Theaters, carried stretchers over No Man's Land, brought in the wounded, gave first aid, yes, and listened to the last requests of men whom they used to see in the seats of these same playhouses.

That is ended now and the band is producing real music. French trumpets have been introduced and other changes made. Each morning at reveille, these men who had played in Alsace, who traveled with their regiment along the many fronts, who were gassed in the Argonne and bombed along the Meuse, play up and down the two streets of the village.

And always, their section is, "The 32nd Division March." It seemed like the old days down in Texas, the days when the hearts of these men were toward the East with a great longing. The biggest excitement now is the arrival of the mail.

And letters with a Michigan postmark receive the quickest, most earnest and most undivided attention of about 700 officers and men.

Pages of Liberty Volume Illustrated by the 119th

(No. 2 of 6) Tuesday, February 25, 1919

This is the second of a series of six articles dealing with the One Hundred and Nineteenth Field Artillery, largely Detroit and other Michigan men, from the old First Michigan Field Artillery (National Guard), now in the Fifty-seventh Brigade as part of the Eighty-eighth Division. (Formerly the regiment was in the Thirty-second Division.)

By L.L. Stevenson (Special Correspondent, *The Detroit News*)

Mauvages, France (By Mail.)—There were three candles burning in the room in which this epic was told me. A flickering light was thrown on a table shown with maps. Two of the candles were dusty bottles and one was in a jam tin, a small German shell being the base. Otherwise, there was little to suggest war, save occasional heavy explosions from a nearby ammunition dump.

The room was the abode of Colonel Chester B. McCormick, commanding the 119th Field Artillery. It was the best room of an old French home, comfortable and almost painfully clean. A big wall clock made so long ago the date was no longer decipherable, gave additional homelike atmosphere. But as the story told by the little group of officers unfolded itself, the walls drew together and dripped dampness; out where the geese disputed over a puddle was a scene of carnage and in the air was threat.

And just as the maps were spread out for the opening of the Odyssey of the 119th Field Artillery, an extra heavy explosion shook the house and almost ripped loose the muslin covering that was substituting for a window pane, glass being scarce.

"They are detonating Boche ammunition," said the colonel, "that fire which makes this place comfortable is kept up with Boche ammunition cases."

NO HORSES; FIGHTING STOPS.

Quite commonplace after all, but it was the one tough needed to add vividness to the striking tale, a story told not for record, but merely a discussion to show the visitor that which had been happening to his friends. For the officers present, the maps were unnecessary. The irregular loop, showing the travels of the 119th from June 11 to November 2, 1918, was burned into their minds. They had lived it. Those not present had died it.

The story has to do with fighting that lasted to within nine days of the armistice and would have continued until 11 a.m., November 11, even though the regiment had virtually no rest, save for the fact that so many animals were lost that the regiment was no longer mobile and had to stay put until it was pulled out by motor trucks.

TWO WEEKS' FIRE BAPTISM.

The 119th Field Artillery, which was and is a part of the 57th Field Artillery Brigade, belched forth its first messages to the foe the night of June 11, up in the Toul sector. The 119th was all Michigan then and more than half the officers and men were from Detroit, the rest being mainly from Lansing and nearby Michigan cities, with a few men from other states. The 119th then was attached to the 26th Division.

Its baptism of fire lasted two weeks, the bombardment being constant day and night, souvenir being returned for souvenir. Then the regiment was sent into Alsace, to join the 32d Division, composed of Michigan and Wisconsin National Guard troops, under Major-General William G. Haan, which was ready to begin writing its part of world history.

Rejoining the 32d was like meeting home-folk, as the 119th was born just after this division was formed, in Waco, Texas.

CHEERED AND KISSED.

Just after the reunion, things began to happen around Chateau-Thierry and all the world now knows what those events portended. So the division climbed into those cars which have become the foundation of about half the jokes in France, those boxes labeled, "8 Chevaux—40 Hommes." The destination was the Soisson front and the route was via Paris. Going through that city, the division was given a Paris welcome, American soldiers being comparatively novel then.

Between the cheers of Paris, the flags, the greetings and kisses and Chateau-Thierry, there was only brief interval. The division detrained at Rivecourt and made a night march of 17 miles to Pont St. Maxine, where it bivouacked a day. Then came the order to reinforce the Allies at Chateau-Thierry, 112 miles away.

TO FRONT IN TRUCKS.

To the great counterattack, the infantry of the 32d Division went in motor trucks. There were 1,200 of these vehicles and they made a mighty train stretching as far as the eye could see, the freight Michigan and Wisconsin boys, tight-lipped and grim—men who were just ordinary boys back home, but who were to write their names in the History of Human Liberty—heroes.

The artillery traveled overland also, but not in motor trucks. Horseback and afoot, these men went across France day and night until their objective was reached. Shorn of detail and the personal touches and giving only a bare record of achievement, here is what that meant:

To Vaumoise, 45 kilometers (36 miles): to Coulomos, 25 kilometers (28 miles) and so on until Chateau-Thierry was reached, the last march being 28 kilometers (22.4 miles).

Nor was that the end. To reach the battery positions, north of Lacharmel, 30 more kilometers (24 miles) had to be covered. The end of that journey had been reached. The artillery was with the 32d Division up in the front line.

It was just in time for that great drive of 20 kilometers, resulting in the capture of Fismes. After that feat, the 32d, the line being stabilized, was withdrawn for a rest, being relieved by the 28th Division. The artillery, including the 119th, stayed right where it was, because it was needed.

The enemy made a stand and the attempt to force the Vesle failed, but the 28th, with its artillery support, captured Fismette, on the north bank of the Vesle. Colonel McCormick was acting chief of light artillery during the capture of Fismes and Fismette.

WITHDRAWN AUGUST 24.

After about a week with the 28th Division, the 119th took a merited rest on the left of the 77th Division and, August 24, was withdrawn, as General Mangin had selected the 32d Division as being one of the best American shock divisions to put on an attack with the French north of Soisson, for the relief of the line along the Vesle. The artillery was then rushed to the vicinity of Juvigny and was again marched overland, covering 30 kilometers at night.

Near Larcharmel, the artillery made a night march of 45 kilometers and bivouacked in a French forest at Faverolles. This was a great natural cathedral, as carefully kept as a parlor, even after four years of war, with trees fully 60 feet high and all regular and symmetrical. There it was as if there was no war—only peace and a sweetness and cleanness of nature, grateful to the war worn men. But this was only for a night.

TO THE FRONT AGAIN.

The next day, the artillery brigade started forth again. The march was to have been 25 kilometers, but from the front came the cry, "Artillery, more artillery!" It was a plea not to be denied. The 25 kilometers stretched into 50 and for 26 hours officers and men were in the saddle, so great was the congestion of the roads, everything traveling toward the front. And the Supply Train, caught in the congestion, was on the way 36 hours. This was August 27, a date which will live in the minds of Michigan men as long as they breathe. The echelon was established at Vingre.

The animals suffered with the men. Their work had been virtually continuous, supplying ammunition on the east front and going forward in the drive. The horses and mules came into Vingre leaning against one another and some of them supported by men who were supposed to ride them.

And the next day, the artillery took its position with the 32d Division in the vicinity of Juvigny.

How War Urge Took 119th, in Rest Billets, to France

The Detroit News, Wednesday, February 26, 1919. (No. 3 of 6)

This is the third of a series of six articles dealing with the 119th Field Artillery, largely Detroit and other Michigan men from the old First Michigan Field Artillery (National Guard), now in the 57th Brigade as part of the 88th Division. Formerly the regiment was in the 32d Division.

By L.L. Stevenson (Special Correspondent, *The Detroit News*)

Mauvages, France (By Mail.)—There is much joking and laughter among the officers and men in the 119th Field Artillery as they go about their daily life here. Greetings, in French, are exchanged between the soldiers and civilians and it is significant that, even now, virtually the only young men in the village are in olive drab. The black dresses among the women show the reason: "C'est la guerre."

Letters from up in Germany, from the infantry of the 32d Division, show the same spirit. As these Michigan men, both here and in Germany go about the never-ending tasks of military life, the thought is uppermost in their minds—the war is over, going home time may come in May. And the belief is universal that the homecoming will be worth the price paid.

If the regiment again is brigaded with the 32d Division, the men will be in Michigan by June.

This series of letters has to do all with the 119th Field Artillery because that was the organization which I encountered here in France. There is no attempt to ignore the infantry. The deeds of our feet soldiers speak for themselves. The name given them by the French, "the workmen of victory," is true. As Lieutenant Garvey, Detroit, himself an artillery officer, put it: "You have to hand it to the infantry."

JOAN'S NATIVE TOWN.

But only artillery officers were present in Mauvages this evening. True, on the 100-kilometer drive from Montigny, where I am stationed at present, up to Mauvages, I encountered Detroit men, and even passed the camp of the 330th Field Artillery, which is composed almost entirely of Detroit and Michigan men, though I didn't know it was in the neighborhood. But there was no chance to stop to visit.

A leave of 24 hours and an 80-mile drive over roads, many of them cut clearly by war traffic do not permit delays. And having been present at the birth of the 119th and being especially interested in the fragments of the old 31st Michigan Infantry therein, I wanted as much time as possible at Mauvages.

There was just one stop on the way—in a little village of Domremy, where Joan of Arc was born, baptized and had those visions which set her out on a mission that made her immortal in France, if not the world. Joan's church, a quaint box like structure, is still standing and her baptismal fount is preserved with great care.

THAT BELLE ISLE BRIDGE.

There a soldier asked me if a new bridge had been built to Belle Isle yet: He was John A. Graves, Detroit, and was convalescing from gas at Rimaucourt and was in Domremy on leave. He had fallen in Argonne.

In a previous letter I told of the 119th Field Artillery reaching the 32d Division in the vicinity of Juvigny. The signal to attack was being waited and August 27 it came and the fight, which lasted until September 1 and resulted in the capture of Juvigny and Tenry-Sorny, began. This attack, which was on the flank, was driven almost straight east. But the division paid the price, particularly on its own left flank.

When the 32d Division was relieved by a Moroccan division, the artillery again remained in the line and, with those wonderful fighters Laffeux was captured. The artillery then was pulled out, taken to Joinville and promised a much needed rest.

But the breathing space was short. At 3 a.m., September 3, the 119th was ordered to be ready to move at daylight. In the wan hours of the dawn the Aisne was crossed at Vic Sur Aisne and, after a march of 40 kilometers (nearly 25 miles), the regiment bivouacked at Mortmont. Early the next day there was a march of 25 kilometers (15 ½ miles), to Villers-Cotterets and there the regiment entrained for Joinville again, thus finishing a march of 402 kilometers (about 250 miles).

"PIECE OF GOOD LUCK."

It was more than mere walking and riding. Mile after mile was tramped in the night and the blacker the night, though it meant more difficult traveling, the better were these Detroit men satisfied. Continually the enemy would fly over with a load of death which he would dump on anything that moved.

This harassing was almost continual, particularly at Lacharmel, and on the Soissons front. There the avions endeavored to machine gun the battalions and would have succeeded had it not been that there was an anti-aircraft battery nearby.

"A piece of good luck," said Colonel McCormick, dismissing the incident.

The heavy detonations continued. The old stone building rocked.

A soldier walked along the street with a child holding fast to each hand. The fighting was over. The 119th was resting at Mauvages. But the candles were renewed. More was to be told. There was to be no rest at Joinville. The Argonne and the Meuse were to come.

Somber and Gay Mingle in 119th's War Picture

The Detroit News, Thursday, February 27, 1919 (No. 4 of 6)

This is the fourth of a series of six articles dealing with the 119th Field Artillery, largely Detroit and other Michigan men from the old First Michigan Field Artillery (National Guard), now in the 57th Brigade as part of the 88th Division. Formerly the regiment was in the Thirty-second Division.

By L.L. Stevenson (Special Correspondent, *The Detroit News*)

Mauvages, France (By Mail.)—"Our men had hardly scattered to the billets at Joinville before there was a cry for more artillery," said Chaplain Atkinson, adjusting the candles so that the map could be read more readily.

Following this appeal for artillery were seven days and seven nights of marching. Then the 119th went into position in No Man's Land, at Aisnes. For four years war had rolled over this part of France. For five kilometers (3 miles) there was naught but devastation. The terrain looked as though it had been wrought by devils. And in digging the positions grim reminders of the cost of war were exposed.

At this point, Lieutenant Picard, Detroit, interrupted to tell a story, one of those grim stories of the front. It seemed that a company of Negroes were working under shell fire repairing roads. They were green and nervous and, when a shell would burst nearby, there would be a panic. Finally, the work being delayed, the captain called them together.

SPEAKING OF RUNNING.

"See here, men, he said. "I've been through this thing a long time and I know when there is danger. Now I don't want any of you men to run until I do. But when you see me run, you boys dig your toes in."

Just then a shell struck so close the rush of air could be felt and an ashen-faced negro leaped to the captain's side.

"Boss," he said, his teeth chattering, "would I be disobeying orders if I done passed you when you run?"

"I can't describe the appearance of the field at Aisnes," said Colonel McCormick. "The earth was ruined. It was as though a giant had burrowed 20 feet below the surface and then raised himself. As far as you could see it was this way. With it was all kinds of debris, rusty wire, broken guns and other waste. What had been villages were now irregular heaps of mortar, brick and stone. Forests were now only blackened splintered stubs."

HORROR BEYOND WORDS.

It was at this point that the 119th was attached to the 79th Division. Mt. Faucon, which had been the observation post of the German Crown Prince in the battle of Verdun, was the objective. To reach it the vast waste had to be crossed. The infantry got over all right, but it was necessary for the Engineers to build roadways for the artillery. The making of these roads revealed a horror tale that cannot be told.

The 119th waited in the saddle while these roads were being built. For 36 hours they endured this wait, a heavy, soaking, persistent rain falling continually. Meanwhile, the infantry was suffering severely from the enemy's artillery. At last there was an aisleway through the wire and debris and the artillery went over, taking a position about a half mile south of Mt. Faucon.

After Mt. Faucon, Nautillois and Cunel were taken, the 79th was withdrawn and the 3d substituted. The stubborn resistance made by the enemy caused heavy losses and the 119th suffered with the infantry. It was at Nautillois that Major Edward W. Thompson, of South Haven, was killed.

YANK METTLE TESTED.

The 32d Division entered the sector on the left, after the capture of the Cunel Wood and the 119th, with the rest of the artillery brigade, was recalled and placed in support of the Michigan-Wisconsin division. Then ensued a test.

The enemy had fallen back to a prepared position, the Kriemhilde-Strellung line, and there waited the smash, confident that the Yanks were stopped. But they only paused seemingly to put more force into a series of smashing blows. When the enemy recovered from his surprise, he found that the Michigan-Wisconsin infantry and artillery had pushed him out of his concrete and wire, had taken the heights of Coute Dame Marie and had captured Cierges, Gaenes, Romanges and Bautheville.

Then the 32d was relieved by the 89th, the 119th and the other artillery remaining in, however, and preparations were made for the final drive of November 1, when the Americans pushed forward, crossed the Meuse and the enemy was convinced that he had met his master, his defense having been smashed.

1,300 HORSES, 300 LEFT.

The 89th Division went on its way, but the 57th Field Artillery Brigade did not. It couldn't; it was unhorsed. The night of the armistice found the 119th quietly camped in echelon west of Mt. Faucon, preparatory to moving to the rear for rest and re-equipping. Out of more than 1,300 horses, less than 300 remained.

More than 300 had been killed in action. The others had died of exhaustion, due to lack of nutrition, because in bringing up supplies men came first, and from grazing in the gassed areas. Virtually all the animals were gassed, as well as the men. So the regiment was pulled down to Mauvages, 62 miles, by motors, and here it remains.

Counting the 32d as a new division each time it was attached to it, the 119th has been with 19 different divisions, 11 of them combat. It has worn out two sets of guns; it has marched all over Northern France. It has had its share of glory—yes, and its share of dead.

CANDLES BURN LOW.

Night now had come; the candles were burned low. The officers lighted cigarettes, the recital was over.

I have given but the outline, yet it suggests that which our men have done. They don't go into detail and decline to make it individual.

They are like workmen who, having done a job, are satisfied with the achievement and are willing to let others do the judging.

Came a few seconds of silence, broken by a bugle announcing that supper was ready.

The war is over; the bugle has come back; all that remains is the home-going.

119th's Holy Pig Absent, if Unit Parades Detroit

The Detroit News, Friday, February 28, 1919 (No. 5 of 6)

This is the fifth of a series of six articles dealing with the 119th Field Artillery, largely Detroit and other Michigan men from the old First Michigan Field Artillery (National Guard), now in the Fifty-seventh Brigade as part of the 88th Division. Formerly the regiment was in the 32d Division. Colonel Chester B. McCormick, Lansing, is the commander.

By L.L. Stevenson (Special Correspondent, *The Detroit News*)

Mauvages, France (By Mail.)—The "Holy Pig" was around begging. He had been fed by every cook in the regiment, but was not satisfied. The Holy Pig is prosperous looking and is quite happy, but his future is not bright. [Insert photo of Colonel Chester B. McCormick.]

If the 119th Field Artillery received orders to go home, the Holy Pig will be served at a banquet. If the order reads to travel to Germany and join the Army of occupation, then the Holy Pig will be eaten because that will be the easiest way to transport him. So, either way, things look bad for the Holy Pig.

PROWLER, BUT ADOPTED.

The Holy Pig was found prowling around among bombs, shells, machine gun bullets and other things neither good for men nor pig, near Mr. Faucon, and attached himself to the supply company, which was a brilliant stroke, as a supply company feeds the regiment. In the midst of all the bother of getting good through shell swept roads, someone found time to put the Holy Pig into an escort wagon and he has been with the company ever since.

The Holy Pig's appetite brought him his name. At first, he was just "the pig." But one night he ate a blanket roll and, as Tom Raymond's Bible was in the roll and was never found afterward, the pig became the Holy Pig. But even with that name, he is not a good risk, because he is due, whether it is Home or Germany.

READY FOR ANY ORDER.

And Home or Germany is the question uppermost in the minds of the men. Not that the 119th wants to quit. If there is work to be done, the 119th is ready to go on. Should the order be Germany, there won't be any complaint.

Nevertheless, in the long hours of peace, while the hot excitement of battle is lacking, there is a wonderment as to what the order really will be. If Colonel McCormick has been given any intimation in advance of what the 119th will do, his men do not know it, naturally, but at least they can speculate—and dream of Michigan.

With this speculation, with this dreaming, is a visualization of the actual homecoming. Based on orders published from time to time, there is a belief that the demobilization will be at Battle Creek, rather than Waco, Texas, where the men were trained. Grayling is considered to be entirely out of the question, though this was the mobilization point of the Michigan brigade.

If the demobilization was at Battle Creek, the train service would be such that the 119th could be transported either to Detroit or to Lansing without difficulty and this would make possible a parade in either or both cities, preferably both. I can say without hesitation that orders for such a march would bring no protest.

BOTH CITIES SUGGESTED.

Speaking as one who accompanied the 31st Michigan Infantry from Detroit to Grayling and from Grayling to Waco, and basing my argument on the ground that at the start, the 119th was built from not only the 31st, but also from the Detroit squadron of cavalry and the South Haven troop, and the Lansing artillery battalion. I believe that place should be made for a welcome for the 119th, both in Detroit and in Lansing and, if possible, the regiment should be reviewed in both cities.

The troops that compose the 119th left Detroit and Lansing without extensive goodbye. Colonel McCormick's home is Lansing. The movement was veiled in as much secrecy as possible. Instead of parading to the stations, as did the selected men, these National Guardsmen were sneaked out of town. Those who informed those nearest and dearest to them that they were about to depart did so against orders.

Now that these men have gone forth and have made good, fighting as I have said, from June 11 to November 2, there is a chance for Detroit and Lansing to make some payment. There will be gaps in the ranks and the cheers will be mingled with tears, because many a brave boy who left his home won't be there for the march of triumph, but it will be worthwhile and will be appreciated by a lot of young fellows who went out as boys, but are men now regardless of their years.

NOT TOO EARLY FOR PLANS.

Nor is it too early to make such plans. The welcome to these former National Guardsmen should be worked out with as much detail as was that memorable national G.A.R. [Grand Army of the Republic from the Civil War] encampment in Detroit. It should be a haphazard thing by no means. No matter how far the headquarters cities of this regiment go, they cannot go too far. The day the regiment arrives in its home state should be a memorial. It has been paid for in bravery and blood.

I wish I could be eloquent in this plea. I know how it would appreciated. I know that there is something of this in the minds of the men of the regiment, though they do not speak of it. Nor are they asking such. They say that just to be back in the old home town—if they are needed here no longer—would be payment enough. But would it?

At any rate, during one of the rehearsals of the minstrel show, one of them remarked:

"I wonder how this would go back in Detroit?" And I wonder with him.

But the Holy Pig won't be there, no matter what happens.

Path of Duty to Death Trod by 119th's Major

The Detroit News, Saturday, March 1, 1919 (No. 6 of 6)

This is the sixth and last article of a series dealing with the 119th Field Artillery, largely Detroit and other Michigan men from the old First Michigan Field Artillery (National Guard), now in the Fifty-seventh Brigade as part of the 88th Division. Formerly the regiment was in the 32d Division. Colonel Chester B. McCormick, Lansing, is the commander.

By L.L. Stevenson (Special Correspondent, *The Detroit News*)

Mauvages, France (By Mail.)—Twice Major Edward W. Thompson, South Haven, Michigan, passed through a shell-swept area on September 29. He had been in the line from June 11 and knew what those two journeys meant—and perhaps even some prescience of that which was to happen—but he was a soldier and his duty took him over the road that was under direct observation of the enemy, and registered with nicety.

I say some forewarning may have come to him. It is a matter of record that such knowledge was vouch safed him when he was in Texas last winter. That letter to his mother, written just after the major had attended church service, is proof.

It seemed as though it were so written that Major Thompson was to die on that day. But the enemy had to expend two shells to take his life.

RECOMMENDED FOR MEDAL.

A recommendation for a Distinguished Service Medal for Major Thompson has been made by Colonel Chester B. McCormick, and with it, recommendations for similar medals for Captain Corwin J. Schneider, Lansing, and Sergeants O'Brien, Rowe and Lamson, and

Corporal Herriman, all of Detroit and Lansing. The official records of the 119th Field Artillery give the reason.

Major Thompson's battalion had been designated to report to the colonel of one of the different elements of infantry supporting the artillery. This was after the capture of Mt. Faucon and—to quote from the record—"on account of the furious enemy bombardment of our own infantry, the leading elements had become somewhat demoralized."

Disregarding his own danger, Major Thompson went among the infantrymen and succeeded in quieting the personnel and starting them on the way. He escaped that time without a scratch. It was 10 a.m.; his hour had not struck. This work concluded, the major sought the colonel of the relief to report.

DEATH WHINES IN AIR.

The sun was shining that day, but air was full of shrieking, whining things and occasionally the earth would heave upward and spray the landscape. Here and there were men who would never return home. With his adjutant, Captain Schneider, Major Thompson continued his search. At last they came to:

"An area which was under direct observation of the enemy and was shell-swept constantly. A fragment struck Major Thompson in the arm. Captain Schneider applied a tourniquet and started to the rear."

But the sand had not run from the glass of Major Thompson's life yet, though nearly so. It was not until half the journey to safety had been completed, before the end came. Then an enemy shell burst nearby and a piece struck the major in the back, a mortal wound.

Then the enemy seemed to concentrate his fire on this one particular spot as though he were determined that the officer having escaped once, was to die where he fell. But the enemy reckoned not of the courage of Michigan soldiers. With the assistance of Sergeants O'Brien, Rowe and Lamson and Corporal Herriman, the dying officer was rescued and taken to a dressing station. Major Thompson died the next day.

The battle continued, but—and this may comfort the many who knew Major Thompson back in Michigan—he received the burial to which he was entitled. The flag for which he had died was wrapped about him and his body was placed in a coffin constructed by men who had served under him.

And, though the shells were bursting around about, the burial was with the rites of religion. Chaplain William A. Atkinson was in a hospital wounded, but a priest was obtained from the 77th Division and, though the major was not of his faith, with an accompaniment of shells instead of the notes of an organ, he prayed for the rest of the soul of a gallant and brave officer who met death in the line of duty.

Major Thompson sleeps on a hill west of Mt. Faucon. His grave is marked with his name, and his rank and daily [illegible] French, who have returned to their homes, attend to this grave as they do to those of the other Americans.

Letter of Commendation to the 32nd Division from General John J. Pershing, Commander-in-Chief, American Expeditionary Forces

HEADQUARTERS THIRTY-SECOND DIVISION
AMERICAN EXPEDITIONARY FORCES,
Rengsdorf, Germany

GENERAL ORDERS
28 March, 1919, NO. 23.

1. It is with sincere pleasure that the Division Commander publishes to the command the following letter from the Commander-in-Chief:

AMERICAN EXPEDITIONARY FORCES
Office of the Commander-in-Chief
France, March 24, 1919

Major General William Lassiter, Commanding, 32d Division, American E. F.

My dear General Lassiter:

Please extend to the officers and men of the 32d Division my sincere compliments upon their appearance and upon the splendid condition of the artillery and transportation at the review and inspection on March 15th. In fact, the condition of your command was what would be expected of a division with such a splendid fighting record.

After training for several months following its arrival in February, 1918, it entered the line in Alsace and held this sector until the time of the Aisne-Marne offensive, when it moved to that active front. On July 30th, it entered the line on the Ourcq, and in the course of its action captured Cierges, Bellevue Farm and the Bois de la Planchette. The attack was resumed on August 1st; the division captured Fismes and pushed ahead until it crossed the Vesle. On August 28th it again entered the line and launched attacks which resulted in the capture of Juvigny at the cost of severe casualties. During the Meuse-Argonne offensive the 32d Division entered the line on September 30th and by its persistence in that sector it penetrated the Kreimhilde Stellung, taking Romagne and following the enemy to the northeastern edge of the Bois de Bantheville. On November 8th, the division took up the pursuit of the enemy east of the Meuse until the time when hostilities were suspended.

Since the signing of the Armistice the 32d Division has had the honor to act as part of the Army of Occupation. For the way in which all ranks have performed their duties in this capacity, I have only the warmest praise and approval. The pride of your officers and men, justified by such a record, will insure the same high morale which has been present in the division during its stay in France. I want each man to know my appreciation of the work he has done and of the admiration in which he is held by the rest of his comrades in the American Expeditionary Forces.

Sincerely yours,
JOHN J. PERSHING.

2. This order will be read to the troops at the first formation following its receipt and will be posted upon bulletin boards.

WM. LASSITER
Major General, Commanding.

Colonel McCormick's Summary of Operations

Throughout the war COL Chester McCormick commanded the 119th FA Regiment. He wrote two detailed summaries of the unit's actions. The first was written in April 1919, on board the U.S.S. Frederick, during the unit's return journey across the Atlantic Ocean. It is included here as it focuses on the unit's combat operations. The second summary was part of the Lansing State Journal's 1920 publication, *Honor Roll and Complete War History of Ingham County in the Great World War*. This summary was very similar but had some slight changes and additional details including a description of the mobilization and training period in the U.S.

HEADQUARTERS 119TH FIELD ARTILLERY
On Board U.S.S. Frederick
At Sea, 27 April, 1919

To The Officers and Men of The 119th F. A.

As a tribute to the gallant performance of the 119th Field Artillery, it is with pleasure I review briefly the exploits of its battle activities in recent military operations on the western front which terminated with the signing of the armistice November 11, 1918.

Submitting conscientiously to the routine training in the United States, you were rushed to France in February, 1918, with the first few hundred thousand-arriving with the fifth American division. Here again the command eagerly and rapidly mastered the technique in modern field artillery of the French school at Camp Coetquidan, which was completed late in May. Early in June sent in to the Toul Sector for preliminary training in support of the 26th Division. On June 11th our batteries sent forth their first ultimatum to the enemy. We suffered our first casualties in this sector. I consider the command was extremely fortunate in having as its tutor the more experienced elements of the 26th Division.

Although the regiment at this time was operating with only 60% of its authorized strength, due to its rapid transformation from horsed to motor artillery and vice versa, in which it lost heavily by transfer practically all its personnel familiar with horseflesh, the situation was met with patience and determination.

Moving to the Alsace sector, the regiment again joined the 32nd Division and after further experience in stabilized warfare, with slight casualties, your roll of the field of battle was incomparable with that which followed.

The latter part of July, you rushed into the Second Battle of the Marne referred to as the Marne-Aisne Offensive. You were suddenly confronted with one of the most severe tests of your career. With new animals and inexperienced drivers, you were forced to march for five days to the vicinity of Chateau Thierry. On account of the shortage of artillery harness, the regiment was compelled to drag 16 American caissons loaded with ammunition this entire distance. To save the animals, everyone except drivers were compelled to walk and carry full pack for which you had no previous training.

Entering the lines July 30th in support of the 32nd Division, by rapid advances August 2d and 3rd the Division forced the enemy from the Ourcq to the Vesle. This was the first rigorous and reliable test of the ability of the regiment in open warfare and it was a matter of pride to me in which each organization acquitted itself so creditably in arriving promptly with the first elements of the infantry and assisting in effecting the capture of Fismes. The 32nd Division was relieved on the 6th and you were left in support of the 28th Division and by the dogged support of your guns, promptly assisted their infantry in the capture of Chateau de Auble and crossing the Vesle and capturing Fismettes. Here the gallant and courageous conduct of your gun crews which time and again were totally wiped out and the guns destroyed by enemy and shell fire, demonstrated that the rigid discipline and details of your early training had not been without avail, the test came and you met it without faltering. Relieved from duty with the 28th Division on the 12th, you were placed in support of the 77th Division where after 10 days constant strenuous service, under many trying conditions, you were relieved.

Joining the 32nd Division which was personally selected by General Mangin to assist the French in a flank attack north of Soissons which, if successful, would relieve the line along the Vesle and gain the Aisne. Consequently, on the 24th of August, the regiment moved out and after four days of hard forced marches, covered approximately 140 kilometers, on the 28th were again in support of the 32nd Division west of Juvigny fighting dead east and suffering flank fire from the north. Here, after bitter and determined fighting, in which the division withstood several powerful counterattacks by some of the best enemy division, sent to "Hold the lines at all costs" you enabled our gallant to capture Juvigny and reach Torny-Sorny. The brilliant support which our artillery brigade gave to the infantry enabled them to gain the heights of the plateau overlooking the Aisne. The 32nd was relieved on September 1st by the 1st Morroccoan Division where the same determined spirit of the officers and enlisted men prevailed much to the admiration of the French Artillery Commander of the sector. I consider the selection and occupation of position in and about Juvigny on the night of September 2nd, one of the most noteworthy features of our career as without any daylight reconnaissance, the battalions moved out into an unknown country after dark and were in position serving their guns near the village of Juvigny before daylight. On September 6th, the regiment was relieved for the Joinville area for the rest and reequipping. However, in our brief stay of five days, little was accomplished in this particular.

Beginning September 16th, there followed seven nights of exhausting forced marches in mud and rain entering the Meuse-Argonne offensive. Not only was this a severe test upon the morale of our organization, but the many hard marches began to tell upon the animals that at this time were weak and exhausted. On the night of the 24th, the regiment entered the lines in support of the 79th Division. On the morning of the 26th, after a tremendous artillery preparation, the infantry went over the top on the same ground where a half a million perished on either side in the operations about Verdun in 1916. After many hours delay in the preparation of roads across "No Man's Land" you succeeded in reaching positions near Montfaucon being the first of the divisional artillery over. After the capture of Montfaucon and Nantillois, both battalions were detailed as supporting artillery under direct command of the infantry colonels. Here the batteries suffered one of the most trying ordeals of their experience in the war. Occupying what were impossible positions in the face of terrible destructive fire of the enemy with its toll death, you, without flinching, again demonstrated as on the Marne, that indomitable dogged spirit of true artillery and stuck to your guns. The 3rd Division relieved the 79th Division on the 4th. Relieved from assignment with 3rd, the regiment moved to the sector on the left and were again in support of the 32nd Division. Then followed the breaking thru of the Kriemhilde Stellung capturing Gesnes, Cote Dame Marie, Romagne, and Bantheville. November 1st found you in support of the 89th Division with the front lines along the north edge of Bois de Bantheville, at which time was launched one of the best organized and most preponderous artillery attacks yet delivered on the western front, covering a front of 25 kilometers, in which your guns assisted in smashing the bone of his resistance, cutting his communications into Belgium and climaxing in his submission to the terms of the armistice 11 November, 1918.

Here after five months continuous fighting in which your assisted in smashing the way for eleven infantry division in combat in recovering a total of 70 kilometers of French territory, you were not only tired and worn mentally from exposure and exhaustion, but were rendered immobile from the loss of horses. For out of a total of 1459 animals received during the summer, only 327 remained, 1057 had been lost from all causes of which 645 were either killed or wounded in action. The entire brigade was sent to the rear areas for rest, recuperation and re-equipping.

You may well feel proud of the distinguished service you have rendered. The record of the regiment stands out brilliantly equaled by few if any. Although our casualties have been heavy as compared with other regiments of artillery, considering the hazardous service rendered I consider we have been extremely fortunate but more so to good discipline and judgment of both officers and men. The mission entrusted to you have been ably performed with a spirit of cheerfulness and steadfast self sacrifice and devotion to duty, serving under conditions of extreme hardship and danger, you have acquitted yourselves in a highly gratifying and satisfactory manner. During the long marches covering over one thousand kilometers, and periods of exposure and hunger, you have accepted all as a matter of duty, even to your conduct and behavior in the rear areas after the armistice where the mental stress was worse than the front line combat, you seemed always embued with that indomitable spirit of "Let's Go."

Let us pause in reverence to our immortal dead who by their courageous sacrifice have permitted us to return victorious in honor. May their souls rest in peace.

It has indeed been an honor to command you. I thank you for your loyal support and congratulate you upon your success.

CHESTER B. McCORMICK,
Colonel, 119th Field Artillery.

IV Corps Commander Recommendation of the 32nd Division Artillery units to receive the French Croix de Guerre

HEADQUARTERS IV ARMY CORPS
AMERICAN EXPEDITIONARY FORCES
GERMANY
May 24, 1919.

From: Major General C.P. Summerall, Comdg. IV Army Corps.

To: Colonel Linard, Chief of the French Military Mission, Hq. A.E.F.

Subject: Decorations.

I am in receipt of a letter which states that prior to the departure of the 32nd Division the colors of the infantry regiments were decorated with the Croix de Guerre, but that no decorations were given to the Artillery Regiments. This was probably due to the fact that on account of exhaustion and lack of horses the 57th Field Artillery Brigade, which belonged to the Division, remained in France when the Division continued to Germany.

The 57th Field Artillery Brigade participated in all of the actions of the 32nd Division and in addition it supported various other American divisions and the First Moroccan Division. It was especially distinguished by its efficiency and by the long and continuous service that it performed. I believe that no Regiments are entitled to greater honor than the 119th, 120th, and 121st Regiments of Field Artillery that constituted this Brigade.

Knowing the generous spirit that has actuated the French Army in honoring the American Regiments, I desire to present this matter for such action as you may consider proper and with the hope that the same decorations may be given to the artillery as were given to their sister regiments of the Infantry of the 32nd Division.

With assurances of my high regards.

C.P. SUMMERALL
Major General, U.S. Army

As previously noted, the 119th FA Regiment had been awarded the French Croix de Guerre on two occasions.

NOTES

1. L.V. Jacks, *Service Record, By An Artilleryman* (New York: Charles Scribner's Sons, 1928), 115-117.

2. Colonel Frank Foster and Lawrence Borts, *Military Medals of the United States* Seventh Edition (Fountain Inn SC: Medals of America Press, 2010), 100.
Paul J. Schultz, Hayes Otoupalik, Dennis Gordon, *World War One Collectors Handbook, Volumes 1 and 2* (GOS Publishing, January 1, 1988), 96, 99.

3. Colonel Frank Foster and Lawrence Borts, *Military Medals of the United States* Seventh Edition (Fountain Inn SC: Medals of America Press, 2010), 12, 63.

4. American Battle Monuments Commission, *American Armies and Battlefields in Europe: A History, Guide, and Reference Book* (Washington, D.C.: U.S. Government Printing Office, 1938), 513-514
Colonel Frank Foster and Lawrence Borts, *Military Medals of the United States* Seventh Edition (Fountain Inn SC: Medals of America Press, 2010), 152.

5. "119th Field Artillery in World War I," Michigan Department of Military and Veteran Affairs, accessed January 12, 2014, http://www.michigan.gov.dmva
Army Distinguished Service Medal Citation for Colonel Chester B. McCormick, Military Times Hall of Valor, accessed January 12, 2014, http://projects.militarytimes.com/citations-medals-awards/recipient.php?recipientid=17908
1930s Army Officer Signed Photo, Wehrmacht Award Militaria Forum, accessed January 12, 2014, http://www.wehrmacht-awards.com/forums/showthread.php?t=633254

Chapter 13
Furlough and Final Months in France

American soldiers not on occupation duty in Germany were granted furlough leaves to various cities in France. Elmer Smith spent a week in Nice, a city in the south of the country, arriving on New Year's Eve. This was a rather popular furlough location and he met two of his friends there. In a subsequent letter Elmer stated to his mother that he would never regret the seven days spent there, though he wished he had visited nearby Monte Carlo, Monaco as well.

After returning from his well-deserved furlough in Nice, France, Elmer settled into routine duties awaiting his unit's return to the United States. This was a relatively quiet time where he and his fellow soldiers reflected on their five months in combat. All were anxiously waiting to cross the Atlantic Ocean again and return home to their families.

Elmer Smith completed the entries in his 1918 "Day by Day" diary on New Year's Eve in Nice. Thereafter, in 1919, we can only glean an understanding of his remaining time in France through the several letters exchanged with his parents and sister.

In early February, the Catholic Church in Mauvages, the town where the 119th was stationed, held a service to thank the unit and recognize the significant contributions the United States and its Army made in maintaining France's freedom against their common enemy. Again, Elmer had the foresight to keep a copy of the priest's sermon that had been translated into English. It was likely given to the soldiers so they could follow and understand what the priest was saying in French to his parishioners and the 119th soldiers. The speech provides a descriptive French perspective on America's role in the world and its assistance to France and the Allies in helping to defeat Germany. These views were likely commonly held by the French people.

Diary Entry Sat. December 28

Got my furlough signed this morning. Walked to Gondrecout (12 kilometers). Did not get out of here until 7 o clock to night. Had to change at Pagny sur Meuse. Waited all night for my train.

Diary Entry Sun. December 29

Caught the Nancy express for Paris at 8 o clock this morning. Arrived in Paris at 3:30 P.M. Had my pass extended until morning here but thot it best to catch the 9:05 out tonight.

Diary Entry Mon. December 30

Woke up near Lyons. The scenery from Lyons to Marseilles is very beautiful. Arrived in Marseilles about 3 o clock. Caught the 4:45 train for Nice.

Final Diary Entry Tue. December 31

Pulled into Nice about 3 o clock. Got to bed about 4:30 at the N. York hotel. Duvall [H. Blair DuVall of McBain, Michigan] and Jarm [William E. "Bill" Jarm of Niles, Michigan] dropped in and awoke me up at 10:00 o clock.

Spent the day with Jarm. Went thru the Natural Museum. Went to the Elderado this evening. After that we also celebrated the old and n. year.

Letter to Mother, January 20, 1919

Mauvages

Dear Mother:

Will drop you a few lines this morning to let you know I am still alive. I haven't written for quite a while but I have been away on a furlough having to good a time to think about writing.

I took my furlough at Nice, France and believe I will never regret the seven days I spent there. The city is surrounded by the Alps making it very warm there during the winter months. The people are of all descriptions from all over the world as Nice is one of the most popular watering places in Europe. I had several chances to go to Monte Carlo while in Nice and now wished I had. But I was bumming around nights and having to good a time to think about going then. I can tell you more about it when I get back. Sometimes I think we will be home soon and sometimes I think it will be another winter before we get back. I understand the 3rd Div. is coming out of Germany. I hope we join them if its true.

Well mother will write again soon. Goodbye

Your Son,
Elmer

Address to 119th FA Regiment by Local Priest in Mauvages, France, February 2, 1919

119th FIELD ARTILLERY
Mauvages, France
February 2nd, 1919

Address by Local Priest of Mauvages, delivered on February 2nd, 1919, at the Patriotic Mass given especially for the 119th Field Artillery on the Feast of the Purification, at which the entire Regiment was present.

My Brothers:

Many times in the course of this terribly long war you have seen the Battalions of France filing through your streets; you have felt your souls vibrate with love and hope during the passage of our heroes; you have bowed with emotion before the glorious emblems of the Motherland; but above all you have paid particular homage to our valiant soldiers each time they have come to pray to the God of the Armies in your old venerable church.

Today it is our allies of American that you are honoring here in such great number. Let them receive our humble congratulations and our thanks, my brothers, at this moment. Is there need of my dwelling long on the common feeling of affection which unites them to you. Let it suffice for me to recall to you the preponderant and decisive role which they have played in this war which thanks to their efforts was brought to such a happy termination.

In entering the lists our American friends did not cease repeating, "We come to fight on your side to pay an old debt and to aid you to triumph in your cause, which is just." No idea of self interest or conquest inspired at any moment this noble people of the UNITED STATES when they took up arms. They proposed from the very first day to avenge completely the violation of the right and the oppression of humanity. They recalled first of all that in the American war for independence which lasted eight years, France favored the noble movement with all her power; by her policy, her resources, by her leaders, such as Rochambeau and Lafayette and her men.

It was to pay this debt contracted with France that the noble soldiers from beyond the Atlantic came so spontaneously to our side. But another consideration also inspired them to take this action. When they knew of the horrors committed in the name of brute force, the contempt, for the rights of treaties, the oppression of the feeble, the martyrdom of innocents, the methodical destruction of the most respectable and inoffensive things, organized pillage and murder, terror and death sown without distinction at the front and in the rear alike; then these men with ideals, proud lovers of Liberty and humanity, understood that the hour for the vengeance of justice and the right had struck, and they resolutely entered into war. All, or almost all, had to be created out of nothing, organization was begun under the most difficult of auspices, but their ingenious spirit overcame all difficulties and at the end of a year the American Army, more than a Million strong had debarked on our continent. Last spring our enemies began their gigantic and supreme effort to pierce our front. They had not counted on the resistance of our Allies. The meeting of our great Military chiefs, in which the use of American troops on all fronts was decided, will remain historic. The Germans had advanced their lines to Montdidier and Chateau-Thierry, and threatened to cross the Oise and the Marne. The Allied Generals were deliberating upon the opportunity and means for waging a successful counteroffensive which should end in complete annihilation of the Barbarian hordes. But for this decisive stroke we needed many men, and we didn't have enough. General Pershing understood this, and on the spot he placed all American troops under his command at the disposition of Marshall Foch. Some days later these troops were on their way to check the German push on the Marne. Then followed the gradual repulse of the Germans to the positions from which they departed. The famous exploits on the banks of the Meuse, including the delivery of St. Mihiel. Since then victory has come—Victory rapid and complete, thanks again to the American sword, which with all its moral weight as well has turned the tide in our favor. Today our Governments have a heavy task to accomplish, to fashion the peace of the world. God, who has visibly aided us to win our victory, will grant a durable peace to our incessant prayers. "Da pacem Domine in diebus et nostris." Let us repeat it without cease, for we have urgent need of peace, and God alone can give it to us. "Non est aluis nisi Deus noster."

Who knows but what the illustrious President of the UNITED STATES, is not the arm of Providence. In the mean time, Mr. Wilson reveals himself as a man of the broadest of concepts and of the strongest of wills. His disinterested honesty recommends him to our confidence as his high degree of personal morality demands all our respect. Honor, then, to the Greatest President and the Chivalrous nation which he so admirably represents. My Brothers, the great war through whose means I have familiarized myself to some degree with our Allies, in Italy, where I have tasted the sweet fruits of the a Latin civilization and in an English Hospital where for three months I received the most gentle and maternal treatment; this same war now privileges me to live a few days with these sons of the New World. It is a joy for me to be able to share with you in doing them the honor which is their due. May this daily contact leave them with a good impression of us and may this religious fete leave in their hearts a kindly memory of this beautiful religion which has cradled us during the course of our poor lives and in whose peace we will sleep our last great sleep.

All our gratitude goes to these dear Allies from America, and it is to testify to this sentiment that we have desired this fete in their honor. Entertain them well in praying here for them and for their noble nation, in rendering them in your homes the little services and attentions which will bring them sweet memories of their own fire sides and the joy of Motherland always present in their thought and in the folds of the Flag which accompanies them. Honor and Benediction to these sacred emblems displayed at this moment at the foot of our Altars. Honor to grand America, represented here in this Church by such noble Officers and valiant soldiers. ET vive toujours la FRANCE.

Letter to Mother, March 2, 1919

Mauvages, France

Dear Mother:

Will drop you a few lines tonight to let you know I am still alive. I am freting and am getting anxious to get back home. By the way things look now if we come home with the 32nd we probably will sail some time in May. If we come home with the 88th [Division] it will be in Sept. I know of a number of fellows from the reg't that have dependents or such parents are getting discharges here and are going back. They get their pull thru their representatives back there.

The last letter Zelma wrote she said you bought a farm. She didn't say where so I take it you bought the Munson farm. I hardly know what I will start to work at when I get back. Frank is determined I will come and work at the machinist job where ever he is working. Well can't think of anything to write so will quit. Goodbye

Your Son,
Elmer

Letter to Sister, March 5, 1919

YMCA Letterhead
Mauvages, France

Dear Sister:

Well this is about one o'clock in the morning. I presume you think it rather a queer time to be writing letters. But you see I am on guard at the stables. I am writing in a little shack filled with horse medicine.

Well sis I will give you a little real honest to God dope when I am coming home. An order came in today stating we are to join the 32nd either at Coblenz or Antwerp some time this month. And the 32nd is to supposed to sail about the third of May. Gee it's going to be a long wait to us for May to roll around. We probably will be mustered out at Camp de Coos [Camp Custer] sometime in June.

Gee watch me eat eggs, warm milk & bread & etc. when I get back.

I suppose the folks are moving out of the farm by this time.

Well Sis this is short & sweet. So goodbye until next time.

Your Brother,
Elmer

Letter to Sister, March 26, 1919

YMCA Letterhead
Mauvages, France

Dear Sis:

Received your letter a few days ago.

It is rather moist outside today. Which is nothing out of the ordinary for this country.

I am sending a few souvenirs home. The shell case is a German 77. The little box is made from two 77s. I had it made for a cigarette humidor. The one pounder I got from a frenchman and have carried it since we came off the last front. The other is a small type of bomb. I suppose you won't receive them for quite awhile. Perhaps I will beat them home.

We are suppose to turn in everything next week and we will go straight to a port with the 32nd. I don't think we sail much before the 1st of May.

Well it is getting near chow time so will quit.

Goodbye
Your Brother,
Elmer

P.S. Do you ever anything from LuLu L. I had a letter from her while she had the "Flu" and that was the last I heard from her alltho I have written since.

E.S.
On Envelope: Censored William Stillwell, 1st Lt USA

Letter to Mother, April 12, 1919

April 12, 1919

Dear Mother:

I am writing to you for the purpose of letting you know it would not be of any use to write to me anymore. I presume this will be the last you will hear from me until you see me.

We were supposed to leave on Monday the 14th for port of embarkation. But I suppose because of the lack of transportation it was delayed until the eighteenth. So I probably will be very near to N. York when you receive this. Will quit as I have another letter to write.

Your Son,
Elmer

Chapter 14
The Return Home to Michigan

THE 119TH FA RECEIVED NOTICE of its return home in March 1919 and the specific details were solidified in April. Elmer, like all the soldiers, was overjoyed to finally be returning home, five months after the war had ended, and a total of 14 months overseas.

In late April the unit boarded the U.S.S. Frederick in Brest, France and arrived in New York harbor on May 3, 1919. During the trip, Colonel McCormick wrote a summary of the unit operations from mobilization through all their training and combat actions.[1] On May 5, a *Detroit Free Press* photograph depicted Elmer's original mates from B Battery as the first soldiers to disembark back onto American soil. The 119th FA stayed at Camp Mills on Long Island for a few days eagerly awaiting train transportation back to Michigan.

A significant amount of newspaper coverage focused on the 119th FA's return. The unit arrived in Lansing on Monday evening, May 12, 1919. A huge welcome home parade occurred in downtown Lansing on Tuesday morning, May 13. Elmer was met by his parents after the parade and was able to spend that night with them. He then proceeded to Camp Custer, near Battle Creek, Michigan, where the Army out-processed and discharged him and the rest of the 119th FA on May 15 and 16.[2] His two-plus years in service to his country had concluded.

As documented in his letters and diary, Elmer's two years in the wartime U.S. Army had been a whirlwind of activity focused on extensive training and preparation for combat followed by five months on the front lines. Those long months in the crucible of war forged a young man into a responsible adult. Although, he was seriously wounded in the unit's initial action, Elmer had a relatively quick recovery, and then returned to the war's horrific final months during the American Army's major combat operations. These were the highlights and primary events of his time in the Army. Elmer had survived the war, remembered its highs and lows, and in the long term was a better person and citizen for the significant experience he lived through.

Newspaper Article, Detroit Free Press, Saturday, May 3, 1919

119th to Land This Morning
Real Apple Pie and Homemade Spread To Be Put Before Wolverine Gunners.
Rousing Welcome is Arranged for Troops.

By William N. Hard, *Free Press* Correspondent.

New York, May 2—With victory after victory emblazoned on their banners for 14 months' service marked throughout with gallantry, Colonel Chester B. McCormick, hailed as one of the greatest artillery chiefs of the United States army and 1,392 gunners of the 119th field artillery will enter a harbor of unfurled flags, crashing bands, and thundering cheers at 6 a.m. Saturday.

The skipper of the cruiser Frederick, bringing home Colonel McCormick and his stalwarts, sent a wireless message to shore tonight, saying he would be at Ambrose channel at 6 a.m. and tie up at Pier 2, Hoboken, at 10 a.m., with the vanguard of the Fighting 32nd.

To Get Real Apple Pie.

The members of the 119th are to be debarked 15 minutes after the ships dock. Immediately, on the Hoboken pier, they are to be treated to real old-fashioned apple pie.

This is a special favor on the part of the Red Cross to Michigan friends of the homecoming gunners.

But apple pie won't be all those Michigan heroes will get. There'll be a regular home cooked meal, the like of which Colonel McCormick's men haven't seen in the months they have been away. The feeding over and the roll called, the men will go on ferries to Long Island City. From there they will ride by train to Camp Mills, L.I. and arrive there at 3 p.m.

May Get Passes Sunday.

They must stay at Mills, until the sanitary authorities complete examinations, probably Sunday afternoon.

According to an estimate of port authorities today the Michigan gunners, or at least 50 percent of them ought to be out on pass by Sunday afternoon and those that do not care to leave Mills will be permitted to have visitors.

To give the homecoming heroes a real Michigan welcome, a party of Michigan mothers, fathers, brothers, sisters and sweethearts of the soldiers will go down the bay on the welcoming boat Patrol leaving Battery wharf at 8 a.m. They will be accompanied by a band and will carry Wolverine greetings on banners prepared at Michigan military headquarters. They expect to meet the Frederick in quarantine and escort her to her pier, all the time throwing good things to their loved ones on the cruiser.

Some of the Greeters.

Among the Michigan people who had registered at headquarters tonight to go down to the bay area: Dr. J.W. Moore, Houghton; Miss Norma M. Loewe, Belding; Miss Theresa Sher, Lansing; Mrs. L.F Otis and Miss Marion Otis, South Haven; Major Walter G. Rogers, Lansing; C.J. Van Haltern and Miss Anna Van Haltern, Lansing; Mrs. Stephen Gauss, Lansing; V.R. Barry, Lansing; W.W. Brown and William Cayan, Lansing; W.W. Murphy, Lansing; Mrs. Floyd H. Randall, Bay City; Mrs. Edward G. Heckel and Miss Betty Heckel, Detroit; Sergeant Stuck, New Buffalo, and Miss Mildred Groom, an army nurse just back from France, Detroit.

The following wireless message was sent to Colonel McCormick from Michigan headquarters this afternoon: "Governor Sleeper welcomes the men of the 119th. Michigan men will find a welcome at 26 West 40th Street, New York.

Military authorities here said tonight they could not hazard a guess as to when the 119th would leave Camp Mills for Camp Custer to be demobilized. It seems likely they will be in the east at least 10 days and perhaps longer.

Some to Land at Boston.

The Wilhelmina, which is bringing the 120th field artillery and the fifty-seventh field artillery brigade headquarters, has been diverted to Boston and is due to arrive there Monday.

Several organizations and a few enlisted men from Michigan are in these organizations.

The transport General Goethals, with 10 officers and 433 men of the 323rd field signal battalion, medical detachment, Companies A, B and C, is due to arrive at Hoboken tomorrow. These troops will be sent to Custer, most of them being Michigan men.

Michigan Men Returning.

Wolverines who are returning:

119th F.A. Michigan Officers.

Colonel Chester B. McCormick, Lansing; Chaplain William A. Atkinson, 2102 West Grand Boulevard, Detroit; Major Joseph H. Lewis, Lansing; Major Harold T. Weber, Royal Oak; Major Murdock M. Kerr, Larium, medical officer; Captain Paul A. Applegate, Lansing; Captain Harold H. Borgman, 30 Edison Street, Detroit; Captain Frank G. Chaddock, Lansing; Lieutenant Jeffrey C. Creegan, 500 25th Street, Detroit; Lieutenant Harold V. Garvey, 684 Morrel Avenue, Detroit; Lieutenant Herman B. Hale, Caledonia; Lieutenant Edwin C. Hamann, New Buffalo; Lieutenant Kenneth W. Hutton, Lansing; Lieutenant Charles H. Jarvis, Ishpeming; Captain Edgar J. Learned, Lansing; Lieutenant Pierce Lewis, Niles; Lieutenant Leslie E. Peek, Fowlerville; Captain Milton Shaw, Lansing; Captain John F. Soraruf, Ironwood; Lieutenant William G. Stilwell, Pellston; Lieutenant Jay P. Sweeney, Mason; Lieutenant Fred A. Battelle, Detroit; Captain Ned F. Stevenson, Detroit; Captain Orlando A. Pickard, Detroit.

Letter to Sister, May 7, 1919

YMCA Letterhead
Camp Mills Long Island

Dear Sister:

I received your letter and the money order this forenoon. I was certainly glad to hear from you. If I keep it up I will certainly owe you quite a debt. But don't worry I am going to pay you back with intrest when I get a job. I think I will work around home for a while until I have most of my clothes. It is going to cost me like the deuce for clothes. I'll have over a months pay and my bonus to help me out. I am figuring on getting some good shoes & some other stuff here if we get paid before leaving for Camp Custer.

We probably will leave here about Sat. or Sun. Possibly sooner but hardly think so.

I hear the people of Lansing are planning on quite a reception for us. But I think if it were up to the men of the regiment we would not parade anywhere. Governor Sleeper is here to speak to us this afternoon but it was called off on account of rain to the satisfaction of the men. He stands about 100% nothing to the personnel of this regiment.

Well Zelma will talk to you soon so will quit writing.

Your Brother,
Elmer

American Red Cross Typed Postcard, May 10, 1919

Bureau Of Communication
American Red Cross
Washington, D.C.

In answer to your inquiry regarding Pvt. Elmer Oscar Smith Hdqts. Co. 119th F.A. AEF. We are glad to inform you that we have received word from our Paris Office that the Headquarters of our Army in France reports him well and on duty on March 21st, 1919. If we can be of further assistance, be sure to let us know.

Yours Very Truly, William R. Castle Jr.

[Handwritten at bottom of postcard]

119 F.A. Arrived N.Y. May 4—and went to Camp Custer

Newspaper Headlines, The State Journal, Monday, May 12, 1919

WELCOME HOME OUR OWN 119TH F.A.

"Lansing's Own" Is Home Again

Monday Lansing welcomes home the 119th F. A. and stages a celebration honoring every Lansing man who served in the World war.

Even the weather man became imbued with the "When-Johnny-Comes-Marching-Home" spirit and did his bit to make the day a success. Bright sunshine, temperature just a bit invigorating and a 50-50 chance that the sun will shine Tuesday is really more than could be expected on the way of Michigan weather at this time of year and encouraged the city to go the final limit in preparing for the boys who come home.

The city has gone the limit in its preparations. Every Lansingite feels pride in the achievements of the home town boys who went to battle and is co-operating to make the celebration in their honor a success.

The largest of Lansing men who served, to return in a body, comprise the 119th Field Artillery, and in the greeting of these Victory heroes, Lansing aims to reflect all the pride, gratitude and glad—your back spirit which the return of sons, sweethearts and brothers makes for in every home, still showing a service flag.

Preparations for the gala days did not lag even on Sunday. Firemen went to the Chamber of Commerce, which serves as a headquarters for the entertainment committee and for men in uniform, and covered the walls of both the Chamber of Commerce and Prudden auditorium with flags, bunting and shields. Bright and early Monday morning, a crew of men started hanging Japanese lanterns from the city lighting poles and replacing the frayed decoration canopying Washington and Michigan Aves.

Business places showed the colors. Never has Lansing been more ablaze with color.

At 2 o'clock, the executive committee, and sub-committee chairmen of the organization arranging the demonstration, the city council and city officials, boarded a special at the Grand Trunk and went to Durand to meet the returning victory heroes. Great banners bearing a big red arrow, the insignia of the 32nd division, and worn by every man in the 119th F.A. and the words, "Lansing's Own" and "119th F. A." were put on the sides of the coaches carrying the men.

The troop train arrives at 5 p. m. Several bands and companies of state troops and one of the largest crowds ever assembled at the station meet the train. A line is thrown around the train by the state troops and the 119th F. A. step on Lansing soil again after an absence of 21 months and are ordered into formation. Then the crowd is let in and greetings are to be said.

After going to the Reo garage for refreshments and to leave luggage, and the 119th Field Artillery men march uptown and 200 of the men go to each of the following places for a banquet; Masonic temple, Elks' home and K. of C. home. Jazz orchestras and cabaret numbers keep things lively.

The 119th Field Artillery band is taken in tow by the Reo band and will be banqueted and entertained at the Hotel Kerns.

Monday evening, the Third Ward park is to be the scene of all festivities. The pavements on each side have been roped off for a big municipal dance. There will be several bands. A midway, blazing with light, colors and sure to be rife with happy humanity, leads east and west across the park, connecting the two dancing street-pavilions.

On a platform at the south side of the park, several big-time vaudeville acts are to be presented, starting at 8:30. Manger J. J. Dewald of the bijou theater has booked the acts for the concert platform. His program starts with Sydney Lachman, the famous baritone, leading in community singing of popular songs. Gilbert & LaPaula, a man and a woman, do some wonderful hand balancing stunts. Cornella & Wilber, two men comedy acrobats, have a very clever novelty. Smiletta sisters, sensational aerialist, will round out the first part of the show. The celebrated 119th Field Artillery band of 60 selected pieces will next render a concert program, when the vaudeville bill be repeated again at 10 a. m.

The housing committee has lined up sleeping quarters for the night for 750 men, according to J. G. Reutter, chairman. As there will not be that many men to be provided for, some who may be expecting boys may not have them for the night. The only way of handling the situation was to provide extra accommodations. Langsingites must not be disappointed if they do not get boys after making plans, and have done their share in agreeing to make provisions for them.

PROGRAM
MONDAY AFTERNOON

5:00 p.m.—

Troops train, 119th due to arrive at Grand Trunk. Platform reserved for relatives of men returning. Bands and State Troops surround train.

5:15 p.m.—

119th Field Artillery marches to Reo garage for refreshments and to leave luggage.

5:30 p.m.—

Bands, 119TH F. A., State troops and crowd march uptown.

6:00 p.m.—

200 men of 119th F. A. go to march of the following places for dinner: Masonic Temple, Elks Home, K. of C. Home. Jazz orchestras and cabaret numbers during "feed."

7:00 p.m.—

Crowd starts to collect at Third Ward Park.

7:30 p.m.—

Midway is ablaze; bands, orchestras, stands, outdoor vaudeville numbers, get started for evening.

8 to 12 p.m.—

Dancing on pavements each side of Third Ward Park; midway features, concerts, outdoor entertainments.

8:30 p.m.—

Program starts on concert stage, Pavese orchestra.

Community singing led by Sydney Lachman, baritone; Gilbert & LaPaula, hand balancing feats; Cornella & Wilber, acrobatics; Simletta Sisters, sensational aerialist; concert 119th F. A. Band until 10 p. m.

10:30 to 1:00—

Autos at Chamber of Commerce, headquarters for celebration, to take 119th F. A. men to homes for night.

TUESDAY

9:00 a.m.—

Assemble, 119th F. A.

All returned soldiers, sailors, and marines meet at Sparrow home, Washington ave. and Lenawee st., to form for parade in honor of them and 119th F. A.

10:00 a.m.—

Parade starts on Capitol ave. at Michigan ave.; south to Main st., east to Washington ave., north to Shiawassee st., west to Capitol ave., south to Michigan ave.

Newspaper Article, The State Journal, Mon. May 12, 1919

LANSING UNIT STARTED 119th
APPELLATION, "LANSING'S OWN" IS DESERVED.
STARTED FROM "GUARD"

First Batteries Starting Regimental Organization Hailed From This City.

Lansing's right to the appellation, "Lansing's Own" in speaking of the 119th F. A., is better realized when one goes back into the history of this artillery organization which distinguished itself so famously in the World war.

The 119th F. A. consists of the regimental headquarters, Headquarters company, supply company, two battalions of artillery and a sanitary detachment of the medical department.

The first battalion of artillery consists of a battalion headquarters company, Batteries A, B, and C.

The second battalion consists of a battalion headquarters company, and Batteries D, E, and F. The regiment is a regiment of horse drawn, light field artillery.

This regiment was organized at Camp MacArthur at Waco, Tex. in the fall of 1917 from the first battalion of Michigan Field artillery commanded by Col. Chester B. McCormick, then Maj. McCormick, from the first squadron of Michigan cavalry, commanded by Maj. Henric Pickert, from the headquarters company and supply company of the 31st Michigan infantry, first squadron of cavalry and field artillery battalion.

Some of these organizations had been in existence for years.

Battery A was organized at Lansing in 1905 as the first battery of field artillery in Michigan.

Battery B was organized at Lansing in 1876 as an infantry company and served during the Spanish-American war as Co. E., 31st Michigan Volunteer infantry. In 1912 it was transformed into field artillery and became Battery B.

Battery C was organized at Lansing in the spring of 1917 on the return of the field artillery from the Mexican border service, the war department desiring the completion of the field artillery battalion.

The second battalion was organized from the first squadron of cavalry consisting of troops A, B, C, and D.

Troop A was organized at South Haven in 1905.

Troop B was organized at Detroit in 1908.

After these two troops had served on the Mexican border and returned in 1917, the war department desired the completion of the squadron, so Troops C and D were at once organized at Detroit.

The headquarters company of the 119th F. A. was organized from the headquarters company of the 31st Michigan infantry, and the supply company from the supply company of the 31st Michigan infantry. Both of these organizations had served on the Mexican border with the 31st Michigan infantry, the supply company being organized in June 1916 and the headquarters company while being organized at the same time, had been in existence in its various component parts as long as the 31st Michigan infantry existed as a regiment.

The sanitary detachment of the 119th Field Artillery, was originally the sanitary detachment of the 31st Michigan infantry, and had served on the Mexican border, its organization really beginning with the organization of the 31st Michigan infantry.

Newspaper Article, The State Journal, Tue. May 13, 1919

MY BOY, MY BOY IS MOTHER CRY
AND EVERYBODY FELT NEAR KIN.
JOY WAS ALMOST SOLEMN

No Outward Manifestation Seemed Quite Equal to Inward Thankfulness.

"My Boy" "Your Boy" "Lansing's Boy" came home. Came with a record of defeats of the Huns, a record of glory, that perhaps will not be equaled in the history of the world. Came home with the realization of a difficult duty, an unpleasant duty done, and mighty well done at that. Came home to Lansing, came home to father and mother and sister and sweetheart, and when they saw the mothers and sisters and fathers and sweethearts, they just forgot that they had faced the Hun in battle, with all of the grimness and determination of veterans, and had turned back a world menacing tide; forgot the horror of the battlefields of Chateau Thierry, of the Argonne, forgot the thunder of the guns, forget war's desolation, and just melted into mother, and sister's, or sweethearts arms, just a plain, common ordinary boy again. Glad that he had been there to help but gladder yet to get back home once more. Father and mother and sweetheart just held the boy and held him tighter and tighter and just wouldn't let him go.

Previous to the time that "My boy" and "Our Boys" came it was a quiet crowd. There were a few jokes to be sure, there was some laughter, but in the main it was a tense, strained silence. It was happy silence to be sure, and underneath reserved was the undercurrent of happiness, of joy. It came to the surface, but did not break quite through. One mother said to another mother in a quiet tone.

"Are you waiting for your boy?" "Yes. I surely am, my boy is in Battery A." Other boys were in Battery B or C whichever it happened to be. The members of the Father's and Mother's Home association, waiting in the depot, talked in almost subdued tones. The crowd outside the depot was silent as well. They were all looking for the train and the chief topic of conversation was the time that the train would come. One mother read a letter, probably for the hundredth time from her son, the last one written before reaching home. One could little surmise from the talk of that went—

It was just "What time did they leave Detroit?" or "Are you sure they will be here tonight?" "Did they parade in Detroit this morning?" but the word most frequently heard was "I just can't wait, I want to see them so badly."

Then the Reo factory whistle blew for 5 o'clock. That was the time that father and mother, sister and sweetheart jumped up and down with cry of "Here they come, here they come," which was just a hint of what was to come.

After the mistaken signal it seemed to be quieter than ever. The suspense grew sharper and the tension harder for those who were waiting to bear. Then, suddenly—"Here they are, here they are," rang out, outside, and there was one grand rush of the fathers and mothers through the depot door that nothing under heaven could stop. There were soldiers there with guns, but that didn't make any difference. "My Boy" was coming home and mother went right out there to see him and all the guns in the army could not stop her. Then the joy broke through the surface. It was a veritable volcano of joy. Man kissed man, and mother held her son with that hug that only mother love knows and, yes, it was a joy of tears. There were tears in plenty. Whole families cried, and the boys, just for a few minutes to be sure, forgot that they were now vets of the 32nd division, one of the proudest divisions in the whole army and shed a few tears too. At least there was a little moisture in the eyes. And it made those who didn't have any close relatives, wipe their eyes as well.

And even after the boys were here, there was no wild, unreasonable jubilation. After the first arm clasp even after the procession was headed up Washington ave. There was no wild, hilarious demonstration. Everybody was happier than they were to be sure, there was more noise than before, yet there was that wonderful surge of happiness that no noisemaking, no whistle blowing, no yelling, no matter how loud, could give expression to. They were home and that was all there was to it. It was realized way down deep inside—-the realization had no outward equivalent.

Men shook hands with men, with grips that almost took the hands off and yet not a word was spoken. It was "how are you, Bill, or Harry" or whatever the name might be. But all the boys did not come back. Some of them are in France, sleeping quietly under French soil, as a sacrifice that Hun domination of the world may forever cease. Mother, sister, father and sweetheart of that boy was at the Grand Trunk depot. She had a gold star. Her boy, her hero, her loved one who marched away so proudly months ago, was not there. She was there that she might hear first hand from the lips of some pal, of her boy, in just the manner in which her son gave up his life in faraway France. She was glad that other boys had come back, but this gladness was as a thread of silver through a dark, dark pattern of woe. They were the ones who hearing that the boys had died bravely in "line of duty" went to think, ponder and marvel, apart from the merrymaking of the evening. Perhaps to these groups came some small token sent by pal or comrade as a last material reminder of love and of a life gone out because duty had called.

The boys who did come back were welcomed by the capital city, and welcomed with such a high, almost solemn joy that will be remembered in the hearts of every member of the 119th Field Artillery for many years to come.

Newspaper Headlines, The State Journal, Tue. May 13, 1919

LANSING POURS OUT ITS HEART TO 119TH
PRIDE, SORROW, LOVE MINGLED
WHOLE CITY GIVES ITSELF OVER TO EXPRESSION OF RECOGNITION OF SOLDIER SERVICE.
THRONG SEES TRIUMPH MARCH

Washington Avenue From Station to Business Center is Lined with People; Dinner and Joyfest in Evening.

A celebration without parallel in the history of gala days in Lansing marked the home coming of the 630 officers and men who comprise the 119th Field Artillery, "Lansing's Own" Monday afternoon.

Being host to the men who were in the thick of the fight on the western front six months ago is an easy task for the home town which hasn't seen these lads in 21 months. A crowd greeted the returning men and joined in the merry making which justified, seemingly, any claim for size one might make for Lansing.

Business was virtually suspended about 4 o'clock when the first band and company of State troops started for the Grand Trunk station. From homes, offices and shops came the folks who were mighty glad the boys were coming back. The crowd came to number thousands.

IS DRAMATIC MOMENT.

Whistles, bands and a cheering mob started a greeting clamor when the smoke of the first section of the regiment train appeared in the distance. Never was there a more dramatic moment for Lansing than when the train came to a halt and the tanned, smiling warriors started to pour from the coaches to the narrow platform space kept clear by State troops.

On August 17, 1917, Lansing had seen a crowd of laughing boys board a train which made the first lap of a tour which has touched Texas, eastern camps, England, France and Germany. It was a more grim, older crowd which filed from the coaches May 12, 1919. Many who had gone 21 months before did not return. Those who did had learned the most grim angles of warfare and had distinguished themselves in the midst of such grimness.

An intangible something—pride, admiration, gladness, sorrow, love—swept up alike in the hearts of those who searched for a relative or friend and those who were merely drawn to the scene by excitement. When Col. McCormick, aged but looking pretty much the same, started up the street at the head of a swinging line of veterans, none who crowded the marching line could remain immune to the contagion of enthusiasm, pride and patriotism.

The reception Lansing staged for her own organization justifies a degree of pride. Few cities have greeted returned heroes more sincerely. A crowd of about 40 committee chairman, city officials and councilmen formed the advance guard of Lansing's greeting and met the troop train at Durand.

IN SCHEDULE FORM.

The delegation went by special train, leaving Lansing shortly after 2 p. m. To have plans arrange themselves according to schedule and have weather ideal for a demonstration of the kind seemed almost too much to expect in one undertaking. But train-dispatchers and the weather men were in line and there was nothing to mar the demonstration.

Bearing Col. McCormick and his staff, the first section of troop train arrived in Durand shortly after 4 o'clock, according to schedule. The train stopped only long enough for huge banners, bearing the red arrow of the 32nd Division and the words, "Lansing's Own" to be roped to each side of all coaches, and for papers, cigarets and half of the advance guard to find places on platforms.

The section of the train arrived within 10 minutes of the time the first had departed, remaining only a short time longer in Durand.

On the trip into Lansing, tickets for all entertainments, directions to a home to spend the night, cigarets and a program of the events planned in their honor, were given each of the men.

The artillerymen had spent the night before in day coaches on their way to Detroit from New York. Kit bags, steel helmets and duffle were piled up in seats and the men were making themselves comfortable as only soldiers can who have spent months sleeping in dug outs and besides their guns.

"Oh Boy! Some program"

It was the remark heard up and down the train.

Enroute from Durand, farmers paused in their fields and waved a greeting. Crowds collected in the stations along the way and prefaced Lansing's greetings and flag-waving.

OFFICERS LEAD MARCHERS

Nearing Lansing, officers left their cars to take charge of their men and headed their batteries through the pressing crowd and up the streets to the Masonic Temple, Elks Home, and K. of C. Home where regular, old-fashioned banquets were served. There was no speech making but plenty of food. Orchestras and special entertainment features had been provided.

Following the evening meal, the streets became alive with humanity. The colorful and plentiful decorations were lighted up far into the night by red and green fire. Boys scouts keeping the color torches blazing from every light pole until the wee hours.

The crowd drifted to and from Third Ward Park. Bands were on stands at each side of the park on the pavement and with their music kept myriad feet a shuffle on the asphalt pavement which had been roped off and cleaned for the occasion.

So great was the press of dancers that the affair resolved itself into a matter of revolving on one spot, being bumped each quarter turn by the couple next. This was not a source of discouragement, however, and all went merrily until the last bar of the goodnight waltz "Home Sweet Home."

MIDWAY ABLAZE

Meanwhile a midway of booths and counter attraction was ablaze with life and light. On a platform at the south side of the park, several good outside vaudeville numbers were given, followed by a concert by the 119th Field Artillery band, only to be repeated again later for a different crowd of joymakers.

The Salvation Army had booths on the midway on the downtown streets and the doughnut kettle sang merrily throughout the evening.

Autos were awaiting at the Chamber of Commerce for the artillery men who were to spend the night in Lansing homes. Business did not start very brisk, for the soldiers' chauffeurs until and then came with a rush.

A big moon made its appearance and soldiers and girls were to be found strolling and occupying porch steps long after the lights on the scene of festivities had been turned out.

Newspaper Article, The State Journal, Tue. May 13, 1919

ARTILLERY BAND DOES MADELONE
MARCH OF SATISFACTION IS CHICKERWARD.
REO BAND IS HOST

Fighting Musicians Are Guests at Feast—Meaning of Marches is Told.

"Oh, gee, real chicken boys" was the remark of Musician William Puckett of Detroit, as he and his comrades sat down to dinner given to the 119th F. A. by the Reo band in the blue room of the Wentworth-Kerns hotel, Monday night.

"THE band boys are real soldiers just like the fellows that manned the guns of the 119th artillery regiment. They go right to the front like the rest of the fellows. When the fight is on they render first aid to the wounded, bury the dead and assist in digging holes and trenches" explained Lieut. E. W. Thomas, the band commander. He told why his band played "Sambre Meuse," "32 Division March" and "Madelone" while on the march up front the station.

"The 'Sambre Meuse' march is the tune that set France on fire. "The 32 Division' march is the tune that set the world on fire. The Madelone' is a march of satisfaction after the job is done" was the explanation.

The dinner arranged by the Reo band in compliment to the visiting musicians, and in honor of 31 men, its own, former members it sent into the service.

The skirmish in the direction of the good things brought by the waiters was at first hesitant. The soldiers awkwardly unfolded their napkins. "These are the first napkins we have seen for a long time" said one. "Real cows milk" said another and before it was realized the (cutoff) style all along the line and nothing withstood the onslaught.

The program rendered was short. Leader Carl Dewey of the Reo band, introduced Carl J. Ruth as toastmaster. Roy Livingston of the Reo company made a short address of welcome and told the fellows that no overseas soldier would want for a job while in Lansing. Then each musician was presented with a gold watch symbolic of the Reo.

Clarence E. Holmes made the main address of welcome. "We are great because you are symbols of real Simon Pure Americanism" said Mr. Holmes. He paid a further tribute to the work accomplished by the American army. "That's a real speech, too, and sounds real home like" came a remark from a modest soldier near where the speaker was standing.

Many of the soldiers were called upon to give short talks but in each case they spoke only a short sentence. "We just can't believe we are back" said Musician Alfred Underwood of Indianapolis. "We really appreciate this kind of reception it is more than we expected" said Sergeant Rage. The soldiers were loathe to talk about their achievements. The toastmaster told the boys that the town was theirs and they were assigned to places where they would be entertained for the night. "Company dismissed" was the command, and the boys filed out to join in the merrymakings. They were face to face with the first real freedom granted to them in months.

Newspaper Article, mid-May, 1919

[This article was likely clipped from the local Ovid newspaper]

Elmer Smith Pays Parents Short Visit

[Photo of PFC Elmer O. Smith]

But Will Be Discharged Soon From 119th Artillery

Elmer Smith, a member of the 119th Artillery, arrived in Lansing with his company, Tuesday [May 13]. The capitol city had a big celebration in honor of this unit of the famous 32nd Division, and the boys were given a rousing reception. His parents, Mr. and Mrs. W.F. Smith went to Lansing Tuesday to meet their son, and they found him in excellent health. He was anxious to spend one night at home, and was allowed to come back with his parents, but returned the next morning as the unit had to go to Camp Custer where they will be mustered out within a few days.

It will be remembered that Elmer was the first Ovid boy to be wounded while engaged in active duty on French soil. He was struck by pieces of a shell on June 16th, 1918, but after a few weeks was able to return to his company. The 32nd is counted the crack division of all the fighting forces. They were in contact with the enemy forces on five fronts and had the honor of defeating Germany's best troops, the Prussian guards, when the latter were sent against them in order to stem the advance of the 32nd. This division never gave up an inch of ground to the enemy and because of their furious onslaughts were called "Les Terribles." [By French Army commanders]

Images of America, Lansing: City on the Grand, 1836-1939, captured the 119th FA Regiment's jubilant return to Michigan with a photograph of the parade that celebrated the memorable occasion in Lansing with the below caption.[3]

"THE RETURN OF "LANSING'S OWN" 119TH FIELD ARTILLERY REGIMENT FROM THEIR SERVICE IN WORLD WAR I. The 630 soldiers of the unit were greeted with a hero's welcome well deserved for service in the "War to End All Wars." On Tuesday May 13, 1919, thousands of Lansing's residents gathered to welcome the returning soldiers. There were several emotional reunions as parents rushed out to embrace their soldier sons while the regiment marched down Washington Avenue. The parade was led by Lansing resident and commanding officer of the regiment Col. Chester B. McCormick." (Photograph from the Forest Parke Memorial Library/Capital Area District Library)

U.S. Army Discharge Work Availability Card, May 1919

Undated

CAMP PERSONNEL OFFICE
Camp Custer, Michigan
To Packard Motor Car Co., Detroit, Michigan
Elmer Smith
has been honorably discharged from the U.S. Army. He is sent to you for employment as
Clerical Work

WILMER T. SCOTT Major, F.A., U.S. A. Camp Personnel Adjutant

C.P.A. 6 [Camp Personnel Adjutant, Form/Card 6]

Western Union Telegram from Frank Nethaway to Mr. Fred Smith, Thursday, May 15, 1919

Elmer O Smith Ovid Mich will leave Detroit for Ovid by earliest train Sunday morning.

Frank

NOTES

1. Colonel Chester B. McCormick, *To The Officers and Men of The 119th F.A.* (Headquarters 119*th* Field Artillery, A.E.F., On Board U.S.S. Frederick, At Sea, April 27, 1919).

2. The 85th Division trained at Camp Custer during World War I before departing for France. Like the 32nd Division, the troops of the 85th Division primarily came from Michigan and Wisconsin. The 85th arrived in France in August 1918, but did not serve as an active combat division.
U.S. War Department, *The War With Germany: A Statistical Summary* (Washington, D.C.: U.S. GPO, May 1919), 26, 28, 33.

3. James MacLean and Craig A. Whitford, *Images of America, Lansing, City on the Grand, 1836-1939* (Great Britain: Arcadia Publishing, 2003), 75.

Epilogue: A Lifetime of Service

In 1919, a grateful nation welcomed back its Doughboys who had helped make the world safe again for democracy. President Wilson led the U.S. delegation to the Paris Peace Conference in January 1919, which resulted in the Versailles Treaty in June 1919. However, the U.S. Senate never ratified the treaty and a separate U.S. peace accord was negotiated directly with Germany in 1921. Although a League of Nations was organized to prevent another conflict of the scope of the World War, Americans soon began to reject the notion of continued involvement and presence in European affairs. The World War was the first major war in Europe the U.S. had been involved in and many thought these civilized countries could take care of and resolve their own problems. Similarly, the war left bitter feelings in Germany. Many Germans resented the Allied occupiers along the Rhine River. They thought the war had ended prematurely and that the German Fatherland would have eventually prevailed in the West. The majority of the German Army felt they had not been truly defeated. Twenty years later, a major war would erupt in Europe again to resolve many of the underlying issues remaining from the earlier World War.[1]

The international politics of the post-World War I era had little meaning for the common American soldiers who returned to the U.S. After returning from the war and being honorably discharged in May 1919, Elmer O. Smith settled down to a humble, quiet life. The two years of intense training and war proved to be a positive experience in a long life of service in Lansing, Michigan. Elmer, widely known as Bob to his friends and colleagues, became active in many civic organizations throughout his life.

Post-War Military Interaction

Official interaction with the military was infrequent for Elmer after his discharge. In October 1920, he applied for and received approval for the World War Victory Medal. In 1921, he applied for and received a bonus from the State of Michigan for his service during the war. In that year he also applied to receive his official military records.[2] In 1932, the U.S. Army established the Purple Heart medal for soldiers wounded in war. Retroactive to the World War, Elmer applied for and received the medal. The Purple Heart replaced the Wound Chevron he wore on the cuff of the right sleeve of his service uniform tunic. His name Elmer O. Smith is inscribed on the back of the medal.

The Purple Heart was the third military medal that Elmer was authorized to wear. As detailed in Chapter 12, the other two were the French Croix de Guerre (Cross of War) and the U.S. Army World War I Victory Medal. The French military had bestowed the Croix de Guerre to the 119th FA Regiment on two occasions for its superior combat actions. The Victory Medal had battle clasps for the main campaigns the Army fought in during the war. Elmer was authorized to wear the four battle clasps that represented the major engagements he and his unit fought in. In 1922, the French government also authorized a commemorative medal to all Allied soldiers who served three months or more in France. The "Medaille Interalliee" was better known as the Allied Medal or Allied Victory Medal.[3]

His Regimental Commander, COL Chester McCormick, continued to serve in National Guard leadership, training, and advisory capacities in Michigan, Hawaii, and New York through the start of World War II. He named many of the prominent terrain features at Camp Grayling for locations or battles the 119th FA fought in. Camp Grayling continues to be the Michigan National Guard's primary field training reservation used by units throughout the Midwest.[4]

In 1923, Congress established the American Battle Monuments Commission to erect memorials at sites of U.S. cemeteries in France. Monuments were established to commemorate the sacrifice and service of American soldiers at three major campaign sites where PFC Elmer Smith and the 119th FA Regiment fought, the Aisne-Marne, Oise-Aisne, and Meuse-Argonne battlefields. Five other World War memorials were also commemorated in France.[5]

In 1938, on the 20th anniversary of the Great War's end, the U.S. established the annual Veterans Day holiday. It coincided with the World War's Armistice, November 11, to recognize veterans of military service from all of the nation's conflicts.

Elmer was a lifelong member of the Veterans of Foreign Wars (VFW) and Disabled American Veterans (DAV). The VFW chapter was in Holt, Michigan, a few miles south of Lansing near where he lived. Many of the men he associated with in these organizations were the former soldiers and leaders within his 119th FA Regiment. Elmer knew and served with these men in war and therefore, felt a close bond with them. A blank application to the 32nd Division Veterans Association was in his papers, indicating he probably did not join this broader Veterans organization.

The main piece of shrapnel he received when wounded remained embedded in his body for his entire life. Occasionally, he coughed up substantial amounts of blood. However, this was more likely due to having inhaled residual mustard gas during the war. One small piece of shrapnel did eventually work its way out onto his back's surface in the 1940s.

Most of his wartime uniforms, documents, and memorabilia were stored in a large trunk in the basement of his home. The small trunk he used during the war became a tool chest and resided in his garage. These items have since been divided among his children and grandchildren.

Family History

When he applied for his Victory Medal in October 1920, Elmer was residing on Washington Avenue near downtown Lansing.

His older sister Zelma and his childhood best friend Frank Nethaway married in 1922.

In 1923, Elmer met and married, Louise M. Kadolph. They were together for ten years, divorcing in 1933. They lived in Lansing. No children came from this marriage and this may have been one of the reasons for their split. Little was shared with his later family about this marriage.

In 1925 Elmer became employed by the U.S. Post Office, a job he held for the next 31 years. This job provided steady income throughout the Great Depression that started in late 1929 and lasted the entire decade of the 1930s. This income allowed him to raise a family during austere economic times.

In 1933, he met and married Marjorie A. Bala. They honeymooned at the World's Fair in Chicago. Marge, as she was known, was 14 years younger than Elmer. Marge Smith was totally devoted to her husband. She took superb care of him, their children, and later their grandchildren.

Their first daughter Sharon K. was born in November 1934, followed by Margo R. in May 1936, and Steven E., known as Steve, in June 1940. They lived on Miller Road near the Bala family store at the corner of Cedar Street and Miller Road in south Lansing. In 1941, the family moved down the road about a ¼ mile into a new house built at 345 East Miller Road. The large lot had a detached two-car garage as well as an area for a large vegetable garden. A cherry tree grew along the back fence line adjacent to the North Elementary School property.

In 1950 Elmer and Marge built a cottage in the northern part of Michigan's Lower Peninsula on Spider Lake near Traverse City. This was the family's haven from the summer heat and humidity of mid-Michigan. It still belongs to the family today.

The primary route to the cottage went through Camp Grayling, the military ground where Elmer trained in 1917. In the town of East Boardman, a World War II Sherman tank is prominently displayed on the main road to Spider Lake. World War II's substantial size and scope quickly caused many Americans to forget the sacrifices and service of soldiers from the World War, a quarter century earlier. During World War II, Elmer's younger brother Dee served in the Army Ordnance Corps and was stationed in the U.S. during the conflict.

Elmer's mother, Olive Irene Smith (Oakes) passed away in September 1952. His father, Wilfred Fred Smith followed 10 months later on Independence Day 1953. His father-in-law, William H. Bala, died in July 1956 and his mother-in-law, Hettie J. Bala (Coultes), died in May 1969.

After working for the U.S. Post Office for 31 years, Elmer retired in 1956 at age 59. It was the same year that Mark, the first of his nine grandchildren, was born. Daniel, Julie, Matthew, John, David, Christopher, Gregg, and Brian followed.

After retirement, Elmer served as a volunteer crossing guard at the neighborhood's North Elementary School. He did this for the next 12 years, ensuring that children were able to safely cross busy Miller Road to get to and from school.

The parents and children recognized Elmer Smith's contributions to the community. In 1967, they honored him as the following article captures:

Crossing 'Helper' Honored

Elmer O. (Bob) Smith, 70, was honored Wednesday afternoon by students and faculty of the North Elementary School for 12 years of service as a crossing guard at Currie Lane and Miller Road.

Students, Parent-Teachers Association members and the school faculty combined to purchase a watch for Smith. It was presented to him by Nick Johnson school safety patrol captain.

Smith served as a crossing guard since he retired from the postal service 12 years ago.

A World War I veteran, Smith has been active as a leader of youth activities sponsored by the Miller Road Optimist Club.

After his death in 1968 the community again recognized him. Another article appeared in the North Elementary School News and was reprinted in Lansing's *State Journal* soon after his passing. It included a fitting poem, entitled *The Coin.*

Tribute to a 'Crossing Man'

Until his retirement in 1967 Elmer (Bob) Smith was the School Crossing Watchman at Miller Road and Curry Lane. There is probably no way of estimating the positive influence this quiet person had upon the lives of the children who crossed there each day. When the children learned of Mr. Smith's death on October 24th they experienced a sense of great loss; and so it should be. For this was their friend who gave security and substance to their daily pattern. Adults may, at times, take friendship for granted, but children rarely do.

Almost 50 years ago a lovely little poem was written by Sara Teasdale. It follows:

THE COIN
Into my heart's treasury
I slipped a coin
That time cannot take
Nor a thief purloin,
Oh, better than the minting
Of a gold-crowned king
Is the safe-kept memory
Of a lovely thing.

North School Children have a lovely thing in the safe-kept memory of their "Crossing Man" who had a kind word for every child he knew.

Elmer Oscar Smith was seventy-one years old when he died on October 24, 1968. Most importantly, he raised a loving and productive family. But he also truly lived a life of service. First, he served his country in dutifully fighting to defend its freedom during war. Second, Elmer served his community while diligently working for the U.S. Postal Service for over three decades. And finally, he served his neighborhood by shepherding its school children to and from their education on a daily basis. He was also active in many community associations including being a Charter Member of the Miller Road Optimist's Club, where he led youth activities programs.

Elmer was the first of his siblings to pass away, followed by Clarence in 1973, Zelma in 1986, Dee in 1999, and Genevieve in 2000. Elmer's best friend and brother-in-law Frank Nethaway passed away in 1970.

His beloved wife Marge lived until September 1993. They are buried beside one another in North Cemetery on Miller Road, Lansing. Their oldest daughter Sharon lies close by after her death in April 2009.

As of 2015, Elmer Smith had two surviving children, nine grandchildren, 16 great-grandchildren, and three great, great-grandchildren.

The Final World War Veterans

The last men and women who fought in the Great War have died in the past several years. In February 2011, Frank Buckles, the last American veteran, died in Charles Town, West Virginia. The war's last combatant, Claude Choules, a British Royal Navy veteran, died in May 2011. Finally, Florence Green, who served in the Women's Royal Air Force in England, the last known veteran of the World War, died in February 2012, two weeks shy of reaching her 111th birthday.[6]

Numerous American World War Memorials still exist in France. Two primary sites continue to commemorate World War I in the U.S. today. The first is the National World War I Museum at Liberty Memorial in Kansas City, Missouri. This impressive museum provides a detailed overview of the historical events highlighting what the soldiers endured in the brutal environment of front line duties in France and elsewhere. The second site is the AEF Memorial on Pennsylvania Avenue near the White House in Washington, D.C. At this site the World War I Centennial Commission will build a fitting tribute to the men and women who honorably served the nation during this major conflict. Currently a statue of AEF Commander-in-Chief, later designated General of the Armies, John J. Pershing stands there along two granite walls. One wall describes the formation and deployment of the AEF to France and the significant contributions it made to the Allied cause. It then describes the massive American effort which culminated with over a million soldiers fighting intensely in the raw conditions of the Meuse-Argonne Offensive that helped lead to Germany's defeat. Inscribed on the back of the second wall is General Pershing's final thank you to the soldiers who served with him in France, stating,

In their devotion, their valor, and in the loyal fulfillment of their obligations, the officers and men of the American Expeditionary Forces have left a heritage of whom those who follow may ever be proud.

NOTES

1. Byron Farwell, *Over There: The United States in the Great War, 1917-1918* (New York: W.W. Norton and Company, 1999), 258-272.

2. "Statement of Service, Smith, Elmer O." (Washington D.C.: War Department, The Adjutant General's Office, May 27, 1921).

3. "Medaille Interalliee dite Medaille de la Victoire", accessed January 13, 2014, http://france-phaleristique.com/accueil.htm

4. "119th Field Artillery in World War I," Michigan Department of Military and Veteran Affairs, accessed January 12, 2014, http://www.michigan.gov.dmva
   1930s Army Officer Signed Photo, Wehrmacht Award Militaria Forum, accessed January 12, 2014, http://www.wehrmacht-awards.com/forums/showthread.php?t=633254

5. American Battle Monuments Commission, *American Armies and Battlefields in Europe: A History, Guide, and Reference Book* (Washington, D.C.: U.S. Government Printing Office, 1938).

6. Emily Brown, "Last American veteran of World War I dies at 110," *USA Today*, March 1, 2011.
   Margalit Fox, "Florence Green, Last World War I Veteran, Dies at 110," *New York Times*, February 7, 2012.

BIBLIOGRAPHY

American Battle Monuments Commission. *American Armies and Battlefields in Europe: A History, Guide, and Reference Book.* Washington, District of Columbia (D.C.): U.S. Government Printing Office (GPO), 1938.

American Battle Monuments Commission, *32^D Division Summary of Operations in the World War* (Washington, D.C.: U.S. GPO, 1943). Also, the 3rd, 26th, 28th, 77th, 79th, and 89th Division Summaries in the same series were primary sources.

Boghardt, Thomas. "Chasing Ghosts in Mexico: The Columbus Raid of 1916 and the Politicization of U.S. Intelligence During World War I," *Army History*. U.S. Army Center of Military History, Fall 2013.

Borgman, Harold H., Captain, 119th F.A. *War Record of Battery F, 119th Field Artillery, 32nd Division*. Lansing MI: Library of Michigan.

Carter, Russell Gordon. *The 101st Field Artillery: AEF 1917-1919*. Boston MA: Houghton Mifflin Company, 1940.

Coffman, Edward M. *The War to End All Wars: The American Military Experience in World War I*. Lexington KY: University of Kentucky Press, 1998.

Dalessandro, Robert J. and Michael G. Knapp. *Organization and Insignia of the American Expeditionary Force, 1917-1923*. Atglen PA: Schiffer Publishing Ltd, 2008.

Farwell, Byron. *Over There: The United States in the Great War, 1917-1918*. New York: W.W. Norton & Company, 1999.

Ferrell, Robert H. *America's Deadliest Battle: Meuse Argonne, 1918*. Lawrence, KS: University Press of Kansas, 2007.

Foster, Frank, Colonel, and Lawrence Borts. *Military Medals of the United States, Seventh Edition*. Fountain Inn, SC: Medals of America Press, 2010.

Historical Committee 120th Field Artillery Association. *The 120th Field Artillery Diary, 1880-1919*. Milwaukee, WI: Hammersmith-Kortmeyer Co., 1928.

Jacks, L.V. *Service Record, By an Artilleryman*. New York: Charles Scribner's Sons, 1928.

Joint War History Commissions of Michigan and Wisconsin. *The 32ND Division in the World War 1917–1919*. Milwaukee, WI: Wisconsin Printing Company, 1920.

Maclean, James and Craig A. Whitford. *Images of America, Lansing, City on the Grand, 1836-1939*. Great Britain: Arcadia Publishing, 2003.

Pictorial Souvenir of Camp MacArthur, Waco, Texas. Waco TX: D.E. Hirshfield, 1917.

Preston, Richard A., Alex Roland, and Sydney F. Wise. *Men In Arms: A History of Warfare and its Interrelationships with Western Society, Fifth Edition*. Fort Worth TX: Harcourt Brace Jovanovich, 1991.

Schultz, Paul J. Hayes Otoupalik and Dennis Gordon, *World War One Collectors Handbook, Volumes 1 and 2*. GOS Publishing, January 1, 1988.

Stallings, Laurence. *The Doughboys: The Story of the AEF, 1917-1918*. Harper & Row, 1963.

Suciu, Peter. "Militaria: World War I Gas Masks," *Military Heritage*. Maclean VA: Sovereign Media, Late Winter 2012.

The State Journal Company. *Honor Roll and Complete War History of Ingham County in the Great World War*. Lansing, MI: The State Journal Company, 1920.

The Thirty Second Division, American Expeditionary Forces, 1917-1919. Coblenz, Germany: Y.M.C.A., 1919.

Tucker, Spencer C., Editor. *World War I: A Student Encyclopedia*. Santa Barbara CA: ABC-CLIO, 2005 and 2006.

U.S. Army Center of Military History. *Order of Battle of the United States Land Forces in the World War, American Expeditionary Forces: Divisions, Volume 2*. Washington, D.C.: U.S. GPO, 1988.

U.S. Army Center of Military History and the Smithsonian Institution National Museum of American History. *Army Art of World War I: Guide to the Print Set*. Washington, D.C.: U.S. GPO, 1993.

U.S. Army, Office of the Chief of Military History. *American Military History*. Washington, D.C.: U.S. GPO, 1973.

U.S. Army, Office of the Chief of Military History. *The Army Flag and Its Streamers*. Washington, D.C.: U.S. GPO, 1964.

United States Military Academy (USMA) Department of History. *Campaign Atlas to Wars of Napoleon, the American Civil War, the Great War, Fourth Edition*. West Point NY: 1980.

USMA Department of History. *The Great War, First Revision*. West Point NY: 1980.

U.S. War Department. *Battle Participation of Organizations of the American Expeditionary Forces in France, Belgium, and Italy 1917-1918*. Washington, D.C.: U.S. GPO, 1920.

U.S. War Department. *The War With Germany: A* Statistical *Summary*. Washington, D.C.: U.S. GPO, 1919.

INDEX

ABOUT THE AUTHOR

A retired U.S. Army Military Intelligence (MI) officer, John DellaGiustina has served the nation in operational and training positions in Germany, Korea, Kuwait, Colombia, Iraq, the Republic of Georgia, and throughout the U.S. southwest. He is a graduate of the U.S. Military Academy at West Point and holds a masters degree in History from West Virginia University. John is the editor of the MI Corps Association journal *The Vanguard,* and currently resides in Tucson, Arizona.